burnout and tedium, and provide a method of self-diagnosis. They explore the causes of burnout among people in the helping professions, describe tedium among people working in large bureaucracies, and discuss special issues concerning dual-career women. They maintain that while burnout can be extraordinarily painful and distressing, it can be overcome and, if properly handled, may be the first step toward self awareness, enriched human understanding, and a precursor of important life changes and growth.

Pines and Aronson offer special strategies for coping to each occupational group. Additional coping strategies are discussed at great length in three subsequent chapters. These include: strategies for combating burnout and tedium on the organizational level, the special functions of social support systems as buffers against burnout, and suggestions for the individual on how to expand and better utilize existing coping strategies.

For the reader interested in research, the book includes an appendix (written by Ditsa Kafry) presenting significant findings. For the reader interested in leading—or participating in—burnout workshops, the book includes an appendix describing the content and impact of such workshops.

About the Authors

AYALA PINES is a Research Associate in the Psychology Department at the University of California, Berkeley. The co-author of *Experiencing Social Psychology,* Dr. Pines has studied burnout and tedium for the last six years. Her research resulted in numerous publications.

ELLIOT ARONSON is Professor of Psychology at the University of California, Santa Cruz and is the author of more than 60 scholarly articles and of 10 books, including *The Social Animal* for which he won the National Media Award of the American Psychological Foundation. He is also the recipient of the distinguished research award of the American Association for the Advancement of Sciences as well as the distinguished teaching award of the American Psychological Foundation.

DITSA KAFRY is presently a Research Psychologist in the Psychology Department at the University of California, Berkeley, where she also received her PhD. Her masters of arts degree was obtained at Hebrew University in Jerusalem.

Burnout

Burnout

from tedium to personal growth

AYALA M. PINES and ELLIOT ARONSON
with DITSA KAFRY

THE FREE PRESS
A Division of Macmillan Publishing Co., Inc.
NEW YORK

THE FREE PRESS
A Division of Macmillan Publishing Co., Inc.
866 Third Avenue, New York, N.Y. 10022

Collier Macmillan Canada, Ltd.

Library of Congress Catalog Card Number: 80-755

Printed in the United States of America

printing number
2   3   4   5   6   7   8   9   10

Library of Congress Cataloging in Publication Data

Pines, Ayala.
  Burnout
  Includes index.
    1. Work—Psychological aspects.
  2. Burnout (Psychology) I. Aronson, Elliot,
joint author. II. Kafry, Ditsa, joint author.
  III. Title.
  BF481. P63   1980   158.7   80-755
  ISBN 0-02-925350-0

Excerpts from the article entitled "Burnout: The Loss of Human Caring" by Christina Maslach
and Ayala Pines, published in *Experiencing Social Psychology,* Pines and Maslach (eds.) (New
York: Random House, 1979), appear in this book on pages 15, 17, 22, 48, 55-61, 110-113, 133, and
165. Much of the excerpted material originally appeared in the following articles or papers
written by Christina Maslach: "Detached Concern in Health and Social Service Professions,"
paper presented at American Psychological Association convention, 1973; "Burned-out,"
Human Behavior, 5, no. 9; (September 1976); "Burnout: The Loss of Human Caring," in
Psychology and Life, Zimbardo (ed.), 9th ed. (Diamond Printing) (Glenview, Ill.: Scott
Foresman, 1977); and "Burn-out: A Social Psychological Analysis," paper presented at the
American Psychological Association convention, 1977.

If I am not for myself, who will be for me, if I am only for myself, what am I, and if not now, when.

Hillel, *Wisdom of Our Fathers*

Contents

Acknowledgments

A great many people contributed directly and indirectly to this volume. First, we are pleased to express out gratitude to our friend and colleague, Christina Maslach. Dr. Maslach's work helped spark our own interest in burnout, and one of us (A.P.) collaborated with her in some of that early work. This volume has benefited from the contributions of our colleague in Israel, Dr. Dalia Etzion, who collaborated with us in the cross-cultural studies and provided many helpful comments on an earlier version of the manuscript. We are also indebted to Isamu Saito of Rissho University in Tokyo, Japan, and Dale Stanley of the Community Health Clinic in Saskatoon, Canada, who worked with us on the cross-cultural research on tedium. Jacob Golan and Edna Eldar studied burnout in Israel and Dov Edden of Tel Aviv University supplied some valuable insights on the conceptualization of the coping process.

Several students at the University of California at Berkeley took an active part in the tedium research: Alan Kanner, who generated and coauthored two different studies, Liz Lopez, Teresa Ramirez, and Susan Rauss. We are indebted to them all. Steve Weinberg and the Management Training Program staff at the University of Alabama collaborated with us on the studies of institutional factors affecting burnout.

We are grateful to all those who provided us with observations, interviews, and personal insights about the burnout process, most notably Sue Gershenson, David Woods, Harriet Herman, Diane Crawford, Sylvia Guendelman, Irene Melnick, Moshe Kafry, and the teachers at Smyth Fernwald Child Care Center.

We wish to thank Linda Steck, who edited the manuscript in an earlier stage, and Carol Hecker, who typed it. Finally, and perhaps most important, we are pleased to express our gratitude to the thousands of former burnt-out individuals who took part in our research and workshops and on whose experiences this volume is based.

part one

What are burnout and tedium?

1

What is burnout?
an overview

We have been studying burnout and life tedium for the past several years. Through formal research and conducting cognitive and experiential workshops for thousands of people, we have discovered what causes burnout, how it affects people, and how best to cope with it. We have found that, while burnout can be an extraordinarily painful and distressing experience, as with any difficult event, if properly handled it can not only be overcome, it can be the first step toward increased self-awareness, enriched human understanding, and a precursor of important life changes, growth, and development. Accordingly, people who have experienced burnout and have learned to overcome it almost invariably end up in a better, fuller, more exciting life space than if they had not experienced burnout at all.

We will present a formal definition of burnout in Chapter 2. For purposes of this overview, we will define burnout informally as a state of mind that frequently afflicts individuals who work with other people (especially but not exclusively in the helping professions) and who pour in much more than they get back from their clients, supervisors, and colleagues. It is accompanied by an array of symptoms that include a general malaise; emotional, physical, and psychological fatigue; feelings of helplessness, hopelessness, and a lack of enthusiasm about work and even about life in general. It is insidious in that it usually does not occur as the result of one or two traumatic events but sneaks up through a general erosion of the spirit. Tragically, burnout impacts precisely those individuals who had once been among the most idealistic and enthusiastic. In other words, if individuals entered a given profession (e.g., nursing) with a cynical attitude, they would be unlikely to burn out; but if those who entered had a strong desire to give of themselves to others—and actually felt helpful, excited, and idealistic during their early years on the job—they would be more susceptible to the most severe burnout. We have found, over and over again, that in order to burn out a person needs to have been on fire at one time. It follows, then, that one of the great costs of burnout is the diminution of the effective service of the very best people in a given profession. Accordingly, everyone is the poorer for the existence of this phenomenon.

Examples of burnout

Perhaps the best way for us to communicate how burnout operates is to provide a few examples.

The most striking cases of burnout that we have ever encountered involved hospital nurses working with terminal cancer patients. We think it can be quickly understood why burnout would be such a severe problem in this setting. First of all, most of the nurses who volunteered for this assignment were incredibly idealistic. They really wanted to help people, and they cared deeply about their patients. Yet they burned out after a relatively brief period of time. This is partly due to the very fact that they care so much about their patients, coupled with the fact that their patients keep dying. The nurses are attentive, become involved—and then their patients disappear. The stress is enormous. Moreover, people dying of cancer are frequently in great pain and, of course, are under a great deal of psychological stress. It goes without saying that most are not in a frame of mind to be considerate, grateful, responsive patients. While this is certainly understandable, it can nonetheless add to the stress of nurses who are giving a great deal and getting little concrete gratification in return.

Without realizing it, most nurses begin to do things to protect themselves from being overwhelmed by their situation. Many begin detaching themselves emotionally from their patients. Others will occasionally engage in a kind of gallows humor in which they might put down or mock their patients whether in their own mind or when talking to their closest friends. The fact that they are experiencing less attachment (for their own protection) to patients who are quite demanding (and relatively lacking in expressions of gratitude) leads

many nurses to begin resenting the very people whom they are supposed to be helping. As this resentment becomes increasingly man-
ifest, the typical nurse will begin to feel guilt and shame about her
behavior, attitudes, and general mental state. The hard work, the
feelings of resentment, helplessness, hopelessness, being trapped, as
well as the guilt and shame, are continually recycled and lead to
feelings of exhaustion and malaise, which in turn increase the feelings
of resentment—and the cycle continues.

Moreover, because, for the most part, these particular nurses were
once idealistic, the guilt and shame are enormous. "I, of all people, am
not supposed to be feeling this way" is a statement we have heard
from a great many nurses. This tends to lead many of them to attempt
to mask the symptoms from one another. Several nurses in such a
situation informed us that, while they felt miserable on the inside,
they tried to look crisp, efficient, sometimes even ebullient on the
outside. And here is the supreme irony: imagine nurses in this situation. They are feeling all the symptoms of burnout, but as they look
around, what do they see? What they *don't* see are other nurses
hurting and feeling anguished and guilty. A few nurses are expressing
gallows humor and resentment, but most nurses are looking crisp,
efficient, and ebullient. Virtually all of them are experiencing inner
turmoil and are desperately trying to mask it—either with sarcasm or
with a show of false valor. Indeed, several of the nurses who look so
valiant, crisp, and efficient are secretly envying others because they
look so valiant, crisp, and efficient.

What would one conclude from such a situation? A great many of
our nurses told us *they* concluded: "Most people around here seem to
be doing O.K., therefore there must be something wrong with me.
Perhaps I'm too delicate or hypersensitive; maybe I'm going crazy; I
must not be cut out to be a nurse." In short, because the nurses were
ashamed to share their innermost feelings, they were ignorant of the
fact that they were not alone. This increased their stress by making
them feel (incorrectly) particularly inadequate. They blamed their
burnout on themselves rather than seeing it for what is: a response to
a highly stress-producing situation that is so powerful it affects *almost*
everyone in a similar manner.

The "causal locus"—that is, the place where individuals perceive
the cause and attribute the "blame"—has enormous consequences for
action. If they make a "dispositional attribution"—identifying the
cause of their burnout to a characterological weakness or inadequacy
in themselves—they will take a certain set of actions: quit the profes-

sion, seek psychotherapy, and so forth. However, if they make a "situational attribution"—seeing the cause as largely a function of the situation—they will strive to change the situation to make it more tolerable. This would lead to a totally different set of remedial actions. In some cases, the primary cause *does* lie in the individual. In these cases, changing jobs or seeking individual therapy may be the best solution. On the other hand, our work has made it clear that, in the vast majority of cases of burnout, the major cause lies in the situation. Clearly, in the example involving nurses in a terminal cancer ward, we cannot do much to change the kernel stressor in the situation: all of the nurses will experience the death of most of their patients. But there are countless ways to reduce the burnout caused by this kernel by impacting the situation surrounding it. These coping strategies have proven to be very helpful and will be discussed in subsequent chapters.

For now, let it suffice to say that the first and most important step would be to change the focus from "What's wrong with me?" to "What can I do about the situation?" Indeed one of the most exciting events that happens in our burnout workshops occurs near the beginning when we simply ask the participants to write down the major sources of stress that they experience on their job. We then ask them to meet in groups of five or six and share what they've written. When we did this during a workshop with the cancer nurses, there were many expressions of excitement and delight as each of the individuals discovered for the first time that she or he was not alone—after years of experiencing the lonely and agonizing feelings of guilt and inadequacy they suddenly became aware that behind the smiling mask of their colleagues were similar feelings of inadequacy. From that point in time they could begin focusing on the problem as a *situational* problem, not as a problem of their own individual failure.

Nurses are, admittedly, an extreme example. At the same time, it would be unfortunate if the reader were to conclude that burnout occurs only among people who are dealing with death while working in a tight bureaucratic organization such as a hospital. Burnout can occur in occupations where, from all outward appearances, the individual seems to have it made. Let us look at just such a group of people—dentists. Dentists are professionals with whom almost all of us have had experience; most people are surprised to learn that dentists suffer from burnout because, on the surface, dentistry seems like a relatively easy, lucrative, relatively nonstressful profession. No one dies on the dental chair; the dentist is captain of his or her own ship—not part of a bureaucracy—he or she has a lot of autonomy, a lot of control, a lot of power. In the past four years, we have conducted workshops involving several hundred dentists. In the course of these workshops, we discovered that the burnout rate among dentists is extremely high.

Why? What causes dentists to burn out? There are several factors. We will focus on the most salient one: dentists are highly skilled, highly trained professionals who are almost always performing routine tasks very well and who almost invariably find themselves in a situation where there is almost no one around who is both able and willing to show appreciation for their work. Neither their patients nor their coworkers are in a good position to express meaningful appreciation. Let us first look at the personnel in a dental office. Typically, dentists work with a staff consisting of a receptionist, a hygienist, and an assistant. Very few dentists collaborate with other dentists. While their staff serves an important and vital function, there is no one who has the expertise to say "Wow, what a wonderful job you did in capping that molar."

But certainly the patients are grateful. Or are they? Let's take a closer look. Most patients when entering a dental office are in a high state of anxiety. Their major concern as patients is to get out of there as fast as possible with as little pain as possible. Most of them do not want to be there—and this gets communicated to dentists in subtle ways. While dentists are cognitively aware that this is so the experience of being feared and even disliked is nevertheless very unpleasant. Moreover, most patients are not in a frame of mind to concern themselves too much about dentists' need for appreciation, respect, and approval. To add to the problem, dentists work on the mouth—a situation that not only produces extreme physical and psychological discomfort for patients but one that makes it difficult for patients to communicate (other than to gasp, groan, or emit an occasional "uh huh" through lips swollen with novacaine). In addition, because dentists work in the mouth, patients don't have a very good view of what the dentists are doing, so they are not very likely to utter sounds of approval even if it were physically possible and even if they were in a frame of mind to do so.

How often do patients phone their dentist the day after their visit to say how well their new filling is fitting and how normal their "bite" feels? Indeed, most dentists we've worked with report that virtually the only instances when they hear from a patient after a visit are when the patient has something to complain about.

The experience, hour after hour, day after day, week after week, of pouring in maximal effort for minimal appreciation is extremely taxing and causes the erosion of the spirit known as burnout.

In discussing this situation with dentists, we learned that many of them respond to this lack of appreciation in a manner that is diametrically opposed to what we would have recommended. The most common response to burnout among dentists is to take on more patients! What dentists are doing is using their autonomy to make a decision that seems reasonable. They are saying in effect, "This job is boring, I'm not getting much appreciation, I might as well become rich." So they live in fancy houses, drive fancy cars—and dread going to work in the morning—longing for the time when their real estate investments will allow them the financial freedom to leave the profession entirely.

Of course, we have oversimplified. But the picture is far too accurate to be easily dismissed. In our work with dentists (and other professionals) we have found that, while money is a very useful commodity (and *might* even buy a modicum of happiness!), it is *not* a good cure for burnout.

Indeed, what we have discovered in working with dentists is that the most successful way of coping with burnout is for them to see fewer patients—and spend more time with them. This time can be spent in helping put them at their ease, reducing the anxiety, and allowing patients and dentists to emerge as three-dimensional people for each other. Let us elaborate: in our workshops, when we asked dentists to describe their most typical unpleasant patients, they used adjectives like "sullen," "uncommunicative," "uninteresting," "unresponsive," "uncooperative," "uninterested," etc. "Of course," as one of us quickly pointed out to them, "you are describing me perfectly! Not the warm, charming, exciting, effervescent personality that my friends know and love, but the me that exists in a dental chair when I'm scared, full of novacaine, and have a mouth stuffed with cotton!"

If dentists had spent more time with patients and allayed their anxiety, they would have reaped a huge benefit. They would have begun to see the kinds of things in patients that their friends see and would have added a great deal of variety to an otherwise routine day. Rather than seeing Mrs. Jones as the uninteresting, sullen possessor of a molar that needs capping and Mr. Smith as the uncooperative, unresponsive owner of a cavity in his incisor (who tends to gag while being x-rayed) dentists would be able to see these two as very different people—each interesting in her or his own right.

Moreover, as their anxiety gets reduced, patients begin looking at dentists as competent and caring people, begin trying to attend more to what the dentists are doing, and are in a better position to show them some honest appreciation, which is one of the things dentists were lacking.

This was our recommendation to many dentists. In addition, we urged them to meet with one another on a monthly basis in order to share ideas, talk about any especially interesting problems they encountered or work they had done during that month. This provided them with the kind of support and professional appreciation that many people in less isolated professions can get more easily from their coworkers.

While admittedly these recommendations are not always easy to follow, they are an effective coping strategy if properly implemented.

Strategies for dealing with burnout

Let us now move from the arena of concrete examples to the more general recommendations. As we do this, we are also, in effect, outlining the progression of chapters in this book.

The major strategies for dealing with burnout consist of: (1) being aware of the problem; (2) taking responsibility for doing something about it; (3) achieving some degree of cognitive clarity; and (4) developing new tools for coping, improving the range and quality of old tools.

As mentioned previously, one of the major escalators of burnout are the dual feelings of hopelessness and helplessness, the feeling that "there are too many things in my life that I don't like and that are beyond my control. I feel helpless about it and I have given up all hope of ever being able to change those things." There are two things involved here: one is the *actual* reality of the situation and the other is the perception of the situation on the person's part. In our work with people experiencing burnout, we have found that in almost all cases people have far more control over at least some aspects of their life and work situation than they realize. Once they begin to understand that they have some modicum of control, the feelings of hopelessness and helplessness begin to diminish even before they begin to assert that control. Two people can be working at the same place doing exactly the same job, and yet one can be feeling utterly helpless and hopeless, while the other feels there is both help and hope. The first person experiences intense burnout; the other does not. For example, suppose some dentists felt that they could not spend more time with their patients because they needed to earn $150,000 a year. Such people would feel trapped in that gilded cage and would experience their plight as being far more helpless and hopeless than reality. For, in reality, they could unlock that cage by simply settling for less money. In some occupations there is less automony. Nevertheless, we have found that almost everyone has more power than he or she realizes.

Some people have learned to develop good coping strategies on their own and thus have avoided or diminished burnout. Others need help—the kind of help we have provided for thousands of people through our workshops and the kind of help we hope this book can provide.

Awareness

Adequate coping consists first of awareness of the fact that there *is* a problem. There are people who hide from the problem and try to avoid thinking about it. These are people who believe that the way things are is the way they have to be; they also believe that the way things are in this job is the way they are in all jobs. "That's life" is a slogan that may reduce pain slightly, but it also prevents finding a solution. This generalized cynicism masquerading as a philosophical outlook makes it impossible for people to develop a special awareness of what is happening to them.

Other people who are somewhat aware of the problem tend to think that it is all their own fault. This is usually only partial awareness and it is almost always misdirected and, therefore, dysfunctional. Take the example of the nurses that we presented earlier. When nurses who work in a very painful, demanding job begin to burn out, they either develop a cynical attitude or they begin to feel guilt and shame about the way they had come to feel towards and treat their patients as a result of their burnout and try to hide these feelings from everybody else. Both the cynicism, on the one hand, and the internalization of the guilt and shame, on the other hand, increase their burnout. Becoming fully aware of the problem includes becoming aware of the locus of the cause. Awareness temporarily increases the pain until action is taken.

To summarize, one part of achieving awareness is the simple realization that there is a problem; the other part is the awareness that the problem is largely a function of the situation rather than a function of one's own dispositional inadequacy.

Taking responsibility for action

Once a person becomes aware that the problem is largely situational, then the coping strategies shift from "What's wrong with me as a person?" to "What can I do about changing my environment to make it more pleasant and facilitative for me to accomplish my personal and professional goals?" But in order to effect a change, a person must be willing to take responsibility for changing the environment. This is usually a difficult stage. While many are willing to take responsibility for something that seems to be *"their* fault," they are reluctant to do something about situational or institutional problems. Somehow if it is a situational problem, the organization should do it. This is not an unreasonable wish—unfortunately one cannot count on an organization to take remedial action. Occasionally an extremely enlightened organization might accomplish this task, but this is a rare exception. People can assume more power and control over their lives through the realization that there are more things that they can do to gain control over the environment than they realize. We have found that once an individual begins to take responsibility for effecting a change in a difficult situation, this, in and of itself, is therapeutic simply because it reduces the debilitating effects of the feelings of helplessness. Moreover, there are specific actions small groups of individuals can take that can make real and concrete changes. These will be discussed at length in subsequent chapters.

Cognitive clarity

When people are aware of the existence of a problem and are ready to take responsibility, the third thing necessary is cognitive clarity. When people are burned out and working in a bureaucratic organization, they usually cannot easily discriminate the things that can be changed from the things that cannot be changed. Burnout often manifests itself in people who assume that everything destructive and dehumanizing can be changed. These people invariably end up banging their heads against the stone wall of a nonresponsive bureaucracy. Some aspects of a bureaucracy simply *cannot* be changed. After trying and failing, they obviously begin feeling hopeless and helpless and come to believe that *nothing* can be changed. There are also people who believe that nothing can be changed from the outset. These individuals quickly develop a cynical attitude and never attempt to change anything. They simply put in their time.

In actuality, there *are* things that cannot be changed or that would

be very difficult to change. In some cases, it is probably not worth the
effort to try. But there are many aspects of a difficult work situation
that *can* be changed with little effort. Part of what we mean by the
achievement of "cognitive clarity" is the development of an ability to
distinguish between those aspects of an organization that can't be
changed and those that can. This allows individuals to channel their
efforts where there will be a great likelihood of important progress.
Again, not only will the change itself be beneficial, but the mere
process of being able to effect a change will reduce the feeling of
helplessness and hopelessness and thereby reduce burnout even
though the situation remains far from ideal.

In one social service agency with which we worked, for example,
we found that the crying need among many of the workers, and a
major source of unease on the job most often mentioned by them, was
that people high up in the hierarchy weren't aware of the great effort
they put into their work. Consequently, they did not feel that their
work was appreciated. But, in the kind of bureaucracy that existed in
that social service organization, to expect appreciation from high-
level officials was very unrealistic. It would have taken a major organizational change to bring about systematic expressions of appreciation from above. Our major intervention was to teach workers
on the same hierarchical level to reward each other and to respect and
value the appreciation of their peers. We taught them ways of paying
attention to and acknowledging the good work of their peers and
developed a system of peer review and communication. This simple
intervention proved to be very effective.

Time and again we have found that, in a given organization,
individuals hunger for appreciation. While these people feel unap-
preciated, they almost never reach out to show appreciation of
someone else's work. In our experience, we have found that one of the
best ways for individuals to encourage other people to pay attention to
their work is to start acknowledging the good work of others. When
individuals, on their own, reach out to give each other needed support
and needed appreciation, the reaching out mushrooms and grows
exponentially. Moreover, the existence of peer appreciation (which is
easy to institute) reduces the need for approval from above (which is
frequently difficult, if not impossible, to institute).

There are other discriminations to be learned: for example, people must learn to make a clear discrimination between the concrete
demands of the job and the demands they place on themselves that
they sometimes erroneously attribute to their "supervisor" or their

"organization." Thus, some people regularly overwork, assuming that this is a demand placed on them by their organization. But if they examine that closely, they would realize that they were much harsher taskmasters than their employer. They would then realize that they *did* have more control than they realized—and would have to deal with the issue of whether or not they wanted to exercise that control.

Developing tools for coping

Some of the major tools necessary for coping have already been alluded to. For example, in order to see the specific problem, one needs to develop some diagnostic and discrimination skills. In the above illustration, the realization that peer review could be an adequate substitute for supervisory praise requires the development of the skill to look for and find alternatives. Similarly, one needs practice in looking inward to be able to articulate clearly what our own needs are in a given situation. If a solution involves meeting with other people to discuss problems and solutions, certain skills such as "active listening" and clear communication need to be developed. It is important to realize that these skills are, at one and the same time, *essential* and *easy to master*. This will become clearer as the reader delves more deeply into this material in subsequent chapters.

One of the major reasons for mentioning the sequence of strategies for dealing with burnout is to make the point that earnest awareness is not enough. But it *is* a good first step. As with any problem (alcoholism, obesity, etc.) it is important to be aware and to desire change, but much more is needed to reverse the problem. This fact can best be illustrated than explained. Last year, we conducted a series of burnout workshops for executives in Isreal. One of the participants (whom we'll call Dov) is a vice-president of one of that country's largest oil companies. We returned several months later to conduct a more intensive follow-up workshop for alumni of the previous one. We were amazed to find Dov in attendance. The reason for our amazement: a few days before the start of the workshop, Israel was hit with a major energy crisis. Important decisions had to be made. We were certain that Dov, a self-confessed "workaholic" who had previously told us that he was indispensable to his organization, would be burning the midnight oil helping to solve the crisis. What was he doing at our workshop?

He informed us that several months before his initial workshop on burnout he had suffered a serious heart attack. His physician ordered him to stay home from work for sixty days to recuperate. While taking long walks in the woods near his home he noticed the trees, the birds, the sky—seeing them as if for the first time. He realized that he was burning out on his job. He became deeply aware of the fact that he was now in his fifties, that he had poured much too much energy into his work. He was working harder and enjoying it less. He vowed that from now on he would spend more time doing things that *he* wanted to do—spend more time on himself and with his family—cease being a workaholic. "I was excited about this discovery," he told us, "so excited that I could hardly wait to put it into effect. In fact, I was in such a hurry to put it into effect that I ended my convalescence two weeks early and returned to work! And within a very short time, I was back to my usual 14 hours a day."

A few months later, he came to the burnout workshop, without expecting much to happen; he was thoroughly convinced that he was too old to change. In the workshop, however, he gained an increase in his understanding of the phenomenon and picked up a few useful skills. Mostly, what he came to realize is that an awareness of the problem was insufficient. Even a rather dramatic awareness such as his own heart attack could not sustain him through an important life change.

The ultimate proof of his change came when the oil crisis happened to coincide with the date of the more intense workshop. The old Dov would have given up the workshop, convinced that he was indispensable. The new Dov had rearranged his priorities so that he and his needs came first. More importantly, he had given up the ego-gratifying conceit that he was indispensable and had trained others to be able to assume more responsibility as he became freer to delegate it. In effect, he became a more successful executive, was more useful to the company and certainly more useful to himself and his family by learning to get gratification from delegating authority rather than from behaving as if he needed to do everything himself. Thus, as frequently happens, as Dov cured his own burnout, he was not the only beneficiary; his organization, his subordinates, as well as his family and friends, benefited from his reorientation.

Our purpose in writing this book is to be able to take what we've learned from our research and our workshops and share them with you. It is our hope that this book will not only help you increase your awareness of burnout in general and your own potential for burnout in particular but in addition will help provide you with the orientation and tools to cope successfully with the problem.

2

Burnout and tedium:

the experience

Tedium and burnout are states of physical, emotional, and mental exhaustion. They are characterized by physical depletion, by feelings of helplessness and hopelessness, by emotional drain, and by the development of negative self-concept and negative attitudes towards work, life, and other people. They are the sense of distress, discontent, and failure in the quest for ideals. In their extreme form tedium and burnout reach a breaking point beyond which the individual loses the ability to cope with and enjoy the environment.

Tedium and burnout are similar in terms of symptomatology but are different in origin. Both are clusters of exhaustion reactions. *Tedium* can be the result of any prolonged *chronic pressures* (mental, physical, or emotional); *burnout* is the result of constant or repeated *emotional pressure* associated with an intense involvement with *people* over long periods of time. Such intense involvement is particularly prevalent in health education and social service occupations, where professionals have a "calling" to take care of other people's psychological, social, and physical problems. Burnout is the painful realization that they no longer can help people in need, that they have nothing left in them to give. Throughout this book we will reserve the term burnout for those situations in which the individual is dealing with other human beings. It should be clear that the experience of tedium is almost always a part and parcel of the burnout syndrome.

Tedium may occur as the result of a sudden change such as a traumatic life event. More often it occurs as a result of a more gradual process—the daily struggles and chronic stresses that are typical of everyday life and work. Tedium is the result of having too many negative and too few positive features in one's environment: too many pressures, conflicts, and demands combined with too few rewards, acknowledgements, and successes.[1] One may be able to stay in a demanding career when one feels valuable and appreciated. But most people will develop tedium when their life imposes much more stress than support.

Our research* on *tedium* found that people develop some degree of tedium at some point in their lives.[2] Our studies on tedium involved 3,916 men and women, including 3,195 Americans, 118 Canadians, 199 Japanese, and 404 Israelis. They represented a wide range of professions and ranged in age from 17 to 87.

In our research on *burnout,*[3] we observed human service professionals at work, collected extensive data, and conducted personal interviews. Our group work[4] involved over one hundred seminars and workshops in ten states, as well as in Israel, with groups ranging in size from 12 to 500. The professionals who participated in the workshops included psychologists; psychiatrists; psychology technicians; counselors; social workers; probation officers; prison personnel; child care workers; teachers of special education, elementary school, high school, community college, and university; doctors; nurses; physical therapists; dentists; dental office staff; managers; supervisors and superintendents of various human service institutions and organiza-

---

*Throughout this volume we will be reporting correlational data that are based on self-reports; that is to say, the data relate one variable (for example, environmental stress) to another variable (for example, degree of burnout). While such data are of some value, their interpretation is not always crystal clear. For example, it is often difficult to be certain which variable is the cause and which is the effect, or indeed if both are the effects of a deeper cause—that is, do certain stressful activities produce burnout, does burnout sensitize the individual to stress, or do certain occupations attract people who both burn out easily and experience a lot of stress? Usually, common sense dictates the most reasonable sequence; in other words, in most of the data that we will be reporting it makes most sense to assume that specific variables (like certain stresses) are antecedents to tedium.

There is one additional problem with data that are based on self-report, It may be that the results are influenced by such general factors as the honesty of the respondents or, conversely, the respondents' desire to say things in order to put themselves in a more favorable light. For example, if it turns out that there is a correlation between burnout and psychological depression, it is conceivable that such a result is influenced by honesty in that those people who are honest enough to admit to experiencing burnout are the same people who are honest enough to admit to being depressed. While such a possibility exists in much of the data we will be reporting, it is our best guess that this factor accounts for only a small portion of the relationship, and the rest are meaningful. This "best guess" is an informed judgement based upon corroborating evidence from hundreds of hours of interviews, and discussions with individuals at workshops. We feel therefore that the paper and pencil tests, while in themselves somewhat sterile, are bolstered by "flesh and blood" interactions with people currently experiencing burnout.

tions; occupational therapists; perinatal workers; welfare workers; dialysis workers; lawyers; policemen; army psychologists; nuns and priests; and organizational development experts.

Burnout is not an isolated phenomenon that characterizes a limited number of individuals. On the contrary, it occurs very frequently to a wide variety of people working in almost all the human services. Burnout has detrimental psychological effects and appears to be a major factor in low morale, absenteeism, tardiness, and high job turnover. It also plays a primary role in the poor delivery of health education and welfare services. People who burn out develop a negative self-concept and negative job attitudes. Their concern and feeling for the people they work with becomes dulled and in some cases they treat their clients in detached, hostile, and uncaring ways.

Burnout is a very costly phenomenon. It is costly for those who quit their jobs in terms of their wasted training, and it is costly for those who stay in terms of the psychological price they pay. It is costly for the organizations in terms of lost talent and poor performance, and it is costly for the clients and patients. As a result of burnout, clients wait longer to receive less attention and concern. The quality of the care they receive is poorer and the experience of obtaining it humiliating.

The three components of tedium and burnout

Although the intensity, duration, frequency, and consequences may vary, both tedium and burnout have three basic components: physical, emotional, and mental exhaustion.

Physical exhaustion

Physical exhaustion is characterized by low energy, chronic fatigue, weakness, and weariness. People who have burned out report such things as accident-proneness, increased susceptibility to illness, frequent headaches, nausea, muscle tension in shoulders and neck, back pains, and changes in eating habits and weight. Also mentioned in the scientific literature are psychosomatic complaints, increased frequency of illness,[5] nagging colds, and frequent attacks of virus or flu.[6]

The paradoxical combination of weariness and sleep problems is often reported.[7] One may be tired during the day but unable to sleep because of tormenting thoughts or nightmares. The content of nightmares is often related to the burned out state of the dreamer. A prison guard had dreams in which he was chased and shot. A waitress dreamed about dozens of starving and angry diners who were shouting at her for not bringing food ordered hours before. A nuclear physicist under pressure to research and publish dreamt about people finding out that his greatest discovery was in fact an error.

Many people attempt to combat tedium by physical and chemical means such as alcohol, cigarettes, barbituates, tranquilizers, and hallucinogens. For some, overeating began in response to tedium. "All I can do at the end of a day is collapse in front of the T.V. and eat a large bowl of ice cream," a burned out teacher told us. Obviously these coping strategies provide only temporary relief, leaving the individual with an even more overwhelming sense of weariness and despair.

Emotional exhaustion

Emotional exhaustion involves feelings of depression, helplessness, hopelessness, and entrapment leading in extreme cases to mental illness or thoughts about suicide.[8] It may cause incessant, uncontrollable crying or the loss of coping and control mechanisms. People who burn out feel that they need all of the little emotional energy they have left to keep going through the motions of life. Professionals in the social services may feel they have nothing left to give to anyone. One social worker stated, "Sometimes I feel like telling my clients, 'Who cares? You think only you have problems? What about me?' "

"A few years ago," said a lawyer, "I felt that life was an eternal feeling of exuberance and joy, I liked my work and I had a very active social life. Now I feel my job is a dead end. My emotional resources are drained, my best friends irritate me, I do not know my children, and I do not have the emotional energy to be their friend. I find it hard to be polite and tolerant of my clients. I became immersed in self-pity and all I want is to be left alone." The burned out person feels emotionally depleted and yet is frequently irritable and nervous. Rather than sources of nourishment, family and friends become just one more demand. Futility and despair increase. Satisfaction from work and other activities diminishes. Feelings of happiness and hope are replaced by loneliness,[9] discouragement, and disenchantment. "I felt like my soul was dying," recalls a welfare worker.

Mental exhaustion

Mental exhaustion is characterized by the development of negative attitudes toward one's self, toward work, and toward life.[10] People who develop tedium often report dissatisfaction with their work and way of life and a lowered self-concept; they feel inadequate, inferior, and incompetent. "My hands are tied and I feel useless and impotent." wrote a manager of a large public agency. "I never have enough information for making a decision in my work. I cannot deal effectively with the requirements of my job. I feel worthless, like a total failure and I resent my subordinates who witness this failure."

In addition to developing negative self-concepts and pessimistic views of their own work, people who burn out also develop negative attitudes toward others. They discover in themselves coldness and nastiness they never knew existed. Workers in the human services at times develop dehumanizing attitudes toward the recipients of their services. Social psychologists have developed a sizable literature on the concept of dehumanization.[11] Dehumanization is defined as a decreased awareness of the human attributes of others and a loss of humanity in interpersonal interactions. People stop perceiving others as having the same feelings, impulses, thoughts, and processes as they have and thus psychologically eliminate any human qualities that these others might share with them. As a result of the process of dehumanization, people are less likely to perceive and respond to the personal identity of other people and are more likely to treat them as if they were not human beings. But people who dehumanize others experience fewer emotions, less empathy, and fewer personal feelings and thus dehumanize themselves as well.[12] Burned out professionals in the human services often come to see their clients as aggregates of problems rather than as individuals. "They are all just animals," a prison guard said. "I no longer want to work with losers," said a welfare worker. "If they have been the victims of society for so long, they probably deserve to be."

Dissatisfaction with work often leads people to arrive late, leave early, extend work breaks, or avoid work entirely.[13] It can also lead to an "I-don't-give-a-damn" attitude in people who once were very idealistic. Katherine L. Armstrong,[14] who studied burnout among personnel treating cases of child abuse and neglect, identified such symptoms of burnout as daily resistance to going to work, clock-watching, postponing client contacts, resisting client phone calls and office visits, stereotyping clients, and inability to concentrate on what the client is saying, feeling intolerant of clients' anger, feeling immobilized and helpless, cynicism regarding clients, and a blaming attitude. Nurses working in intensive care units were found[15] to be significantly more depressed, hostile, and anxious than nurses in less

stressful units. They showed high incidents of dropout and absenteeism due to minor illness and vague somatic complaints (such as
headaches, upset stomachs, and fatigue). Nurses in high-emotional-
risk settings also had high incidents of hyperactivity and restlessness,
frequent requests for transfers to other work sites, interstaff conflict,
and depersonalization in the nurse-patient relationship. In a study of
mental health workers[16] it was found that, as a result of investing a
great amount of time and energy in patients and meeting with
repeated failure, staff members felt defeated and hopeless. In some
situations, if, after much hard work on the part of the staff member, a
patient regressed, especially after there had been some success at first,
the personnel became bitter or angry and grew indifferent or uninterested in the patient. In studying the characteristics of staff burnout in
mental health settings[17] we found that the longer the staff had worked
in the mental health field the less they liked working with patients, the
more they avoided direct contact with them, the less successful they
felt in their work, and the more custodial rather than humanistic were
their attitudes toward mental illness. They stopped looking for self-
fulfillment in their work, good days became very infrequent, and the
only good thing about their work was now the money and security it
provided. Herbert T. Freudenberger,[18] a psychoanalyst who studied
burnout in alternative institutions, lists such symptoms as cynicism,
negativism, and a tendency to be inflexible. Workers may discuss
clients in intellectual terms and jargon and thereby distance themselves from emotional involvement; they may rarely communicate
with others, may become loners and may withdraw.[19]

   This attitude change happens often to new teachers. A newly
appointed college professor promised herself she would be caring and
helpful as the teachers she always wished she had. She made herself
available to students, encouraged them to come to her office, and
allowed them to call her at home. The students responded enthusias-
tically. They were in her office at all hours of the day and called her
home at night. They would get her in the supermarket, the movies,
and the swimming pool. There was no escape from them. Gradually
her office hours became shorter, and now she sees students by appointment only. Her door, like all other doors in the department, is
locked. She developed the usual "undergraduatitis" (i.e., student
phobia) that so many college teachers show symptoms of: "I find
myself crossing the street whenever I see someone in their twenties
approaching. I do not think I like teaching anymore."

   Often the experience of burnout not only leads to the development
of negative attitudes toward oneself and one's clients but also spills

over to affect attitudes towards one's colleagues, friends, and family members, many times resulting in marital conflict and deteriorating personal relationships. Since one does not get one's needs met at work, the typical reaction is to make more demands of the spouse or the friends at home. Very few relationships can withstand the continual pressure of these excessive and unfair demands. Eventually one comes to resent behaviors of people one either enjoyed or ignored previously. A burned out physician said, "Everything my colleagues do gets on my nerves: their vocabulary, the way they talk, the way they walk, and the way they think. They all seem so stupid to me now, and to think that I once thought they were an exciting, stimulating bunch is quite inconceivable."

Recognizing danger signs

Some people's reaction to burnout is primarily somatic; other people's reaction may be more emotional. If one is having all these physical, emotional, and mental exhaustion reactions, one is in the midst of a severe burnout or tedium crisis. But only a few of these symptoms or only occasional symptoms can serve as warning signs. They are an indication that it is time to examine and evaluate one's priorities at work and home, the stresses stemming from the environment, and the adequacy of one's coping strategies. At the end of this chapter we have included a self-diagnosis test that can help readers identify their own level of tedium.

It is important to note that one can also recognize danger signs in other people. One hundred and eighteen participants in two of our workshops were asked, after diagnosing themselves, to estimate the degree of tedium reported by one of their close colleagues. The correlation between the self-diagnosis and the tedium assessed by the colleagues was highly significant.[20] In other words, people's burnout is almost never a secret from their colleagues; that is, if people are burning out, whether or not they know it, others around them are quite aware of it. Becoming aware that one is burning out, developing cognitive clarity, and identifying the major causes for the burnout are the first steps towards effective coping.

When do burnout and tedium occur?

The timing, manifestations, and consequences of burnout or tedium depend both on the individual and on the environment in which the individual works and lives. In certain professions burnout often occurs shortly after entering the job, sometimes within serveral months or a year. A nurse who works with burned children told us that after a few months she, and most other nurses on the ward, could not tolerate the emotional burden of their work, and they asked to be transferred. Reported turnover rates among nurses as a whole have been exceptionally high. The National Commission for the Study of Nursing and Nursing Education states that 70 percent of staff nurses in Amercian hospitals resigned from their jobs during the year of their investigation.[21] In the child protection field certain departments turn over workers at 50 to 100 percent each year.[22] Poverty lawyers claim that within two years most newcomers burnout. The same percentage was reported for such diverse professions as inner-city teaching, social work, flight controling, and television producing. People in the human services who live on the job (e.g., people working in residential treatment centers) tend to burnout within a year or two. Other professionals, such as doctors, dentists, teachers, and private entrepreneurs, frequently report longer periods of time—four to five years—before the onset of burnout.

Sometimes an episode of burnout or tedium lasts only a few days or weeks and people are able to recover without help. Other times a crisis can last for months or years without solution or recovery.

Herbert Freudenberger[23] found variations in burnout even in the same individual. He claims there are longer periods between each burnout episode after the first one. The first is apt to happen quickly but in time one learns how to pace oneself. One becomes more self-protective, more cautious. One develops more of a self-interested attitude and becomes less intimately and emotionally involved. Eventually one may burn out again, but Freudenberger believes it is not as devastating.

Only rarely does burnout or tedium immediately affect all spheres of a person's life. Many people begin to burnout in their work but enjoy their family life and daily activities. Others may feel burned out about their collapsing family relations, while their job provides them with many moments of happiness and a sense of pride and significance. Often, however, burnout spills over from one category of life to another.

The consequences of tedium and burnout

People deal with tedium and burnout in different ways. Some burned out workers leave their professions. Quitting one's career,

especially after long years in training, is frequently associated with a
sense of failure, guilt and waste. It is also costly for the organization
and for society as a whole.

Other people leave their specific jobs but stay in the same profession or in the same organization. Often, however, people quit one
place of work only to find the same problems in a new job. Sometimes
after burning out in a series of jobs they develop a chronic sense of
hopelessness and failure.

Still other people climb up the administrative ladder as a way of
escaping a job in which they burned out. In our work we have come
into contact with many instances of case workers who burned out in
their work with clients and went back to school to receive a higher
degree so they could become administrators far removed from any
direct contact with clients. On the surface this may seem like a reasonable solution, however, it has been our experience that there is
nothing quite as burnout producing as a burned out worker who is
now supervising other workers. Picture the scene: a young case worker
full of enthusiasm and idealism about the work he is starting. What
could be more devastating for him or her than to run into a supervisor
who instead of encouraging that idealism says, "Just wait, you'll
find out"?

There are also those who never quit. These people are often
motivated by a need for security and when a job offers them tenure
and acceptable retirement benefits they stay as "deadwood."[24] They
do as little as possible and their response to most inquiries is: "I don't
know, I just work here." In one department of social services we heard
about a "phantom" probation officer. No one knew who he was, what
his schedule was, or what he was doing. However, his reports, all
similar and all short, were always presented on time. Sometimes
people who become "dead wood" lose their motivation for change
and improvement and even when offered a more satisfying position
they do not take it.

There is another way of surviving burnout and tedium. Such a
crisis can be a trigger for personal growth. It can be a time for
becoming aware of problems, for examining demands imposed by the
environment, including work and home. It can be a time for taking
responsibility for building support systems and developing other
coping strategies. It can be an opportunity for reorganizing one's
priorities and for learning about one's strengths and weaknesses. It
can be a time for expanding skills and abilities. "This experience
involved incredible pain and suffering," said a television producer
who had a short but severe tedium crisis. "Yet, it was very important

for me as a learning experience. It forced me to examine my priorities. I became aware of the things which were most stressful for me, and the positive things I could not do without. Now I see both my vulnerabilities and strengths very clearly, and I have a more realistic view of myself. I have a deep conviction that I will not repeat the mistakes of the past. And I realize how much strength I could find in myself."

Burnout and tedium are complex human experiences that are affected by the variability of human nature. The case study method can do more justice to this richness than can abstract descriptions. Accordingly, we will present six detailed cases to illustrate the major responses to burnout and tedium: a case of a broken spirit, a case of leaving the profession forever, a case of a prisoner in a gilded cage, a case of deadwood, a case of quitting up the career ladder, and a case of tedium as a trigger for growth. These studies all describe normal, well-adjusted people who had typical clusters of symptoms as a result of both a chronic presence of negative features and a consistent lack of positive features in their environments.

A broken spirit

Charlie was permanently affected by tedium. He had been a creative, energetic, and ambitious man. When he graduated from college he wanted his own fashion business and he was sure he was going to "make it big." Nothing could stop him. He loved the creative aspect of the job and business seemed like a great challenge. But things did not happen quite as fast as he planned, nor in quite the right way. He found himself caught in the trivia of managing a business with little time for creative fashion design. He felt he could not trust his employees to do anything right, so by himself he advertised his products, handled the books, answered the phone, ordered materials, made sure the designs were done properly, and called patrons who did not pay their bills.

When Charlie gained a reputation for producing well-designed, high-quality garments, his life actually seemed to get worse. All of his energies and most of his earnings went back into expanding the business, while his family had problems making ends meet. There was never a sense of achievement and success because, as Charlie described it, "In this type of business you are only as good as your last product, and no one will ever remember the excellent samples you produced in the past."

Anxiety and anger changed Charlie from a friendly person to a man suspicious that everyone was out to ruin him. He was constantly anxious about something's going wrong at work, and something almost always did go wrong. Every day brought another crisis to claim his attention. He entered his office at six o'clock in the morning and after getting home late at night continued working on his books until the early hours of the next morning. He hardly ever saw his family and would never take a day off or a vacation. He felt guilty about his family and resented the fact that they made him feel guilty.

After four years, Charlie had spent all of his physical, mental, and emotional resources on his business. He felt as though his nerves were tied into one large knot. Not even the increasing doses of tranquilizers his doctor prescribed could calm him down. He hated the government for the taxes it imposed, he hated his incompetent employees, he hated the competition, he hated his patrons, but most of all he hated himself. He could not sleep and could not eat. There was never time for laughter nor for releasing tension. Charlie collapsed and was brought to the hospital in a state of complete exhaustion. He was kept in the intensive care unit for five days. After being released from the hospital he was ordered to rest for several weeks.

After his release and recuperation he moved with his family to the suburbs. Charlie felt he could no longer handle either creative or managerial responsibilities on a job. He took a position as clerk in a big clothing company and never regained his ambition or his creative spark. His ability to cope with the world was severely hampered, his spirit broken.

Leaving the profession forever

Some people believe burnout indicates that they have chosen the wrong career. Many teachers, for instance, realize they hate teaching soon after first standing alone before a class of pupils. Carol was such a teacher. Her family had expected that Carol would be an elementary school teacher because "Carol is so good with children" and "Elementary school teaching is a good profession for a woman." Carol never questioned this career choice until her last year in college. At that time, when she first became a student teacher, some doubts entered her mind. The whole situation—the lively, noisy children, her insecurity and lack of control—was extremely frightening and unpleasant. But it was difficult to quit so close to graduation so she finished college. After two years of teaching she realized that she could not go on. She felt unable to fulfill the great, and sometimes conflicting, expectations of the children's parents without more support from them or from the school administration. Standing in front of the class she felt weak, helpless, and miserable. When the school day was over she was physically and emotionally drained; she said she needed "someone to scrape me off the floor." She could not find energy in herself for anything but coping with the daily stress of teaching. Her social life deterioriated, she spent most of her time alone in her room, she was frequently sick and almost always depressed. Carol realized that unless she wanted to spend the rest of her life in misery she had to get out of teaching. She became a secretary in a manufacturing company and found herself very content with her life. She felt glad not to be a teacher and wondered how she could have endured it for as long as she did.

Trapped in a gilded cage

Some people quit their jobs when they realize that they are burned out and have made the wrong career choice. Others stay, particularly those who cannot financially afford to quit and those who believe that quitting would waste their investment in their career.

Michael was one who had doubts about his career choice but could not afford to quit. He was a pediatrician who chose his profession because he loved medicine and loved children. After finishing medical school he started his own private practice and what he hoped would be a successful and an exciting medical career.

In time, Michael found that running a medical office can be very lonely. His office included two nurses and a receptionist but no other pediatricians who could appreciate his work and skill. He found few challenges. Most work was routine and after a while became boring. He had not envisioned medicine as endless cases of flu and diaper rash. He felt he knew how to practice far better medicine than he did, but since his work became a routine he was putting less and less into it. Gradually he was losing interest both in his young patients and in medicine. All this drained any enjoyment from his work. He lost his enthusiasm and his energy, he lost satisfaction from his work and knew it was affecting his home life and his view of himself.[25]

Since Michael was 50 years old and successful, he found it difficult to change what he was doing. He had to pay for a suburban house, two cars, yearly vacations, and private school for two children. Money had become the only part of his work that was gratifying. Rather than find outside activities to balance his work, like the dentists described in Chapter 1, he expanded his office and started seeing more patients. As his work became more scheduled, he had time for fewer conversations

with his young patients or their parents, thereby eliminating all possibility of having any personal contact. Chatting with a patient, which
is one way to increase variety in the daily routine of a doctor, seemed
like a waste of valuable time, and time was money. Michael was
frequently unhappy and started questioning the value and purpose of
his life. He felt trapped in his own gilded cage. But he stayed in it,
longing for the day when he could live off his investments and forget
about pediatrics.

Deadwood

Ichak Adizes, who wrote about deadwood as a type of mismanagement style,[26] wrote, "The deadwood is apathetic. He waits to be
told what to do. . . . He is mostly worried about how to survive until
retirement and how to keep intact the little he has. He has no complaints about anything. He fears that any complaint will reflect on
him." In our experience when people become deadwood, they do as
little as possible for so long that they seem to become part of the
organization's physical structure. No one knows what they do becuase
their interaction with other employees is minimal. They just exist until
they can live off their pension.

Joseph is an example of "deadwood." He had been a clerk in the
same large organization for twenty-three years and now had "only"
eleven years left before he could retire. He counted the years, the
months, and the weeks until his retirement. Soon he would start
counting the days.

It had not always been like this. When Joseph started working in
the organization he was "bright-eyed and bushy-tailed," enthusiastic
and ambitious. Because he was an employee who could be trusted, a
disproportionate amount of work was assigned to him. At first he did
not mind because he was sure his extra work would be appreciated.
But he only heard from his superiors when things went wrong or when
he crossed the authority lines. He felt discouraged and defeated, "like
a little useless bolt in the machine." He started experiencing nightmares, anxiety attacks, and panic and once contemplated suicide. One
day he simply decided to give up. He needed the job and was not
going to quit, but he was not going to put in any effort either. He
would do the minimum required in order to keep his job.

Joseph loathed his work. Something in him died every day when
he climbed the stairs to his office. He punched his time card exactly at
eight and at five, but no one knew what he did between those hours.
Joseph avoided contact with his coworkers. His manner was polite but

distant. He developed a way of making himself invisible that is easy in a large, complex organization. He looked busy at his desk and when approached with a question or request, his answer was always "I am really sorry but I can't right now, I'm very busy." People eventually stopped making requests of him and only a few still wondered from time to time what exactly he was busy doing.

People who knew him away from work described Joseph very differently. They said he was interesting, lively, and knowledgeable about music; he read a lot and could spend hours with his coin collection. He enjoyed time with his friends and with his family. But Joseph hated his work. He had only one goal left: to make it to retirement, doing as little as possible without being fired.

Quitting upward

Some burned out people do not leave their organizations but rather go up the organizational ladder. Jeanne chose this quitting upward path. All her life people had told Jeanne their most private problems because she was genuinely interested and concerned. Becoming a social worker in a welfare department was a natural career choice for her.

To her first cases she gave all of herself—time, attention, and action. But after each client came another one with as great a need and as terrible a story. Jeanne gradually realized that all her effort could never have a significant impact on either the lives of the welfare families or the causes of their poverty. Bureaucratic inertia, endless paper work, and poorly planned policy changes were pressures that added to her eventual burnout.

Her morale was low. She comforted herself with food and gained an enormous amount of weight, which only depressed her more. She was absent from work as often as she could manage to be. She came late to the office and prolonged field visits by stops at local stores. She minimized interaction with her clients, cutting short their appointments, not listening, and avoiding eye contact while talking with them. She began dehumanizing her clients, calling them "society's losers," blaming them for their living conditions, and making fun of them to her coworkers.

As her attitude toward her job changed, so did her view of herself. She realized she was growing cynical and disillusioned and she hated people in general and herself in particular. She knew she had to do something to change her life.

Jeanne went back to school to get her master's degree, then returned to the welfare department as a supervisor. In that position she would never have to interact with poor people again. She liked the power her new position provided and liked the paper work. "Papers have no emotional demands and no physical needs. They are never irate and are very easy to put aside." Jeanne felt detached from the young social workers who were starting their careers with her old enthusiasm. She was more comfortable with other supervisors who had chosen the path up.

A trigger for growth

The myth of Sisyphus tells how as punishment Sisyphus was condemned to push a large stone to the top of a mountain whence the rock would roll down again. The gods had thought that "there is no more dreadful punishment than futile and hopeless labor." Albert Camus wrote, "If this myth is tragic, that is because its hero is conscious. Where would his torture be, indeed if at every step the hope of succeeding upheld him? The workman of today works everyday of his life at the same tasks, and this fate is no less absurd. But it is tragic only at the rare moments when he becomes conscious."[27]

Harriet had this consciousness and it was indeed painful. Harriet was 41, married, and the mother of two girls. She was a successful actress, receiving leading roles and positive reviews, but she had to face many problems. She found some roles to be emotionally draining, especially because her approach to the theater included using her own experiences to deepen her involvement in a role. Harriet was also upset about working with people who were not as serious about the theater as she was. When she started acting in a one-woman show, which she both wrote and produced, Harriet's involvement in the theater became all-encompassing. She was appearing six nights a week and she hardly ever saw her family.

Like many professional women, Harriet felt the burden of her roles as mother and wife. Pressured by time and her tasks as a homemaker, she lost all joy in her family. "All my interaction with my children involved orders: 'Close the door.' 'Practice the piano.' I didn't like being a mother. I resented the children's intrusions."

After months of balancing among her roles as mother, wife, and professional, Harriet noticed the warning signs of tedium. "I felt a tremendous burden on my shoulders. I was exhausted all the time and frequently depressed. I had no energy at all, and yet I was physically tense, irritable, and upset." Just at this time, she was injured in a car accident. Then remodeling work began on her home, her husband discovered a suspicious lump on his chest, and her daughter became ill. Harriet felt she could not take any more.

"I got a migraine headache and felt nauseous and dizzy. There was an enormous amount of tension in my body. Later I developed laryngitis. I couldn't talk, and I didn't want to talk to anyone. I found myself crying a lot. I got to the point where I couldn't leave the house."

Harriet did not run from her crisis. "My style is to throw myself totally into what I do and to experience everything to the fullest. I want to get anything I can out of it." She wanted to face the pain, understand it, and learn from it. She let herself feel the fear, the anger, the frustration, and the craziness.

Harriet realized she needed time to regain control of herself and her life, so she went away alone for a few days. She spent that time examining her roles as a mother, a wife, an actress, and a person. She examined the demands she thought were imposed on her by these roles and the rewards they provided. She knew she had to reorganize her priorities and one of the first was learning to take care of herself. She learned to assert herself, to set limits on how much she could do, and to ask for what she needed.

A few weeks after the crisis Harriet started preparing for a new show that was the highlight of her days, but she knew how important her family was. "It is the family which grounds me and gives me strength and energy to go out and experiment." To avoid conflicts, she tried to keep her professional life separate from her personal life. "I feel I am on the right track," she said, "I feel wonderful. I feel strong. I feel I could do anything." Harriet's crisis was probably not the last time she would develop symptoms of tedium. But in the future she may know what the signs mean and be better able to cope with them. For Harriet the experience of tedium became an experience of growth.

In all the above examples the individual took some action in response to the events that caused burnout of tedium. These actions can be called *coping strategies*. Coping strategies will be discussed in great detail in subsequent sections of this volume. For now it is important to point out that some coping strategies can be useful, others can be disasterous, and still others fall somewhere in between, where they serve merely to delay the inevitable. For example, Charlie's coping strategy after his hospitalization involved a total rejection of his creative abilities and skills. We can easily conclude that while this prevented a further disaster it was almost certainly not the best strategy for Charlie because his present occupation does not begin to fulfill his potential.

In Carol's case she seemed to have coped adequately because as it turned out she herself probably would never have been content as a teacher. On the other hand, we have encountered numerous individuals who were gifted and excited about their profession, but who were burning out because they happened to be located in an organization that did not provide the proper environment or reward system for their efforts. In these cases a lateral job change in which these individuals continue in their professional activity in a different organization is a much better coping strategy than leaving the profession.

In still other cases the problem is not specific to a given organization but is indigenous to the work itself. Here much more subtle and complex coping strategies would be called for. These will be discussed subsequently.

Focus on the environment

Why do some people quit, others stay, and yet others grow with the experience? The specific answer depends on a complex combination of variables involving the person and the environment. For example, in a management workshop we conducted in Israel, we found that the greatest need shared by all the participating managers was a need for freedom on the job—to do things the way they felt things should be done. Situations in which that freedom was undermined were intolerable for them and they said they would rather quit than stay. Because they were not willing or able to accept the lack of autonomy as inevitable, it is unlikely that any of them would end up as deadwood in the organization. On the orther hand, in a social service organization in the United States we found many workers experiencing prolonged tedium but staying on as deadwood, because working for government provided them with the security of a good pension plan. Their need for security was greater than their need for control and autonomy.

People experience tedium and burnout differently and react differently to the experience because people also approach the inevitable stresses of life and work in different ways. Some people seem dramatically affected by nearly everything. These are people who view the world as a place dominated by evil forces where one is best prepared if always ready for the worst. Each problem is exaggerated and seen as evidence that things are bad and will naturally become worse. Other people believe that when left to themselves, things will naturally turn out for the best. The most important thing to these people is being happy and experiencing life to its fullest. Because they can recognize the real tragedies, no trivia are exaggerated or perceived as traumatic. An individual process of cognitive appraisal mediates for all people the effect of environmental pressures.

Cognitive appraisal is a key concept in the stress research of Richard Lazarus,[28] a psychology professor at the University of California. According to Lazarus, all emotions depend on cognitive appraisals (in terms of their significance for one's well-being) of transactions with the environment. Appraisal takes five key forms. A transaction with the environment may be (1) relevant or irrelevant to one's well-being, (2) already harmful, (3) potentially harmful, (4) challenging, or (5) potentially positive in outcome. The same stimulus configuration can produce quite different patterns of stress response in different individuals, depending on their history and characteristics. Thus, one person may react with anger, another with depression, and another with fear or guilt. Still others may feel challenged rather than threatened under comparable conditions. For example, one person may cope with terminal illness by denial and another by depression; one person may handle an insult by ignoring it and another by getting angry and planning revenge. In order to understand such patterning and the stabilities of emotion and coping within an individual, Lazarus examined what mediates between the stimulus configuration and the reaction patterns. In an organism with highly symbolic thought such as man, he reasoned, the most important of such mediators are bound to be cognitive ones.

Individual differences mediate tedium and burnout. People differ in their hierarchy of needs, their view of the world, their appraisal of stresses, and their ability to cope. These and other intervening variables can influence when burnout will occur, how long it will last, and how severe its consequences will be. But the causes primarily reside in the environment rather than in the individual. For example, organizations can encourage choices of quitting upwards, lateral job changes, or quitting all together—depending on the stresses they impose, the rewards they provide, and their flexibility. If the rewards are very high, people may stay even in otherwise stressful occupations. Similarly, the availability of jobs in a certain field enables people with a high need for variety to change their job setting with the first signs of burnout. The point we stress is that if chronic pressures are put on the individual without adequate support, everyone will experience a certain degree of physical, emotional, and mental exhaustion. Thus a focus, on the environment is more useful, both theoretically and practically, than a focus on the individual.

The environment consists of the settings in which the individual is embedded, including the occupational, organizational, social, home, and recreational environments. As much as enviroments differ, common stresses can be identified.[29] All occupational groups that participated in our workshops were able to identify both a shared most stressful and a shared most rewarding feature of their work. For people in the human services, the shared pressures were often emotional, the result of working with the sick, the needy, and the maladjusted. In large organizations, clerks and administrators noted mainly mental pressures resulting from overloads of paper work, routine tasks, red tape, and administrative inertia. Fire fighters, police officers, and soldiers reported tedium caused by physical pressures such as fatiguing exercises or dangerous work situations. Many working women described guilt and anxiety over conflicts between their work and home obligations. People in business were often stressed by the pressure of competition and the need to make important decisions without sufficient time or information. In general these are oversimplifications of occupational stresses, and the chapters devoted to some of these occupational groups will provide a more detailed account of their specific problems.

Just as habitual ways of looking at the world mediate the effects of tedium and burnout for the individual, the organizational setting in which a person works mediates their effect for the occupational group. The organizational environment involves the physical setting and, more importantly, the social setting. Working in a small enterprise is different from working in a large organization. Even among similar organizations there are differences in the problems individuals face and in the prevalence of employees' tedium.

Two family service agencies we worked with had a similar number of psychiatrists, clinical psychologists, social workers, and trainees. Both were located in suburban communities and served a similar clientele. In one agency most employees did not stay longer than two or three years. There was a high level of absenteeism; employees came to work late and left early. Their home visits tended to be very short but the route to them as long as possible. The atmosphere in the agency was hostile and competitive. Staff members were reserved and cautious, especially about admitting less-than-perfect knowledge. Even students who interned in the agency were criticized for asking questions. No one dared admit not knowing how to deal with a case, and staff meetings were "crocodile sessions" with people "biting" each other. However, in the other agency professionals stayed for many years. They felt the agency to be a "home," a warm, supportive, and exciting place. In this agency even the chief psychologist presented cases to the staff for suggestions and feedback.

Tedium and burnout may occur as a result of a stressful organizational setting, a combination of stresses particular to a certain profession, or certain stressful role definitions. The absence of positive aspects in the work environment also makes burnout and tedium more likely to occur. Variety, significance, and autonomy are examples of positive conditions the lack of which was found[30] to be a major contributor to tedium and disatisfaction from life and work. These positive variables when present can serve as buffers against burnout.

Burnout and other concepts

Almost everyone will burn out given a certain combination of environmental conditions. The people who start out with the highest ideals (unless they managed to develop effective coping strategies on their own) are likely to experience the most severe burnout. This prerequisite, initial idealism and excitement, differentiates burnout from the job alienation of blue-collar workers. Alienation can happen to people who have never expected anything from their work except a paycheck. Burnout most often happens to people who initially cared the least about their paychecks.

Burnout is a social-psychological concept and thus different from a concept such as clinical depression. In depression the individual and the individual's personal history are the source of symptoms and the focus of therapy. In burnout the search for the antecedents of symptoms and modes of coping is located in the environment. In all but the most extreme cases, in which the individual burning out becomes depressed, the experience is seen within a social rather than an individual perspective.

In burned out organizations everybody is tired, but, of course, burnout is more than simple fatigue. Obviously people who work hard are going to get fatigued. For example, we once interviewed a high-ranking Israeli combat officer who held a very exciting job of great power, challenge, and significance. He told us that at the end of his full day (frequently lasting from twelve to twenty hours) he felt totally exhausted, and yet he referred to it as "a good exhaustion," full of feelings of power and accomplishment—like a juggler who manages to keep twelve balls in the air all at once. Obviously this is not burnout. Why? He was clearly not experiencing the key elements of burnout—the feelings of helplessness, hopelessness, and entrapment. Indeed, people burn out not only from being overstressed with a great deal of work to do, but they can also burn out from being underchallenged, from having less to do than they have training to do; from not really feeling well utilized.

The reasons for writing this book

While conducting burnout seminars, lectures, and workshops, we discovered that merely identifying the concept of burnout had therapeutic value for participants. One participant's reaction was typical: "So it's burnout! And I thought it was only me! I thought there was something seriously wrong with me!" Participants felt their guilt and confusion replaced by relief simply by labeling this phenomenon as burnout.

In our society it is often undesirable to admit one's limitations, vulnerabilities, ignorance, and problems, especially in one's work. A professional is expected to be impeccable and in control. When problems do arise most people feel at fault and hide the problems from others, feeling that "everybody else" is coping effectively and they alone are failing. The result is what social psychologists call "the fallacy of uniqueness" or "pluralistic ignorance": the individual's false assumption that he or she is the only one responding in this way.

An example will illustrate the impact of a burnout workshop on breaking this fallacy of uniqueness. Welfare workers, like the nurses described in Chapter 1, are particularly vulnerable to burnout, especially those dealing with emotionally demanding cases such as those involving child abuse and neglect. Many welfare workers who choose that work are idealistic, but in a short time, usually a year or two, they begin burning out: the pain of watching the abused children is particularly debilitating because these case workers care so deeply about them. When the pressures become unbearable the workers who are caring and involved begin to protect themselves against their pain by detaching themselves from the situation. They may care less about individual cases, they may even resent the very people they once wanted to help; all these are forms of self-protection. But their resentment breeds guilt and shame because of their idealistic self-images. As with the nurses working on a terminal cancer ward, this becomes a vicious circle: burnout produces resentment which produces guilt which increases burnout. In this situation welfare workers may attribute their unhappiness to personal reasons because they were not trained to look for causes of their personal distress in the environment, and, not having obvious external causes for their unhappiness, it is all the more unbearable because it appears inescapable.[31] The sense of isolation increases the unhappiness, the shame, and the guilt. It also increases each case worker's efforts to hide from others his or her own burnout. A workshop can break the cycle.

When people get together in burnout workshops and are given the opportunity to share their experiences, they break this fallacy of uniqueness, this pluralistic ignorance. They discover that they are not alone, that nearly everyone in their field is having some of the same feelings of burnout or tedium. They shift from searching for answers by finding deficiencies inside themselves to looking for answers in their work situation.

When participants realized that often the most committed workers burn out most severely, it freed them to admit their burnout without shame or embarrassment. In one study[32] we found that people admit higher levels of tedium after finding out about the relationship between tedium and initial idealism. In this study, which was carried out in Israel, sixty-six managers who simply filled out the tedium questionnaire were compared to twenty-one managers who were first told that "the most idealistic burnout most" and then asked to fill out the questionnaire. Results indicated that the second group reported a significantly higher degree of tedium. The mere realization that almost everybody burns out to some degree often caused excitement and a release of energy among workshop participants. All the energy that had been used for hiding the symptoms of burnout could now be used for better coping.

In our work we had two focuses: research on the antecedents and correlates of tedium and burnout, and group work aimed at better coping with these experiences. This book combines both these features; its main purpose is to introduce the concepts of burnout and tedium in the hope that people burning out will realize they are not alone. Another purpose (to which the next chapters are devoted) is to describe common antecedents of burnout and tedium in social service work, in complex organizations, and in women. Focusing on the antecedents and correlates of the experience can suggest both causes and coping devices. We devote three chapters to "what to do about it" because we strongly believe that it is not enough to be aware of a problem. It is not enough to identify the phenomenon and its causes. The crucial step is to find and apply solutions.

Self-diagnosis

You can compute your tedium score by completing the following questionnaire. You can use it for diagnosing how you feel about your work or for diagnosing how you feel about your life. You can use it for diagnosing how you feel in general or for diagnosing how you feel today.

How often do you have any of the following experiences? Please use the scale.

1	2	3	4	5	6	7
Never	Once or twice	Rarely	Sometimes	Often	Usually	Always

___ 1. Being tired
___ 2. Feeling depressed
___ 3. Having a good day
___ 4. Being physically exhausted
___ 5. Being emotionally exhausted
___ 6. Being happy
___ 7. Being "wiped out"
___ 8. Feeling "burned out"
___ 9. Being unhappy
___ 10. Feeling rundown

___ 11. Feeling trapped
___ 12. Feeling worthless
___ 13. Being weary
___ 14. Being troubled
___ 15. Feeling disillusioned and resentful about people
___ 16. Feeling weak and helpless
___ 17. Feeling hopeless
___ 18. Feeling rejected
___ 19. Feeling optimistic
___ 20. Feeling energetic
___ 21. Feeling anxious

Computation of score:

Add the values you wrote next to the following items:

1, 2, 4, 5, 7, 8, 9, 10, 11, 12, 13, 14, 15, 16, 17, 18, 21, (A)_____.

Add the values you wrote next to the following items:

3, 6, 19, 20 (B)_____ , subtract (B) from 32 (C) _____.

Add A and C (D) _____.

Divide D by 21 _____. This is your tedium score.

Of the thousands who responded to this self-diagnosis instrument, none scored either 1 or 7. The reason is obvious. It is unlikely for one to be in a state of eternal euphoria implied by the score 1, and it is unlikely the a person who scores 7 will be able to cope with the world well enough to participate in a burnout workshop or a research project.

If your score is between 2 and 3 you are doing well. The only suggestion we make is that you go over your score sheet to be sure you have been honest in your responses.

If your score is between 3 and 4, it would be wise for you to examine your work and life and evaluate your priorities and consider possible changes. If your score is higher than 4, your are experiencing burnout or tedium to the extent that it is mandatory that you do something about it. A score of higher than five indicates an acute state and a need for immediate help.

Notes

1. A. D. Kanner, D. Kafry, and A. Pines, "Lack of Positive Conditions as a Source of Stress," *Journal of Human Stress* 4, no. 4 (1978): 33–39.
2. For a detailed account of this research see Appendix II, "The Research."
3. This research was inspired by Christina Maslach and described in: C. Maslach and A. Pines, "Burnout, the Loss of Human Caring," in A. Pines and C. Maslach, *Experiencing Social Psychology*, (New York: Random House, 1979), pp. 246–252; C. Maslach and A. Pines, "The Burnout Syndrome in Day Care Settings," *Child Care Quarterly* 6 (Summer 1977): 100–113; A. Pines, "Burnout and Life Tedium in Three Generations of Professional Women." Paper presented at the Annual Convention of the American Psychological Association, San Francisco, 1977; A. Pines and C. Maslach, "Characteristics of Staff Burnout in Mental Health Settings," *Hospital and Community Psychiatry* 29 (1978): 233–237; A Pines and C. Maslach, "Combating Burnout in One Child Care Center: A Case Study," *Child Care Quarterly* 9 (Spring 1980): 5–16; A. Pines, D. Kafry, and D. Etzion, "Job Stress from a Cross-cultural Perspective," in *Burnout in the Helping Professions*, ed. K. Reid (Kalamazoo: Western Michigan University Press, 1980).
4. For a more detailed account of this group work see Appendix I, "Burnout Workshops."
5. J. J. Freudenberger, "Burnout: Occupational Hazard of the Child Care Worker," *Child Care Quarterly* 6, no. 2 (Spring 1980): 5–16 1977): 90–99.

6. K. L. Armstrong, "How Can We Avoid Burnout?" *Child Abuse and Neglect: Issues on Innovation and Implementation*, DHEW Publication no. (OHOS) 78-30148, 2, (1978): 230–238.

7. In our studies the correlations between tedium and sleep disturbances ranged from $r = .28$ ($p < .01$) to $r = .47$ ($p < .001$). The correlations between tedium and physical health ranged from $r = -.20$ to $r = -.46$ ($p < .001$).

8. In a study involving 130 subjects who responded to a hopelessness questionnaire (A. T. Beck, A. Weissman, D. Lester, and L. Trenxler, "The Measurement of Pessimism: The Hopelessness Scale," *Journal of Consulting and Clinical Psychology* 42 [1974]: 861–865), the correlation between the combined tedium score and hopelessness was $r = .59$ $p < .001$.

9. In one study it was found that for men (n = 33) the correlation between tedium and loneliness was $r = .40$. For women (n = 73), the correlation was $r = .27$. Both are statistically significant at the .01 level.

10. We examined the correlation between tedium and satisfaction from self, from work, and from life in most of our samples. The correlation between tedium and satisfaction from work ranged from $-.24$ to 63 (with an average correlation of $-.45$). The correlation between tedium and satisfaction from life ranged from $-.32$ to $-.70$ (with an average correlation of $-.51$). The correlation between tedium and satisfaction from self ranged from $-.32$ to $-.73$ (with an average correlation of $-.51$). All the correlations were statistically significant.

11. For example, V. Bernard, P. Ottenberg, and F. Redle, "Dehumanization: A Composite Psychological Defense in Relation to Modern War," in *Behavioral Science and Human Survival*, ed. M. Schwebel (Palo Alto: Science and Behavior Books, 1965); M . C. Kelman, "Violence without Moral Restraint: Reflections on the Dehumanization of Victims and Victimizers," *Journal of Social Issues* 29 (1973): 25–61; D. J. Vail, *Dehumanization and the Institutional Career* (Springfield, Ill.: Charles C. Thomas, 1966); A. Pines and T. Solomon, "Perception of Self as a Mediator of the Dehumanization Process," *Personality and Social Psychology Bulletin* 3, no. 2 (1977): 219–223; P. G. Zimbardo, "The Human Choice: Individuation, Reason and Order versus Deindividuation, Impulse and Chaos," in *Nebraska Symposium on Motivation*: 1969, ed. W. J. Arnold and D. Levine (Lincoln, Neb.: University of Nebraska Press, 1970).

12. M. Buber, *I and Thou*, 2d ed. (New York: Scribner's, 1958).

13. In a sample of 129 social service workers the correlation between tedium and wanting to leave the job was .58 $p < .01$. In another sample of 181 Israeli telephone operators the correlation between tedium and tardiness (the number of days a year in which employees were late for work) was .30 $p < .001$. The study was done by J. Golan. Correlations of burnout

with new job searches ($r = .49$), extension of work breaks ($r = .47$), days absent ($r = .52$), and days late ($r = .37$) were also reported by J. W. Jones in "The Staff Burnout Scale: A Validity Study," paper presented at the 52d annual meeting of the Midwestern Psychological Association, St. Louis, May 1–3, 1980.

14. Armstrong, "How Can We Avoid Burnout?"
15. W. D. Gentry, S. B. Foster, and S. Fruehling, "Psychological Response to Situational Stress in Intensive Care Nursing," *Heart and Lung* 1 (1972): 793–796.
16. A. H. Stanton and M. S. Schwarts, *The Mental Hospital: A Study of Institutional Participation in Psychiatric Illness and Treatment* (New York: Basic Books, 1954).
17. See note 3 above.
18. See note 5 above.
19. H. J. Freudenberger, "The Staff Burnout Syndrome in Alternative Institutions," *Psychotherapy: Theory, Research and Practice* 12A (Spring 1975): 73–82.
20. The correlation between self-assessment and assessment of tedium by colleagues for the two samples combines was $r = .37, p < .001$.
21. J. P. Lysaught, *An Abstract for Action. National Commission for the Study of Nursing and Nursing Education* (New York: McGraw-Hill, 1970); also, Mitzi Duxbury of the School of Nursing at the University of Minnesota is currently conducting a study of turnover and burnout among nurses in intensive care units all over the United States.
22. C. H. Kempe, "Child Protective Services: Where Have We Been? What are We Now and Where are We Going?" *Child Abuse and Neglect: Issues on Innovation and Implementation,* DHEW Publication no. 78-30147, 5 (1978): 19–28.
23. Freudenberger, "Staff Burnout Syndrome."
24. I. Adizes, "Mismanagement Styles," *California Management Review* 19, no. 2 (1976): 5–30.
25. Martin Lipp, M.D., has also described this process in the chapter on coping and occupational hazards of physicianhood in his book *Respectful Treatment—The Human Side of Medical Care* (New York: Harper and Row, 1977), pp. 206–215.
26. Adizes, "Mismanagement Styles."
27. A. Camus, *The Myth of Sisyphus* (New York: Vintage Books, 1955).
28. R. S. Lazarus, *Psychological Stress and the Coping Process* (New York: McGraw-Hill, 1966).
29. Such variables as overload, conflicting demands, decision load, and guilt are examples of stresses shared by most people. For example, in one study involving 724 human service professionals, the correlation between tedium and overload was $r = .35$; Tedium and conflicting demands was $r = .31$, decision load $r = .30$, and guilt $r = .42$ (all correlations are statistically significant).

30. For example, in one study involving 198 mental retardation workers the correlation found between tedium and variety was $r = -.23$, tedium and autonomy $r = -.32$, tedium and signifficance $r = -.18$ (all correlations are statistically significant).

31. B. Russell, *The Conquest of Happiness* (New York: Liveright, 1971), p. 16.

32. The study was done in collaboration with the Israeli psychologist Dalia Etzion. The mean tedium for the sixty-six managers who simply filled out the tedium questionnaire was $\bar{x} = 2.8$. The mean tedium for the twenty-one managers who were first told that "the most idealistic burnout most" and then asked to fill out the questionnaire was $\bar{x} = 3.5$. The difference is significant at .01 level.

part two

Causes of burnout and tedium

3

Burnout among people in
the helping professions

Sue was 32, bright, warm, sensitive. She wanted to "help people" and
to "make the world a better place," but, although she received a
master's degree in social welfare, nothing in her background or her
formal training prepared her for the stresses she would face in her
work.

Sue's first job was in a residential program for psychiatric patients
who were making the transition from hospital life back into the
community. After three years Sue felt she had to leave the job. "I got
tired of working with chronic patients," she said. "I was still interested
in being a therapist but there was a limit to the amount of therapy that
could be done with these patients. Work with them involved mostly
maintaining them on medication and helping them to manage in the
community. They were very needy people, very dependent, and it was
draining. I did see some changes with a few of the young clients, but
for the most part the improvement I saw was miniscule." Sue felt she
was ready for a change.

Sue accepted a job as family counselor for a police department.
Her unit was responsible for responding to domestic disturbance calls
and for training police officers in family crisis intervention. "In the
beginning it was really fascinating. It was exciting, pioneering terri-
tory. We had a lot of publicity. There were T.V. shows, newspaper
articles, and a film. But there were also many problems."

Sue felt that she needed to distance herself from some of the situations she worked with. "Part of it was in self-protection because some of the things were so grim. I saw *so much* horrible stuff. Not only domestic violence, but child abuse and horrible ways that people lived, going into filthy homes, seeing so many crazy people who weren't coping. It was just too much. After a while I had to shut some of it off."

Sue felt a sense of frustration and futility.

> The situations started looking so much alike to me. I could never see changes. It was always the same people, in the same situations. I would get angry when I'd go in. After a while, I stopped listening. I stopped being empathetic. I had to lose my compassion in order to survive emotionally. It wasn't a job where you got many thanks from the clients. It was a vicious circle; because the more angry I became, the less I felt like putting out in the counseling sessions, so of course the less happened with the clients.

Sue also felt isolated and frustrated on her job. She felt there was no flexibility and no encouragement of personal development by the department or by her boss. The atmosphere in the office was one of suspicion; staff members were reporting each other and Sue felt betrayed by people she had been fond of. "I was so upset I got to the point that I refused to associate with anyone on the staff. I saw things that were wrong and unethical, things that had to do with basic values that were more important to me than anything else. It was very distrubing to me, but I was getting no support from within the staff or the department. I felt alone in it. That was the hardest part."

After two years Sue noticed the signs of burnout. Her response was to work harder. She started teaching at a community college one course each quarter. "I had to get some rewards so I could feel like I was competent in some way. I derived a lot of gratification from my teaching." Teaching involved much time, little money, and no security, but there were intrinsic rewards. "I could see students learning and getting excited. I was teaching things that I enjoyed talking about." Sue tried to balance these rewards against the stress of her job. But with two jobs she had little time off. "One of the patterns I always had was that when things are going on that I can't cope with, or don't want to face, I get even busier. I would work the whole day, teach from seven to ten, and get back home at eleven at night too tired and too depressed to sleep."

Living this way increased Sue's burnout. "I didn't want one more person to ask anything of me. Instead of listening to my friends and trying to be helpful I would feel like screaming. It seemed like I cried the whole time. I was really depressed."

In her work Sue tried to avoid contact with her clients.

> Sometimes I would be late for home appointments. I would make stops on my way to home visits and do my errands just to have time that had noting to do with my work. I sometimes spaced out during interviews with clients and I started referring people to other agencies or counselors. I would have a negative attitude before I even went in; I would be very curt, with no warmth at all. In retrospect I think that I was fighting to create this distance so the clients wouldn't like me. I thought that if I wasn't helpful and I wasn't sympathetic, when I asked if they wanted another appointment, they would say no.

One of the ways Sue dealt with her burnout was humor. "I felt that if I couldn't at least laugh at myself and my work, I was really in trouble. So I did a lot of it. I would make fun of the clients, not maliciously, but as a kind of catharsis. This constantly got me into trouble."

Sue felt she could not take any more, and after four years with the police department she quit her job. She had to sort out what she wanted to do with her life. She knew she was burned out as a public servant. "I don't have any more to give to needy, dependent, victimized people. I have done my stint as a 'do-gooder.' I have really paid my dues." Sue wanted to use her teaching and analytical skills. She wanted to work in pleasant surroundings with people who enjoyed their work. She looked for work in a company that encouraged creativity and was both supportive and challenging. After a long search, she found such a job.

A brief case analysis

Sue's case presents many of the elements that characterize burnout of professionals in the human services. She chose social welfare because she wanted to help people in need and, as is typical, she did not receive any formal preparation for the inevitable job stresses. Sue burned out on her first job after three years and on her second job after two years. This time period before burnout has been reported by many of the human service professionals with whom we have worked.

The causes of Sue's burnout are common. In her first job burnout was mainly a result of the futility of working with needy and chronically ill people and seeing little change or improvement. In the second job it resulted from the hopeless situations she encountered daily and the interpersonal conflicts on the job. Both of these are frequent causes of burnout. Sue's responses to the experience of burnout itself are typical: the initial flight to "workaholism" and the subsequent exhaustion, emotional attrition, anger at coworkers, and resentment toward clients. She felt she had paid her dues as a "do-gooder." This is also common among many formerly idealistic human service professionals. Often they turn to teaching as a way to replenish themselves; the rewards of facilitating change and growth seem more accessible in a teaching career. We stress the typicality of Sue's experience to emphasize that it was primarily the emotional demands imposed by her work, and not personal idiosyncracies, that caused her burnout.

Three common antecedents of burnout in the human services

In modern industrial societies professional organizations perform many of the functions traditionally met by the extended family or the community. This is particularly true in the treatment of personal and interpersonal problems. The result is a large number of medical, educational, social, and psychological services. These human services are performed by millions of professionals who share three basic characteristics: (1) they perform emotionally taxing work; (2) they share certain personality characteristics that made them choose human service as a career; and (3) they share a "client-centered" orientation. These three characteristics are the classic antecedents of burnout.

Emotionally taxing work

In the human service professions, people work with others in emotionally demanding situations over long periods of time. The professionals are exposed to their clients' psychological, social, and physical problems and are expected to be both skilled and personally concerned.

A job in which a person helps others involves a certain degree of stress. The specific degree and kind of stress depend on the particular demands of that job and on the resources available to the professional. Each occupation has its unique pressures, anxieties, and conflicts inherent to the work itself and to the context in which the work is done.

EXAMPLE: EMOTIONAL STRESS IN MEDICAL SERVICES

Medical personnel encounter some intensely emotional situations. These can be especially difficult among physicians. According to Harold Lief and Renee Fox, who studied the psychological basis of medical practice, these emotion-laden experiences include "exploring, examining, and cutting into the human body; dealing with fears, anger, sense of helplessness, and despair of patients; meeting emergency situations; accepting the limitations of medical science in dealing with chronic or incurable disease; being confronted with death itself."[1] Another stress for medical professionals is the knowledge that they are going to fail to conquer death and disease. Other stresses shared by doctors and nurses include the fear of contracting disease by contact with contagious patients, talking to patients about marital and sexual problems, and carrying out physical examinations.

As Dr. Daniel Federman, the chairman of Stanford's Department of Medicine, described it: "Within a few minutes you are granted physical access to the patient with an intimacy and a potential for embarrassment unique in human relationships. The patient offers you vulnerability, accepting medication from you, physical abuse, even the ultimate subservience, the unconsciousness of general anesthesia, and physical alteration of the body through surgery."[2]

Dr. Donald Oken, Chairman of Psychiatry at the State University of New York, noted that providing medical services requires the professional to be regularly exposed to the most forbidden aspects of human functioning, including the sight, sound, and touch of all parts of the nude body and its products, even in private or unpleasant states. Doctors and nurses are also exposed to the most personal intimacies and conflicts and are frequently the focus of intense, primitive transference reactions, both affectionate and hostile, to which they dare not respond in kind.[3]

EXAMPLE: EMOTIONAL STRESS IN EDUCATION

Teachers burn out at all levels of the educational system, from kindergarten to college. One of the antecedents of burnout shared by many educators is the assumption that if students do not learn it is because the teacher did not teach. This assumption is frequently false and is the basis of unrealistic expectations that educators share with students, parents, administration, and the public. These expectations are a source of frustration, guilt, and a sense of failure.

A second stress for many teachers is maintaining discipline in the classroom. Nationwide studies show that since 1972 classroom murders have increased by 18 percent, rapes by 40 percent, robberies by 37 percent, and physical assaults on teachers by 77 percent.[4] The Senate subcommittee on juvenile delinquency reported that, during the academic year 1975, vandalism and violence in school continued to increase, annual destruction of school properties exceeded 600 million dollars, and 70,000 classroom teachers reported serious injuries from physical assault by students. The result for teachers in inner-city schools, where the problem of classroom violence is most prevalent, may be "teacher's combat neurosis."[5]

Teachers may also have to deal with psychological and emotional stress. At all levels of the education system teachers face uninterested, unmotivated students. The teachers may feel alone in their struggle to maintain discipline and minimal standards of education without the support of parents or administration. These problems are particularly painful for those who see their major role as that of educators but find themselves instead policing, testing, and physically managing their students.

EXAMPLE: EMOTIONAL STRESSES IN
SOCIAL AND PSYCHOLOGICAL SERVICES

In many social service occupations the danger of burnout and emotional exhaustion results from the constant demand to give emotionally on the job. As Alfred Kadushin, a leading social work scholar, noted, the flow of emotional supplies goes only one way—from the workers to the client—and may lead to the emotional depletion in the workers. The most important tool for professionals providing psychological help is the professionals themselves. Workers may feel that failure with a client reflects both on their competence as technicians and on their competence as people.[6]

Jobs that are closely allied to life may make the separation of work from other areas of life exceptionally difficult. The interpenetration of life and work, according to Kadushin, is one of the most significant occupational problems faced by the worker dealing with emotionally evocative experiences. Exposure to others' intense feelings is a stress peculiar to the task of extending psychological help.[7] It is, in a sense, an occupational hazard.[8] When the emotional stresses inherent in providing social and psychological help are not acknowledged and dealt with, they often lead to burnout.

OTHER OCCUPATION-SPECIFIC STRESSES

All work with people involves some degree of stress. Certain categories of human services, such as medical, educational, and social-psychological services, share particular kinds of emotional stresses. Specific occupations within each of these categories have their unique stresses.

For Sue, whom we met at the beginning of this chapter, the main emotional pressure in her job as a family counselor resulted from witnessing domestic violence. This pressure was compounded by the fact that she could not change the destructive living conditions of the families she saw.

Nurses who work in children's leukemia wards experience great emotional stress in dealing daily with the pain of their young patients. They feel helpless against the unfairness of inevitable death. Nurses who work with chronic patients talked about the emotional stress of the right-to-die issue. One nurse told of hurrying with emergency equipment to fight for the life of an 87-year-old woman who had previously begged to be allowed to die. Dialysis workers discussed the difficulty of accepting patients' decisions to give up on life. A teacher of blind, deaf, and retarded children talked about the drain involved in working with youngsters who show little progress. "After months of teaching Sandy to tie her shoe laces, she had an epileptic seizure and forgot everything," recounted the teacher. A high-ranking Army officer talked about the stress of having limited time and information to make decisions that can cost people's lives. A priest who had survived a tornado told of having to explain God's will to the mourners in his parish, when he himself felt he could not understand it. A policeman talked about his helpless rage after visiting the home of an abused child. He said he knew he was leaving the child in danger, but there was nothing he could do legally to prevent it.

In each of these jobs the emotional stress is inherent because the work is with people. Yet each "people profession" has its own unique stresses that contribute to burnout.

The people who chose to work in the human services

Another source of stress stems from the special characteristics of the professionals themselves. Most times those who choose to help others as a profession are individuals who are particularly sensitive toward others. If emotional arousal is a taxing experience for any human being, it is particularly disruptive to people who choose such work; these people tend to have especially great empathy to the suffering of others.

Occupational identity can be enhanced by the homogeneity of people selecting an occupation. The nature of the occupational task acts as a screening device, attracting people with particular kinds of personality attributes. Most human service professionals are essentially humanitarian. Their dominant approach is to help people in trouble. They tend to be oriented more toward people than toward things.[9] Social workers, for instance, tend to value themselves most as sympathetic, understanding, unselfish, and helpful to others.[10] In almost every encounter we had with human service professionals, we asked participants to list their reasons for choosing their profession. With almost no exception, whatever their occupation, their lists included such items as "I like people," "I am a people's kind of person," "All my life I wanted to work with people."

People who enter human service careers have other traits that make them vulnerable to the emotional stresses inherent to their professions. For example, in one language school preparing foreign students for American colleges, all teachers and staff had themselves been foreigners in another country. They were all sympathetic to the difficulties of their foreign students, but they still had difficulty dealing with some of the cultural behaviors of their students. Similarly, empathy hampers people who choose to work with children and the elderly. Aides in homes for the elderly must deal with the thoughts, "This could be my mother" or "What if this happens to me?" Professionals working with children often report the emotional pain associated with the thought, "That could have been my child." They also must face their limitations in helping suffering or dying children. Some professionals who work with child abuse have had personal experiences that motivated their choice of career. Similarly people working with alcoholics are sometimes themselves recovered alcoholics or had an alcoholic parent. This personal history serves to intensify both their empathy and their pain.

A "client-centered" orientation

A third antecedent of burnout is the "client-centered" orientation that characterizes human service professions almost exclusively.

In a client-centered orientation, the focus is on the people receiving service. The professionals' role of help, understanding, and support is defined by the clients' needs. The professionals' presence is justified only as long as they continue to serve. Feelings are legitimate only when expressed by the clients.

Most human relationships are symmetrical, but the therapeutic relationship is not; it is complementary: the professionals give and the clients receive. Kadushin sees social service workers as responsive to a "dedicatory ethic" that elevates service motives.[11] In many of these professions, work is seen not as a job but as a calling, and the reward is supposed to be inherent in giving.

In scientific literature and course material relevant to human service fields, little attention is given to the emotional stresses experienced by the professionals. Instead the focus is almost exclusively on the recipients of services and their problems. Thus, in training, the students learn the implicit lesson that it is illegitimate for them to have needs while in the professional role. In her book, "Reality Shock," Marlene Kramer, a nursing professor, writes about the devastating impact work has on unprepared novice nurses.[12] The reality shock often results in an induction crises which refers to the ubiquitous finding that turnover is particularly high in the first few months on the job.[13]

Training schools deal almost exclusively with cognitive material, and traditionally no attention has been given to developing skills for dealing with people or with the stresses experienced by the professionals. More recently there has been a trend to provide practitioners with more concrete skills and practical training.[14] And yet there is still no mention of the stresses the workers should expect and how to deal with them. Even in modern, more enlightened, training manuals in which the professionals are asked to engage in role-taking activities (these activities involve taking the *role of the client* as a way of building empathy), never is it the case that these training exercises are directed toward building empathy for the plight of the professionals who are forever giving and never receiving.

The absurdity of an orientation that is exclusively client centered was dramatically demonstrated in a case reported by Martin Lipp in his book *The Wounded Healer*.[15] It was the case of a psychiatrist who committed suicide, which according to Doctor Lipp, a psychiatrist himself, is not that unusual; many psychiatrists commit suicide. But it was nevertheless a shock to all his friends and especially to his colleagues who, despite their expertise in recognizing depression, did not notice anything unusual about his behavior prior to the suicide. He was young, at the prime of his life. Even though he went through a painful divorce, he seemed to be doing well. He was very successful professionally, and a brilliant future lay ahead of him. No one suspected he was as depressed as his suicide note indicated. The only people who seemed to have any indication of what he was going through were his patients. One patient said she had noticed that he was upset and sensed that something was very wrong. So she asked him about it. The psychiatrist's response was to smile at her gently and say that her job was to look after herself, not after him. Even at his most desperate hour he could not break the client-doctor relationship and take the hand that was offered to rescue him.

A client-centered orientation defines an asymmetry in the therapeutic relationship and can become stressful for the professional providing help. Its effects are doubled when combined with the emotional intensity characterizing most human service work and with the selective sample of people who chose to work in the human services. And since all three elements are present in nearly all human service work, they make the process of burnout almost inevitable.

The goal: detached concern

Human service professionals struggle to obtain "detached concern." Harold Lief and Renee Fox coined the term "detached concern" for a stance in which "the empathic physician is sufficiently detached or objective in his attitudes toward the patient to exercise sound medical judgment and keep his equanimity, yet he also has enough concern for the patient to give him sensitive understanding care." In this way "the patient, rather than just his liver, heart or even psyche, is the concern of the physician."[16]

Professions differ in the ideal balance between detachment and concern. Most people agree that it would be inappropriate for a bank teller to inquire what people intend to do with the money they withdraw from their accounts, but most people become distressed when a physician treats them primarily as their disease.

Detached concern is a balance that is hard to achieve and hard to maintain. There is the danger of becomeing overly involved, losing objectivity, and therefore the ability to help. "Once you are in the shoes of your patient, you cannot possibly be of any help," said one clinical psychologist, "because he has been in his shoes all along, and obviously not done too well. In order to help you have to be able to see more and understand more than the person who seeks your help." At the same time, the opposite danger of complete detachment is always present and with it the loss of concern and the dehumanizing attitudes that characterize burnout. With excessive detachment there is not enough involvement to motivate successful help. Research has shown that the clients themselves also demand a certain balance between personal support and understanding on the one hand, and expertise guidance and decisiveness on the other.[17]

Within the same organization some professionals need to detach themselves more than others. For example, in one mental hospital, psychologists and social workers were burning out on the locked ward because relationships with patients were so difficult and changes so minimal. One physician, however, loved working there. He said that the psychotic patients in their drugged state were easier to work with than his regular patients. "Usually I have to small-talk with patients and be careful about their feelings, which I hate. With these guys I didn't have to talk or be concerned about their feelings. I could concentrate on their sick organs which is really why I was there to begin with."

In our experience the most idealistic and highly committed "social servants" are the ones who have the greatest difficulty detaching themselves and as a result tend to burn out relatively soon. They end up detaching too much as a defense against the power of their own emotions. Psychologist Bruno Bettelheim describes that process:

> One becomes worried about being drawn into the maelstrom of the patient's anger, anxiety, despair; fear for one's own sanity emerges; one may even begin to question which of their delusions are delusions, and which may be reasonable. The most "natural" defense against this is a near automatic response of buttressing one's defenses to avoid the impact of such experiences; and of closing one's heart, if not one's mind, to those who apparently threaten to overwhelm us with the power of their emotions.[18]

Human service professionals may attempt to achieve the ideal balance of detached concern in many different ways. Some try physical withdrawal, some try emotional withdrawal, and some try mental withdrawal. Often people use elements of all three. Unfortunately, as the following examples show, the mode of detachment of professional uses for self-protection is frequently felt as dehumanizing by the recipients.

Physical withdrawal

Some of the most difficult jobs are those in which professionals cannot distance themselves even after working hours. For many physicians and psychiatrists one of the drawbacks of private practice is that the distinction between job and private life cannot be maintained because they are always on call. One physician told us, "Everytime you hear the telephone ring at night, you think, 'Oh, no, I hope it's not a patient.' At times it seems like you can never even get away from your patient's problems for some peace and quiet for yourself." Some psychiatrists who could have made more money in private practice chose to work in a hospital setting because "at the end of the day I can close the door behind me and know that somebody else will take care of the emergency cases." Counselors and educators who live on the job tend to have unusually high rates of burnout. At residential treatment centers the turnover rate is typically very high. Often the centers are run democratically, and both staff and patients are involved in the therapeutic process day and night. Counselors cannot tolerate the emotional intensity and the lack of the time off, and burnout leads them to quit, often within one or two years.

Physical distancing also shows up during work hours. For example, a psychiatrist noticed that as he was burning out in his private practice, he used his desk as a barrier between himself and his clients. Many administrators who start a job with an "open-door" policy begin to close their doors when they feel imposed on; they develop a need to get away from everyone, to be alone and work. Another example of how people may avoid human interaction in their work is the professor who remained on campus during his sabbatical year to finish writing a book. To avoid disturbances he put a card on his office door bearing the name of a nonexistent person. It worked: no one knocked. Three years after his sabbatical the phony name is still on his door! Office hours by appointment only, a secretary to scrutinize visitors, and distance-creating furniture arrangements are a few of the techniques used by professionals to minimize physical involvement in stressful interactions.

Other professionals simply spend less time with their service recipients. Many cut to a minimum the time they spend in direct contact. For example, one pediatrician took as long as possible getting from her office to her first appointment in the morning. Because she was late for the first appointment she could justify cutting short any stressful encounter she had during the day. In a college counseling office counselors found every excuse to look into the students' files because the files were housed in an adjacent building and the walk was a welcome relief from encounters with students.

Two independent studies found that workers experiencing physical, emotional, and mental exhaustion tended to be consistently late for work, to take extended work breaks, and to have a high frequency of unexplained absences from work.[19] In mental health settings it was found[20] that the longer workers have been in the field of mental health the less they liked working with patients and the more custodial rather than humanistic their attitudes became. Those who worked with schizophrenics in the past tried to avoid, as much as possible, direct contact with them. In one hospital, nurses who were burning out gradually spent more time socializing with other staff members and less time with patients. They became almost hostile when a patient approached them, seeing it as an intrusion into "their" time. A child-care worker told us she used her sick leave to get away from people in general and "knee-high people who talk in single syllables" in particular. Clerks in health and welfare departments started "cutting corners" in their interaction with clients by taking increasingly long lunch breaks. Taking longer lunch breaks, spending longer time on paperwork, leaving work early, or being absent are all examples of withdrawal by means of spending less time with clients.

Professionals also distance themselves physically from their clients by standing far away, avoiding eye contact, or keeping their hand on the door-knob. They communicate with clients in impersonal ways, such a superficial generalities and form letters.

Finally, a less common distancing technique was described by a social science consultant, who said that when sitting in boring meetings with particularly difficult clients, she would develop "telescopic visions." She saw her clients as very small and far away, so far that it became impossible to hear what they said.

Emotional withdrawal

When physical distancing is impossible, people who are burning out use emotional withdrawal. Lief and Fox found that during the first two years of medical school the primary problem for students is that of acquiring greater emotional detachment.[21] "To protect myself from my own emotions I feel like I am putting on emotional armor every time I walk into the emergency room," said a young intern. Other professionals who encounter clients' pain use similar modes of emotional detachment. In the case presented earlier, Sue distanced herself by "turning off" her compassion, empathy, and warmth, and by "spacing out" during interviews with clients.

A welfare department worker described her growing emotional detachment:

When I started I was deeply involved in every aspect of the sixty families I had. I really cared and was supportive of everything that went on. But if you continue at this level of involvement you get to be crazy very soon. So I started to withdraw a bit and see things as the client's problem. I went from total involvement to a kind of standing back. In the end I developed a callousness towards the people I was working with. I was so emotionally detached that I might as well not have been there. I was earning money, but I didn't feel the work was part of my life.

In order to protect themselves from the emotional stresses of their work, some professionals make sharp distinctions between their jobs and their personal lives. One prison psychologist said that when he meets new people socially he refuses to tell them what his job is. In response to questions he only says, "I am a civil servant" or "I work for the state." A policeman said that he made an explicit agreement with his wife and friends not to "talk shop." He said he encounters crime and filth all day and wants none of that, not even talk, at home. Such emotional compartmentalization enables professionals to limit their occupational stress to the time and place of their work.

Although professionals detach themselves in self-defense to avoid overinvolvement, this emotional withdrawal may escalate and result in total detachment and the loss of concern for the recipients of their services. It is also difficult to turn on and off one's emotions at will, and as a result the detachment often spreads into relationships outside of work as well.

Mental withdrawal

Mental withdrawal is a set of attitudes that protects the service providers from overinvolvement and justifies detachment from the recipients of their services. In different ways these attitudes help the professional to see the other person as less human, to view the relationship with the other person in objective and analytic terms, and to reduce the intensity and scope of emotional arousal. One such attitude includes reliance on rules to define relationships with service recipients. For example, a parole officer, who was asked to cosign a loan for a parolee as an indication of trust, found to her relief that there was a rule against it. That made it easier for her to say, "No, but it is nothing personal. It is the rule." A formerly enthusiastic teaching assistant in a large course said he burned out when the 313th student came to him after an exam asking for a change of grade. "This particular student explained that his mother was seriously ill and that's why he was upset and confused at the time of the test and misunderstood the question, and he really needs those extra three points, otherwise he is going to flunk the course and be kicked out of the University." Hearing this the teaching assistant got a "glassy look" in his eyes and said, "Sorry, but I can't change your grade. It's a university rule. . . ." He reduced his own emotional overload by making his response to the request impersonal and rule-governed.

The medical profession provides numerous examples of this mental detachment. Physicians, in order to deal with their feelings, tend to use intellectualization and place a premium on "pure rationality." A patient may become an interesting diagnostic problem rather than a human being in pain. Nurses who burn out become more technical and custodial; their primary concern may become the disease, not the patients.

Marcia Millman, a sociologist who studied the work of physicians, described medical work as demanding exceptional emotional risks because mistakes in the line of duty may cost human life.[22] To protect themselves, those in the medical profession have delveloped group techniques for justifying their errors and minimizing the appearance of injury to the patient. One of the best places to observe this collective rationalization, according to Millman, is the mortality conference, where patient deaths may be reviewed in such a way as to justify retrospectively decisions that physicians had made. Physicians may excuse their errors by blaming the patient: if a patient can be discredited as crazy, alcoholic, uncooperative, or otherwise undeserving, the responsibility for the medical error may be shifted off the physician. Collective rationalization and blaming the victim can be seen as protective devices used by physicians to defend themselves from the emotional stress of guilt about medical mistakes.

Another way mental withdrawal shows up is in the use of terminology. Generalizations enable professionals to detach themselves from the individual with whom they empathize; people they know individually become "deprived masses" and "sick and needy victims of society." Other terminology is more derogatory: one teacher called her students "monsters," a drug rehabilitation worker referred to her clients as "junkies." Another way of distancing oneself from people's pain is to identify them by their problems rather than their names, such as the "root canal case" or "the kidney in room 202." Terminology enables professionals to deny the humanity of the recipients of their services and thus to minimize their emotional involvement.

Another way professionals defend themselves against emotional stress is humor. One example is the "sick" humor of medical students in particularly stressful situations such as the anatomy lab. According to Lief and Fox, medical students anxious about cadaver dissection generally name the cadaver on which they work, often giving it an amusing name such as "Elbow" or "Bones." This helps the students reduce the seriousness of "cutting into" or "taking apart" a human body.[23]

Many employees collect funny stories to tell about their clients. A woman who works in a boutique told how she and the other employees privately mock difficult customers. Two group leaders, after a demanding three-day workshop, found relief in hysterical laughter about themselves, the participants, and the situation as a whole. Being able to joke and laugh about a stressful event reduces the tension and anxiety that the professional feels. It also serves to make the situation less serious and less overwhelming.

All the modes of detachment described above—physical, emotional, and mental—are used by professionals working with people to reduce the intensity of the emotional arousal inherent in their work. The detachment techniques are most useful when they aid the professional in achieving the ideal balance of detached concern. They become dysfunctional when used to an extreme and when they produce the dehumanizing attitudes associated with burnout. Unfortunately, even when detachment is useful as a self-protective device, it tends to make professionals less helpful to their clients. The emphasis should be on achieving the *ideal* balance—a balance that is not only desirable for the professional but is also preferred by the clients. Some balance can be attempted by situational mechanisms. For example, the professional can create a very formal situation and then afford to have an emotional approach. Or else the professional can create an intimate situation combined with a more rational goal-oriented approach.[24] In Chapters 7, 8, and 9 we will introduce coping strategies that help professionals achieve relief from burnout in ways that do not diminish the quality of the service they provide for their clients. These coping strategies enable the professionals to replenish themselves emotionally by accepting their own needs as legitimate.

Bad situations, not bad people

People often turn to "trait" theories to explain the ills of society. They believe that antisocial behaviors are committed by people who are basically "bad." In psychological terms these are dispositional attributes of behavior. For example, a professional's indifferent, rude, or dehumanizing behavior may be attributed to such internal traits as coldness or cruelty. This interpretation is frequently erroneous. Social psychological research has helped bring a more accurate and useful perspective to these problems by emphasizing situational attributes.[25] Rather than attributing behavior to a deficiency in character, it is often more helpful to focus on environmental factors, both social and physical, that cause people to act in particular ways. Such an approach does not deny the importance of individual traits and personality characteristics. Rather, it suggests that antisocial behavior may also have a strong situational component. Thus, although a person who behaves rudely may simply be a "rude person," it is more likely that he is an average person currently under pressure. If we view him as a rude person we can do little except to despair, to avoid him, or to get angry at him. If we think of him as a well-meaning person working under pressure, perhaps we can alleviate the pressure. Burnout is not a function of bad people who are cold and uncaring. It is a function of bad situations in which once-idealistic people must operate. It is then the situations that must be modified so that they promote, rather than destroy, human values.[26]

Notes

1. H. O. Lief and D. C. Fox, "Training for 'Detached Concern' in Medical Students," in *The Psychological Basis of Medical Practice*, ed. H. I. Lief, V. I. Lief, and N. R. Lief (New York: Harper and Row, 1963), p. 13.
2. D. D. Federman, "Can Compassion Survive? Pressures Imperil M.D.'s Conscience and Motivation," *Stanford Observer*, March 1976, p. 5. The article was adapted from Professor Federman's address to the Stanford School of Medicine, 1975.
3. D. Oken, "The Unknown Factor: The Doctor and How He Does His Doctoring," *Frontiers of Psychiatry*, June 15, 1978, p. 12.
4. "The 'Jungle' Today," in *Education*, Maclean's (Canada), March 8, 1976, p. 52.
5. A. M. Bloch, "Combat Neurosis in Inner City Schools." Paper presented at the 130th annual meeting of the American Psychiatric Association, May 4, 1977.
6. A. Kadushin, *Child Welfare Services* (New York: Macmillan, 1974).
7. For example, Jim Coins, a clinical psychologist at the University of California in Berkeley, has shown that talking on the phone to depressed clients has a negative effect on the mood of the therapist.

8. Y. Feldman, H. Spotnitz, and L. Nagelberg, "One Aspect of Case Work Training through Supervisors," *Social Casework* 34 (April 1953): 153.

9. Kadushin, *Child Welfare Services.*

10. W. Regiatt, "The Occupational Culture of Policemen and Social Workers" (Washington, D. C.: American Psychological Association, 1970), p. 11.

11. Kadushin, *Child Welfare Services.*

12. M. Kramer, *Reality Shock* (St. Louis; Mosby Co., 1974).

13. J. M. M. Hill, "The Representation of Labor Turnover as a Social Form," in *Labor Turnover and Retention,* ed. B.O. Pettman (New York: Wiley, 1975), pp. 73–93.

14. For example, A. E. Ivey and J. A. Authier, *Microcounseling* (Springfield, Ill.: Charles Thomas, 1978).

15. M. Lipp, *The Wounded Healer* (New York: Harper and Row, 1980).

16. Lief and Fox, "Training for 'Detached Concern.' "

17. D. Etzion, "Achieving Balance in a Consultation Setting," *Group and Organization Studies* 4, no. 3 (1979): 366–376.

18. B. Bettelheim, *A Home for the Heart* (New York: Bantam Books, 1974), p. 280.

19. J. Golan, "Attitudes, Personal Characteristics, and Organizational Factors and Their Relationships with Absenteeism among Telephone Operators." Thesis for M.Sc. degree in Management Sciences, Organizational Behavior, submitted to the Faculty of Management, Tel Aviv University, 1979; J. W. Jones, "The Staff Burnout Scale: A Validity Study." Paper presented at the 52nd annual meeting of the Midwestern Psychological Association, St. Louis, May 1-3, 1980.

20. A. Pines and C. Maslach, "Characteristics of Staff Burnout in Mental Health Settings," *Hospital and Community Psychiarty* 29, no. 4 (1978): 233–337.

21. Lief and Fox, "Training for 'Detached Concern.' "

22. M. Millman, *The Unkindest Cut: Life in the Backrooms of Medicine* (New York: Morrow, 1977).

23. Lief and Fox, "Training for 'Detached Concern.' "

24. Etzion, "Achieving Balance in a Consultation Setting."

25. E. E. Jones, D. E. Kanause, H. H. Kelley, R. E. Nisbett, S. Valins, and B. Weiner, eds., *Attribution: Perceiving the Causes of Behavior* (Morristown, N.J.: General Learning Press, 1972).

26. C. Maslach, "Burnout: The Loss of Human Caring," *Human Behavior* 5 (September 1976): 16–22.

4

Occupational tedium among
people in bureaucracies

Work for most people is central to life. One-third of our waking lives is spent in work. Vocational roles define lifestyles, social networks, self-image, and general health and happiness. Albert Camus said, "Without work all life goes rotten. But when work is soulless, life stifles and dies." There is a growing awareness in this country of the enormous cost of workers' dissatisfaction both for the individual and the organization. A great proportion of this dissatisfaction is found in bureaucratic organizations.

"Bureaucracy" stems from the French "bureau," which has come to mean a department or a subdivision of a department, usually of government. Bureaucratic organizations are gaining control over vocational life in most industrial societies. Their impact on workers is of great theoretical and practical importance. The study of bureaucracies has been greatly influenced by the pioneering work of the German scholar Max Weber who first described a model of "ideal bureaucracy": a social institution of professionals organized in a hierarchy and applying uniform norms to the handling of individual cases. Weber believed that bureaucracies had a "rational character, with rules, means-end calculus, and matter of factness predominating."[1] He perceived bureaucracies as a means of translating social actions—relationships between individuals that were sufficient to guide simple societies—into rational relationships, a form of activity necessary in complex societies.

Recently this positive view of bureaucracies has undergone dramatic changes. In their size and complexity bureaucratic organizations are slow and unresponsive. Usually they are considered equipped to solve problems that existed two years earlier. They are blamed for being self-serving instead of public-serving. Work in these bureaucracies can be frustrating and tedium-causing, especially for energetic and ambitious people who want to see quick changes.

The second and third chapters of this book presented case studies of people. This chapter presents a case study of an organization because the organization is the "patient." We chose the Welfare Department because it demonstrates the impact of working both within a bureaucracy (tedium) and with people (burnout).

A case study: the welfare department as a
bureaucratic social service organization

In the Welfare Department, approximately 381,000 employees interact with over 23,241,000 welfare recipients. Employees are required to work with large numbers of people in situations that can be very demanding. In addition, they contend with paperwork, changing regulations, and a downward channel of communication. Welfare programs include aid to families with dependent children, food, stamps medical aid, general assistance, and supplemental security income for the aged, blind, and disabled.

As a social service organization, the Welfare Department imposes two kinds of stress on its employees: tedium-causing stress inherent in its bureaucratic nature and burnout-causing stress inherent in the services it provides.

Stress inherent in the bureaucratic
nature of the organization

A recent investigation of the Welfare Department described it as "an entrenched bureaucracy so complex and so inefficient that it seems to invite cheating and other abuses." Excessive red tape, inept management, poorly trained frontline personnel, and careless investigative policies are costing taxpayers billions of dollars every year.[2] The picture painted is one of "chaos, confusion and conflict in the management of welfare, particularly in big urban areas." The degree of administrative morass within welfare departments in large cities is almost beyond description," Robert Reed, director of Michigan's Legal Services, told a Senate subcommittee.

Identifying "The Boss" is difficult in any large bureaucracy, and in a government agency it can be nearly impossible. The source of welfare policy can be the federal government, the state government, the courts, or the agency itself. This unclear responsibility keeps workers from effectively stating and correcting their grievances. There are many levels of administrators and many employees in the system. Caseworkers are monitored by supervisors who are in turn monitored by other supervisors. At the top are administrators who often are not familiar with the problems of the workers seven steps below. As a result, although there are many supervisors, case workers often complain that direction is inadequate.

Workers are often bewildered about how to do their jobs. There are frequent alterations of old programs and additions of new programs that create confusion. "Just keeping abreast of policies that are forever being revised by Congress, HEW, state legislatures and state and local administrators can be a full time job. By the time you understand one regulation, another is coming down the pike," said Patricia Johnson, head of Georgia's Division of Family and Children Services. Some rules are vague; others are set forth in minute detail: to implement one program that began as a four-page law, HEW drafted 70 pages of regulations followed by a 1,200-page instruction manual.

The welfare bureaucracy generates so much paperwork that case workers say they are shuffling paper instead of investigating clients. New York State processes three billion pieces of social service paperwork annually. Certain states may require up to sixty forms for a single welfare application The Commission on Federal Paper Work examined the welfare application process and found it "needlessly complex, unduly burdensome, inefficient, inequitable and unnecessarily costly."[3]

Stress inherent in the service provided by the organization

Caseworkers in the Welfare Department screen applications, determine eligibility and benefit levels, and decide when a person no longer needs public aid. "In many parts of the country workers are overburdened by trying to manage loads double or triple the 60-case limit once prescribed by the Department of Health, Education and Welfare. Many labor under pressure in offices that tend to be tense, crowded and rundown, and that may lack even the basic equipment needed to keep track of the work."[4]

Despite such conditions, caseworkers are expected to offer informed assistance to people who require their services. Urged to show compassion, they are also responsible for guarding the public interest by accurately appraising aid applications and staying alert for mistakes and fraud. Employees must answer to their own supervisors, to their clients, and to state and federal governments.

Such work demands skill and training, but in twenty-seven states only a high school education is required to become a caseworker. Most eligibility workers are young, two out of three are women, and relatively few have an education beyond the college level. Inexperienced caseworkers with minimal training are the ones most likely to be fooled by people out to defraud the system. Instead of receiving formal training from supervisors, many caseworkers are trained by fellow workers. It takes new workers about six months to learn their jobs, but many do not stay in the department that long.

Compounding the abundance of negative features in welfare work is a dramatic lack of positive features. The pay is inadequate for such demanding work. In New York in 1978, the starting salary for an interviewer ranged from $9,600 to $13,000, less than the income of some welfare families.[5] Promotions are not a source of satisfaction because local policies often require officials to promote everyone whenever a vacancy occurs, without concern for the individual's performance. Official concern for forms and routines also creates problems for welfare workers who feel they have become clerks instead of social servants.

When these pressures are not dealt with they can lead to the physical, emotional, and mental exhaustion of tedium. Consequently in some welfare offices turnover exceeds 40 percent a year. Many employees quit when they realize that they cannot handle the bureaucratic pressures combined with the job demands. A few change careers after being threatened or physically assaulted by welfare clients. Often caseworkers say they are driven out by the frustration of trying to make an inert system responsive to clients' needs. They know they can continue working with minimal effort even after they burn out, but some feel that when they burn out it is time to leave.

Workers' tedium can be traumatic for the individual, unpleasant for the service recipients, and disruptive and costly for the organization. In the Wefare Department at least four billion dollars are paid out "erroneously" every year. Bureaucratic error, as opposed to outright fraud by aid recipients and others, is responsible for more than half the errors.[6] The welfare bureaucracy begins to falter at the level of the caseworkers. They are supposed to be the first line of defense against welfare abuse, but tedium weakens their resistance and alterness. Inadequately trained, overburdened, underpaid, many quit the field.

Antecedents of tedium in bureaucratic organizations

In his classic book, *Democracy in America,* Alexis de Tocqueville discussed the steady erosion that might develop as a result of a bureaucratic government that "covers the whole of social life with a network of petty, complicated rules that are both minute and uniform"—a situation that, according to de Tocqueville, does not break the human will but rather "softens, bends and guides it."[7]

In one research project,[8] organizational structure was described as a major determinant of job performance, satisfaction, and burnout. Large agencies that are formal, centralized in decision making, and hierarchial were found to have high turnover, low job satisfaction, and rapid burnout.

Consistent with this description is our own work with a bureaucratic organization in which we found high levels of employee tedium.[9] Tedium increased as many job satisfaction measures decreased, and as tedium increased, so did employees' desires to leave the job.[10]

Training schools rarely teach students how to be "good bureaucrats," although most of their graduates will end up working for large organizations. Thus people who work in bureaucracies are generally unprepared for dealing with the stress they generate. This is especially true in the human services where people often choose their careers for altruistic reasons but find themselves filling out forms rather than working with people. Bureaucratic organizations in general share three antecedents of tedium: (1) overload, (2) lack of autonomy, and (3) lack of rewards.

Overload

One characteristic of work in technologically advanced organizations is overload. John R. D. French and Robert D. Caplan, studying occupational stress at the Institute of Social Research, University of Michigan, have done extensive research on the effects of the organizational work environment on psychological and physiological variables; the effect of organizational stress or individual strain.[11] They use the concept of role overload as a key variable in job stress and its effect on health.

French and Caplan distinguish between objective and subjective as well as quantitative and qualitative overload. Objective overload is the actual volume of information that the individuals are expected to process per unit of time. The number of telephone calls to answer, letters to write, office visits to receive, or patients to examine in a day are quantifiable indicators of objective overload. Subjective overload, in contrast, refers to people feeling that they have too much work to do or that the work is too hard for them. Quantitative overload implies that they have more work than they can do in a given time period. Qualitative overload implies that the job requires skills and knowledge exceeding those of the workers. Individuals experience quantitative overload when they have the skills to perform the tasks but do not have the time to get them done. Individuals have qualitative overload when, no matter how much time they are given, they do not have the skills to perform the tasks at acceptable levels.

Many studies have documented the prevalence of overload. In a national survey, 44 percent of the male white-collar employees reported some degree of overload. A study of university professors showed that many of them suffer from a quantitative overload that is mostly self-induced and related to their achievement orientation.[12] In one of our own studies, 724 human service workers were asked to identify the most stressful aspects of their work. Over 50 percent of the stresses mentioned pertained to overload.[13]

Both quantitative and qualitative overload are correlated with psychological and physiological indices of stress. Overloaded subjects show increased heart rate and serum cholesterol levels; they smoke more, have more job dissatisfaction and tension, and show lower self-esteem.[14]

J. G. Miller, a pioneer in the work on information-input overload, has developed an apparatus to study the psychological response to overload.[15] He described several mechanisms of adjustment to information overload, including omission of information; error in processing information; delaying responses during heavy load periods and catching up during lull periods; filtering some items of information; giving an imprecise response; and escape either by leaving the situation or by cutting off the information input. Miller suggested that excessive information overload can cause cognitive and behavioral disorganization.

The specific job components that contribute to overload differ for different professions. Robert L. Kahn, director of the Survey Research Center at the University of Michigan, found overload to be one of the most frequent forms of role conflict in organizations. He summarized the response of people he studied as, "We don't object to the things we're asked to do, and we don't find them inappropriate or unreasonable, but we can't meet all the demands simultaneously within the constraints of time and resources."[16] On the other hand, in police work, qualitative overload may occur as a result of unrealistic expectations placed on police by society. "Society demands too much of its policemen. Not only are they expected to enforce the law, they must also be curbside psychiatrists, marriage counselors, social workers—even ministers and doctors. A good street officer combines in his daily work splinters of each one of these complex professions, and many more."[17] An informal survey found that over 70 percent of police officers feel that they are under the stress of overload.[18]

In a study of one social service bureaucracy, we asked fifty-two employees to identify the most stressful aspects of their jobs.[19] Their most frequent responses were: "There is a heavy work load"; "There is not enough time in the day or enough people to handle the work load so service to the public is not as positive as it could be"; "Folders pile up and clients have to wait excessive lengths of time and I don't see an end to it." Such overload was found to be highly correlated with tedium[20]

Similarly, studies of child-care workers and mental health workers found that the larger the ratio of children or patients to staff, the less staff members liked their jobs and the more frequently they reported cognitive, emotional, and sensory overload. As the ratio decreased, the quality of care improved.[21]

The experience of overload can be aggravated for people in social service organizations by the imposition of tasks that have high priority for the organization but low priority for the service recipients. Paperwork and red tape are more difficult to deal with when there are people waiting for help. We have heard social workers, counselors, policemen, and probation officers say that it is not the contact with clients that is most stressful for them but "writing a report in six copies that I know for sure no one will ever look at." A survey of over 4,500 police officers found that they consider "too much paperwork" as their major job-related problem. [22] Our studies also found excessive paperwork and red tape to be highly correlated with tedium;[23] the more paperwork and red tape, the more tedium.

Lack of autonomy

Lack of control over one's environment is a highly stressful experience. Martin Seligman suggested that when animals and people repeatedly undergo negative experiences over which they have no control, the result is "learned helplessness" and depression.[24] The exposure to uncrontollable events leads to motivational and effective debilitation. Seligman reported, for example, that subjects who were given unsolvable anagrams later could not solve solvable anagrams, and subjects who were exposed to inescapable noise did not attempt to escape later when escape was possible. People who develop "learned helplessness" do not believe that success is the result of their performance but attribute failure to themselves. They develop low self-esteem and become passive and sad. Learned helplessness can explain some of the symptoms of tedium experienced by employees of bureaucratic organizations as a result of lack of autonomy.

Social psychologists[25] have found that people can stand more pain when they have control over its duration and intensity than when they do not. It has also been reported[26] that the mortality rate in old age homes is higher among those residents who had no choice in the decision to be there than among those who made that choice themselves. A study of homemakers found that housewives who chose their career tended to be healthy, happy, and comfortable in their role.[27] They did not want to work, took pride in what they did, felt in control, and were satisfied with their lives. Homemakers who wanted to work away from home, but did not, exhibited the "bitter housewife" syndrome: they were dissatisfied with their lives. had low self-esteem, and often masked their loneliness and worry with drugs. In one study we asked people to indicate if they did professional and personal activities mainly because they wanted to or because they had to. Those who answered "have to" showed far more tedium than those who answered "want to."[28]

A perceived lack of autonomy appears to be a powerful antecedent of tedium. The need for autonomy is so great that people will even blame themselves for accidents in order to maintain their sense of control. The underlying reasoning in such self-blame is: "If it was my fault that it happened, then it is within my control to make sure it doesn't happen again."

Frustration resulting from the lack of autonomy is a common antecedent of tedium in bureaucratic organizations.[29] In a study of one social service organization, two of the most frequently mentioned sources of stress were the frequent changes in rules and the poorly planned agency changes with little advance notice.[30] In all of our work we found that tedium increased as autonomy, sense of control, and discretionary time decreased.

Lack of autonomy in bureaucracies is also apparent in administrative pressures on the individual worker, unnecessary rules, and lack of voice in decisions that affect one's job and life. William Kroes, a psychologist who worked extensively with police officers, wrote about the stress inherent in situations in which patrolmen were transferred from one partner, assignment, or district to another without advance notice.[31] Police officers generally have no say in their assignment to direct traffic, write parking citations, or investigate such petty complaints as too many weeds growing in a property owner's lawn.

Dan Gowler and Karen Legge, who wrote about managerial stress, see it as the product of three factors: uncertainty of outcome, importance of that outcome to the individuals, and the individuals' perception of their ability to influence that outcome.[32] All three uncertainties are clearly related to lack of control and autonomy. One source of uncertainty and stress that Gowler and Legge see as common to many managerial jobs stems from a lack of clear criteria for success. In many organizations, managerial success is equated with implementation of organizational objectives such as increased profits or business expansion. Attainment of these objectives, however, may depend on external factors—like the health of the national economy, the availability of raw materials, and the development of new technology—as much as on the skill of individual managers. Thus managers may feel unable to control their success through their own performance.

Brian Sarata, a professor of Psychology at the University of Nebraska, notes that the feasibility of providing most staff with a significant degree of autonomy is limited by at least two considerations: first, many decisions are made only by professional staff; second, providing good care requires that the efforts of all disciplines be well coordinated and that treatment plans be implemented in a consistent manner. This necessarily limits the autonomy of the individual staff members' involvement in the process.

Lack of autonomy can be aggravated by a communication gap between those at the top and those at the bottom of the organization hierarchy. This gap may be due to the inherent inefficiencies of communication in large organizations or to the different perspectives available to management. The lack of personal control is more clear and stressful in the lower ranks of the organization. As a result, employees often feel a loss of individuality, "like little insignificant wheels in a gigantic machine." Characteristics of complex organizations such as circumscribed authority, downward channels of command, specialization, formal accountability and hierarchy, and broad-base participation all contribute to feelings of helplessness and lack of autonomy and control, and thus to tedium.

Lack of rewards

Complex organizations are inefficient distributors of rewards, appreciation, and recognition. This contributes to discouragement and demoralization and eventually to tedium. In some complex organizations, we found employees were able to withstand great work stress when they felt appreciated and adequately rewarded. Unfortunately, that was rarely the case.

In the Welfare Department, employees developed tedium both because of the negative features in their work and because of the lack of positive features. Their pay was inadequate for the work they were expected to do, they received little positive feedback from supervisors, and promotions were given for political considerations rather than as an acknowledgment of superior performance. And in the study of a social service organization, the lack of rewards, such as pay, benefits, and promotion, was a significant contributor to tedium.[33]

But it turns out that appreciation on the job is more important than dollars for most people. Indeed it seems to be the case that phenomenologically the ideal income tends to remain 10 to 20 percent above a person's current income, even at the very highest socioeconomic status. For example, physicians we interviewed were as likely to complain about financial strain as were social workers and clerks. But people who received appreciation, satisfaction, and a sense of significance from their work were more likely to be content with their income, no matter how low it was. And tedium was more highly correlated with lack of a sense of success and significance than it was with salary. Tedium was also more correlated with poor physical health and lack of self-actualization than it was with salary.[34]

An antecedent of tedium is therefore the subjective sense of inadequate reward rather than the reward itself. Tedium comes in part from the feeling that one is working hard, beyond the requirements of the job, and yet one's efforts are not appreciated. One employee expressed this sense of frustration by saying, "You never hear a good word from management, no matter how consistently excellent your performance is. The only thing you will ever get from them is a cold memo when something goes wrong." The lack of recognition and appreciation is an important antecedent of tedium, and bureaucracies can only benefit by providing positive feedback to employees.

Two cases of tedium

The next part of this chapter presents two cases of people who have experienced tedium working within bureaucratic organizations. The cases demonstrate better than abstract discussion the impact of bureaucracies on their employees. The people presented here played very different roles in very different organizations. They both developed tedium as the result of features inherent in their work environments and work roles.

Employee's tedium

David was 50 years old. He had been developing training programs in a government laboratory for thirteen years when he was told he would be transferred to another department the next day. David was shaken by the transfer and more so by the way the transfer was carried out:

> I felt devastated, I felt a total lack of self worth. I did not trust the person I was transferred to and resented the unfair and inconsiderate way the transfer was done. But I had no choice. I know this is not at all uncommon in industry. But it is devastating to the individual. I found it very difficult to take. I felt that my former boss and the one I was transferred to were playing games with my life. I felt angry, humiliated and used; they were going to pick my brains and then dump me. I never resolved these feelings.

After the transfer David remained in the new department for three years, but his relationship with his boss only became worse. He felt uncertain about what his job consisted of and he felt criticized for the work he did.

> Things that went well went unnoticed, but errors were amplified. Whatever I did was devalued. Year in and year out I experienced the slow eroding away of my soul. I felt like I didn't exist. After a while I was doing my job like a machine, like a warm mannequin, not a person. When you are treated like a nonperson you just keep doing the same thing over and over again. You turn into a paper mover.

Most difficult of all was the feeling of being trapped.

> I wanted to escape at any cost, but there was no way out. The obligations of a large family didn't give me the latitude to simply walk out. And there was the pressure of having put all these years into a retirement system that I knew I was far enough into it so that I couldn't go somewhere else. I knew that if I left I was throwing a lot of my future away. As

the pressure was building up I started making more errors, and as I was making more errors there was more pressure building up. Pretty soon the pressure was so great that I couldn't make decisions, and I couldn't set priorities. I was under so much stress I couldn't find comfort in anything. My feeling of worthlessness was all consuming. I was so miserable I seriously contemplated suicide. I was in no shape to be a loving husband and father. At times I even thought about murder. The pressure is so immense you know that something has to give.

Administrator's tedium

When Susan was hired as the executive director of a victim witness program, she knew it was a political job. It was part of a federal grant to the district attorney's office and involved working with a variety of community groups. Susan was responsible for designing a program to help victims and witnesses of violent crimes. She was given a small budget with which to serve the entire city and pay her staff. The enormity of the job as defined was overwhelming. "Many people had warned me that it was an impossible job," said Susan, "but I felt it was a challenge and a great opportunity."

All the salaries on the grant were low. The staff resented this and projected a great deal of anger onto Susan. As director, Susan had to answer to her staff, the district attorney's office, community and minority groups, the city system, and a policy committee. This committee was composed of representatives from various community agencies and interest groups and there was no agreement among them on the goals of the program. Susan worked sixty hours a week, nights, and weekends. She tried to do everything: business management, financial accounting, reports, training staff and volunteers, community outreach, and service to victims and witnesses. There was simply not enough money or time for everything.

Susan found one of the most frustrating aspects of her job was dealing with the "system." The bureaucracy did not provide candidates for staff positions so Susan had to recruit and select her own staff. The state government made service to victims difficult by complicated forms and requirements. Susan had to provide financial accounting to four agencies responsible for the program. "If the wrong form was submitted, or if a form was submitted to the wrong agency, it took weeks before it was returned and then the whole process had to start again. It often took three additional forms to correct an error. To get anything accomplished in the city took ten times longer than it was supposed to take."

In spite of all these obstacles Susan was committed to the program. She felt it was an important social service and she wanted to help the victims. In ten months the program served 1,000 clients with a staff of three and a few volunteers. But Susan felt that what mattered was what had not been done, although what was expected was humanly impossible, given the resources of the program.

Susan began to develop the classic symptoms of tedium.

> As the pressures and frustrations increased and I felt less effective in what I was doing, my self-concept became more negative. I was a terrible administrator, I wasn't smart enough to do the job, I had let the people down who had helped me get the job. I thought that there was something wrong with me that I was having so much trouble in the situation. The negative self-concept carried over into other aspects of my life, my personal relationships, athletic activities, relationships with my family. Once that sort of concept begins to develop, it almost develops a will of its own and it becomes difficult to let in any information that might allow for a more positive self-evaluation.
>
> I was so fed up with public employment. I was fed up with the way people are exploited or the way I felt I was exploited. I was so tired of having to work with stupid, inept people, and deal with city bureaucracy. I was tired of the politics of community groups and agencies. I was tired of clients who were demanding *everything immediately*!

Susan was mentally, emotionally, and physically exhausted, the hallmarks of tedium. She resigned.

David and Susan had very different positions within their organizations. David was an employee with pressures from above and Susan was an administrator with pressures from all directions. Yet there were common stresses in their jobs that resulted in both of them feeling the impact of tedium. Each had uncertainty about the nature of their work, each lacked the power to make decisions affecting their own life and work, each felt isolated, each lacked occupational support systems, and each felt insufficient appreciation and recognition from the organization.

How to avoid tedium by being a "good bureaucrat"

Despite the increasing number of complex bureaucratic organizations, most people who work in them never learn how to be "good bureaucrats." For many the phrase "good bureaucrat" is a contradiction in terms. In popular speech, a "bureaucrat" is identified with all that is antihuman. Furthermore, the role of a bureaucrat has been almost totally ignored by educators, practitioners, and researchers. But Robert Pruger, a professor of social welfare at the University of California, contends that achieving one's professional goals in a complex organization requires great competence. He recommends that workers develop the skills needed to cope with a bureaucracy rather than try to escape the organization. As bureaucrats, workers are required to negotiate the stresses, opportunities, and constraints that permeate organizational life. Competent bureaucrats have identified the following skills that enable them to avoid the common antecedents of tedium.[35]

Avoiding overload by getting to know the organization and acquiring skills

Overload is built into the size and complexity of bureaucratic organizations. Some overload will dissipate when one learns the work routines and the organizational structure. This requires staying on the job long enough to master the initial stresses.

Employees in social service organizations reported an overwhelming overload during their first six months at work. The information to be learned in that period was enormous and the training inadequate. This initial overload was associated with feelings of inadequacy, guilt, and failure which for some employees never disappeared.

Adequate training for employees is necessary to reduce this initial overload. Effective training programs and supportive supervision are two methods for skill acquisition and improvement that reduce overload and tedium. Again, this requires the employee to remain in the organization long enough to learn whatever skills are needed to be efficient. These may include general skills increasingly required by organizations but for which formal training is frequently unavailable, such as proposal writing, budgeting, or problem analysis. They may also include specific abilities such as clerical, computer, or communication skills.

Organizations can reduce employee overload by defining their priorities for employees. The priority list includes both internal organizational goals and more general goals such as service to the public and a good image for the organization. A priority list for work activities can also ease overload. This job analysis includes all the activities to be performed and identifies which ones are causes of overload. These activities can be divided into necessary activities that create overload and activities that create self-imposed overload. The necessary activities are accepted as such and time is organized accordingly: more time to the more important activities and less time to the less important activities. Priorities are established among the self-imposed activities also. Those deemed important are alloted time, and the others are minimized or eliminated.

These techniques do reduce overload but they rarely eliminate it. The basic strategy is to help people live with overload, set priorities, and reduce the stress caused by worry or guilt. When overload is accepted as a necessary evil and is not accompanied by worry and strain, it is easier to cope with.

Exercising autonomy and remembering goals

In bureaucratic organizations, processes of decision and action move forward at a measured pace. One characteristic of a good bureaucrat, according to Robert Pruger, is staying in power. "Whatever ideas, changes, projects, or other professional aspirations the worker may have, he will not be able to realize them unless he stays in the organization and keeps working for his goals over a sufficient period of time. But it is not enough merely to survive as a physical presense. The good bureaucrat must maintain his vitality of action and independence of thought. He must continue to be led by some progressive vision of what the organization might accomplish and nurture the scope and consciousness of discretionary behavior."[36] Individual employees can almost always preserve and enlarge the discretionary scope of their activities and, by extension, their sense of autonomy and control. Research shows that when staff authority is decentralized and workers at all levels are involved in decision making, there is a significant improvement in performance as well as staff morale.[37]

To achieve these objectives the good bureaucrat is attentive to authority and avoids behavior that earns dismissal. To the astute bureaucrat, things are always more flexible than they seem at first glance. Because authority is most commonly expressed in rules, job descriptions, and work schedules, such statements are general in character and employees can interpret them to their advantage. That built-in degree of generality requires the exercise of discretion. In this sense, skillfull bureaucrats have more control over the content of their jobs than does the organization.

Burnout and tedium are associated with feelings of helplessness and lack of control. Many people in bureaucracies believe and act as if nothing can be done about anything around them; they feel they must perform their duties with little or no autonomy. These are the "dead wood," the "paper-pushers," the "yes men," or the "bureaucrats" in the colloquial meaning of the word. As mentioned previously, people like that, when standing at the head of an organization, can cause burnout in new employees by discouraging them and by derogating their enthusiam. Managers' tactics of discouraging idealistic employees are frequently motivated by their need to insure that subordinates will burn out, thus justifying their own burnout. Other people, usually recently hired, are overly optimistic about the possibilities of change in the organization. These people often end up angry, frustrated, and despairing.

To avoid the pitfalls of overoptimism and overpessimism, employees can evaluate each aspect of the job for its possibilities for change. Those changes that seem impossible after close scrutiny are written off. Energy is then usefully directed toward those elements of the job and the organization that can be changed. Focusing attention on the possible increases one's sense of power and control.

The need for control and autonomy is the other side of the need for security. As described previously, employees who were attracted to large organizations were often motivated by needs for security and retirement benefits. For this reason they remained on their jobs despite high levels of tedium.

Employees of a bureaucracy can use their sense of autonomy and control as a buffer against tedium. They can maximize their discretionary ability to define their roles and establish their priorities at work. We draw a distinction between what serves the organizational purpose and what merely serves the organization. The good bureaucrat does not yield unnecessarily to the requirements of administrative convenience. As a result, the good bureaucrat is less likely to experience tedium. The good bureaucrat, says Pruger, also knows that the most useful skill against inflexibility, officiousness, and the other frustrations of organizational life is a sense of humor.[38]

Not expecting rewards only from above

Employees of an organization can make the work more satisfying by refusing to rely exclusively on their supervisors for praise. This will increase their own freedom to take the initiative and to develop innovations that may keep the individual and the organization alive. Employees who expect to gain their sense of achievement from management's praise alone will most likely be disappointed. Superiors will rarely comment on an employee's work except when things go wrong. Instead of expecting recognition only from above, workers can look for alternative sources. They can give and receive it from coworkers and clients and can achieve a sense of success from the work itself.

Management can help relieve tedium by recognizing rewards and appreciation as powerful buffers against tedium. Understanding employees' needs for rewards and appreciation, and understanding their impact when coming from a superior, can give managers great power to alleviate tedium in the organization. Managers can also increase the staff's sense of power by decentralizing authority and involving people in all levels of the organizational structure in decision making.[39]

Organizational development experts are trying to intervene and affect the reality of bureaucratic life on the organizational level and report success in their efforts.[40] Employees who find themselves working in such an enlightened organization are lucky and most probably feeling less tedium.

Obviously some organizations are better than others on the dimensions of overload, power structure, and rewards. To the extent that an organization is structured in ways that increase such positive features as communication and autonomy, there will be a general reduction in tedium. At the same time even the most enlightened organizations cannot solve this problem for all of their employees. Individuals require sensible and useful coping strategies. These are discussed at some length in Chapters 7, 8, and 9 of this volume.

Notes

1. M. Weber, *Economy and Society: An Outline of Interpretative Sociology,* ed. G. Roth and C. Witlich (New York: Bedminster Press, 1968), p. 1002.
2. D. Bacon, "Mess in Welfare—The Inside Story," *U.S. News and World Report,* February 20, 1978, pp. 21–24. The case study is based on this report. The other quotes in the case study are also from this source.
3. Ibid.
4. Ibid.
5. Ibid.
6. Ibid.

7. Alexis de Tocqueville, *Democracy in America* (Garden City, N.Y.: Doubleday, 1969).

8. K. L. Armstrong, "How Can We Avoid Burnout?" *Child Abuse and Neglect: Issues in Innovation and Implementation*, DHEW Publication no. (OHDS) 78-30148, 2 (1978): 230–238.

9. In the study, which involved fifty-two employees of a large bureaucratic organization, their mean tedium was 3.6. In a study of 205 professionals the mean tedium scores for human service were 3.1, business 3.2, science 3.3, art 3.2.

10. The correlation between tedium and overall satisfaction from work was $r = -.58$,* with overall satisfaction from self $r = -.45$,* with overall satisfaction from life $r = -.44$,* with satisfaction from supervisors $r = -.32$,* with satisfaction from the department $r = -.26$, with satisfaction from the public $r = -.22$, with satisfaction from clients $r = -.53$,* with satisfaction from coworkers $r = -.17$, with satisfaction from work $r = -.43$,* with mean satisfaction from various work activities $r = -.57$,* with wanting to leave the job $r = +.44$* (* indicated that the correlation is statistically significant at .01 level).

11. J. R. D. French and R. D. Kaplan, "Organizational Stress and Individual Strain," in *The Failure of Success*, ed. A. J. Marrow (New York: AMACOM 1973).

12. Both studies are quoted in Z. L. Lipowski, "Sensory and Information Inputs Overload: Behavioral Effects," *Comprehensive Psychiatry* 16, no. 3 (1975): 199–221.

13. The study was conducted in collaboration with Steve Weinberg in the Management Training Program of the University of Alabama in Birmingham.

14. French and Kaplan, "Organizational Stress and Individual Strain."

15. J. G. Miller, in *Communication in Clinical Practice*, ed. R. W. Waggoner and D. J. Carek (Boston: Little, Brown, 1964), pp. 201–224.

16. R. L. Kahn, "Job Burnout, Prevention and Remedies," *Public Welfare* (Spring 1978), pp. 61–63.

17. G. Kirkham, "From Professor to Patrolmen: A Fresh Perspective on the Police," *Journal of Police Science and Administration* 2, no. 2 (1977): 127–137.

18. The study is quoted by W. Kroes in *Society's Victim—The Policeman: An Analysis of Job Stress in Policing* (Springfield, Ill.: Charles Thomas, 1976), p. 27.

19. A. Pines and D. Kafry, *The Impact of a Burnout Workshop on Occupational Tedium*, Technical Report, Berkeley, Calif., 1979.

20. The correlation between tedium and overload in this particular study was $r = .30, p = \leq .05$.

21. The study of child-care workers is described in C. Maslach and A. Pines, "The Burnout Syndrome in Day Care Settings," *Child Care Quarterly*, 6, no. 2 (1977): 100–113. The study of mental health workers is described

in A. Pines and C. Maslach, "Characteristics of Staff Burnout in Mental Health Settings," *Hospital and Community Psychiatry* 29, no. 4 (1978): 233–237.

22. N. Watson and J. Sterling, *Police and Their Opinions* (Gaithersburg, Md.: International Association of Chiefs of Police, 1969).

23. In the study, involving fifty-two employees of a bureaucratic organization, the correlation between tedium and administrative hassles such as paperwork, red tape, and communication problems was $r = .25$. $p < .05$.

24. M. E. Seligman, *Helplessness: On Depression Development and Death* (San Francisco: Freeman Press, 1979).

25. J. E. Singer and D. C. Glass, *Urban Stress* (New York: Academic Press, 1972).

26. P. G. Zimbardo, private communication.

27. The study was done by L. Fidell and J. Prather at California State University, Northridge. It was reported by Carol Tavris in *Psychology Today* 10, no. 4 (1976): 78.

28. In the study involving 205 professionals, the mean tedium for the "have to" respondents was $\bar{x} = 3.5$, for the "want to" respondents $\bar{x} = 3.1$. The difference is statistically significant at $p < .0001$. In a study involving eighty-four students the means were $\bar{x} = 3.8$ for "have to" and $\bar{x} = 3.3$ for "want to," $p < .001$.

29. In a study of fifty-two employees of a bureaucratic organization the correlation between tedium and autonomy was $r = -35$. In a study of 205 professionals (human service, business, service, art, etc.) the correlation was $r = -.28$. Both results are significant at .05 level.

30. Pines and Kafry, *Impact of a Burnout Workshop*.

31. Kroes, *Society's Victim*.

32. D. Gowler and K. Legge, eds., *Managerial Stress* (Epping, England: Grower Press, 1975).

33. Pines and Kafry, *Impact of a Burnout Workshop*.

34. In a study involving 205 professionals the following correlations with tedium were found: with rewards $r = -.33$, with appreciation $r = -.32$, with a sense of significance $r = -.21$, with a sense of success $r = -.24$, with physical health $r = -.39$, with satisfaction from pay $r = .01$.

35. R. Pruger, "The Good Bureaucrat," *Social Work* (July 1973): 26–32.

36. Ibid.

37. N. V. Rayner, M. W. Pratt, and S. Roses, "Aids Involvement in Decision Making and the Quality of Care in Institutional Settings," *American Journal of Mental Deficiency* 81, no. 6 (1977): 570–577.

38. Pruger, "The Good Bureaucrat."

39. Rayner, Pratt, and Roses, "Aids Involvement in Decision Making."

40. W. L. French and C. A. Bell, *Organizational Development: Behavioral Science Interventions for Organizational Improvement,* 2d ed. (Englewood Cliffs, N.J.: Prentice-Hall, 1978).

5

Special issues
concerning women

Rose was 29, sensitive, and exceptionally bright. She graduated first in her high school class and Phi Beta Kappa from college. She met her husband while working toward her Ph.D., which she received with highest honors. Throughout her education she was supported by the most prestigious grants, fellowships, and scholarships. In addition to her graduate school career, Rose pursued interests in sports and music. She ran several miles every day and played competitive tennis. She also played the violin and appeared with local amateur orchestras.

When her husband took a position with a law firm on the East Coast, Rose moved with him. Because they both wanted a child she became pregnant as soon as they settled in their new community. A few months after her child was born Rose received a job offer from a prestigious university that was located sixty miles away. It was a great compliment and an ideal job for her, but now there was a baby with whom she wanted to spend her time. Rose was torn. When she stayed with her child she felt she was disappointing the people who believed in her and who helped her get the job offer. When she worked on a manuscript she was preparing for publication she felt guilty about leaving her baby at home. Her conscience tormented her: "Why did I have a child if I was going to leave her with strangers? She is changing every day now, and I am missing it. Why did I take advantage of all these scholarships when I am never going to publish the research anyway? How can I even talk to my professor again if I turn the offer down?"

The conflict drained Rose of her mental and emotional engergy. As her conflict increased she was less able to separate the issues involved. Her sleep was disrupted and she was frequently upset and nervous. Occasionally she lost her temper and screamed at her child or her husband and then was tormented by guilt and despair. She felt alienated from her family and sometimes cried for hours. She questioned the value of life and her own adequency as a women. She knew she could not stand the situation much longer.

Rose finally turned down the job offer. Two years later she had another baby and took a part-time teaching position at a community college. She received great satisfaction from students' enthusiastic responses to her classes but she devoted so much time to preparation for her lectures that there was little left for sports, music, or her own research. She remained torn between her roles as a professional and a mother, and her role conflict continued as a source of great emotional strain.

Role conflict is a major stress for most women who are combining the careers of a homemaker and a professional. For some women this role conflict is the main antecedent of burnout and tedium. We will discuss such role conflict after discussing separately the stress of the homemaker and the stress of the professional woman.

The homemaker's work stress

More individuals contribute goods and services as homemakers than as any other single occupation. Although these goods and services are not accounted for in the gross national product, they are a necessary part of our economy.[1] But although the role of the housewife and mother may be important for society, for some women it holds little opportunity for a sense of significance and success.

Until recently the role of homemakers was not the subject of much research. In recent years the growing interest in women's issues has prompted a review of the homemaker's role, and social scientists have begun to study it as they study other jobs. According to industrial psychologist Richard Arvey, there are important distinctions between the homemaker's jobs and jobs outside the home. One difference is

that the homemaker receives no pay for the goods produced or services rendered. Another distinction is that the homemaker has little, if
any, separation between her employment role and her other roles.
The roles of housewife, mother, and wife are closely intertwined,
perhaps inextricably so.[2]

Myra Marx Ferree, a sociologist at the University of Connecticut,[3]
described the American housewife as "besieged." On one side stand
the traditionalists who tell her that her greatest pleasures come from
satisfying the needs of others: making a home for her family, raising
healthy children, and pleasing her husband. On the other side stand
the egalitarians who tell her that her own needs are important too.
Marx Ferree, who interviewed 135 women, found that almost twice as
many housewives as employed wives said they were dissatisfied with
their lives. More houswives also claimed that they had not had a fair
opportunity in life and wanted their daughters to be "mostly different
from themselves."

The reasons for the housewives' dissatisfaction were found in the
characteristics of their work:

> A housewife's day is never done and her tasks often bring neither tangi-
> ble rewards nor social connections. Husbands and wives alike have an
> uncertain idea of how much housework is work. Housewives expend
> great effort but don't get recognition for it: their husbands accuse them of
> "doing nothing all day" and in the next breath remind them that their
> duty is to stay home and keep house. As a result many housewives have
> an uncertain idea of what their occupation requires, and how well or
> poorly they are doing it.[4]

Not long ago, writes Marx Ferree, housewives shared a social
network. They were likely to live near their mothers, relatives, and
friends and to establish close-knit groups. Within these groups there
was no doubt whether someone was or was not a good homemaker. In
recent decades, however, a rise in mobility and in the number of
working women has made housewife networks less common and
more difficult to maintain. With husbands at work and children in
school, wives may become isolated. Women who were interviewed by
Marx Ferree felt they were going crazy staying home, "not seeing
anyone but four walls all day." "Staying home all day," said one
woman, "is like being in jail."[5]

Many portraits of the housewife in the literature describe her as
neurotic, bored, depressed, and anxious. They depict her work as the
essence of boredom and triviality, work that is degrading, unpleasant,

and self-negating. Housework has been described as consisting mainly of drudgery, with no formal wages, no social support, and no recognition, resulting in dissatisfaction among homemakers. In Jessie Bernard's words, "being a housewife makes women sick."[6]

Ann Oakley, who conducted in-depth interviews of British homemakers,[7] found that 70 percent of the women she interviewed were dissatisfied with their homemakers' role. In other studies, Richard Arvey reported much lower percentages of dissatisfaction than did Oakley.[8] Psychologist Linda Fidel and Sociologist Jane Prather suggested that the new stereotype of the neurotic housewife may be just as distorted as the old stereotype of the happy homemaker.[9] Fidel and Prather distinguished between those homemakers who do not want work and those who want to work but do not do so because of family responsibilities, lack of child care, a limited job market, or illness. The latter are the ones who fit the "unhappy housewife" stereotype. They are dissatisfied with their lives, have low self-esteem, feel trapped by circumstances, and mask their loneliness and worry with drugs. In contrast, the housewives who do not want to work outside the home are happy, healthy, and comfortable in their role. They often come from high-income families so they do not need a salaried job and they fill their days with housework and time for themselves. They have happy marriages, feel in control of their lives, and have very good physical and mental health.

In working with homemakers[10] we found, as did Fidel and Prather, that they were concentrated in two groups in terms of their tedium. Those exhibiting the "neurotic housewife syndrome" ranked very high in tedium. They were chronically exhausted and emotionally drained. They felt that spending their days with children was making their minds "shrink." They felt trapped and depressed. Many of them had burned out in their roles as wives and mothers. Those women who ranked low in burnout and tedium took pride in their roles as wives and mothers, were creative about their homemaking tasks, and were involved in adult education classes and community politics. Terry and Sara are two women who exemplify these extremes.

Terry had a bachelors degree in English. She was married and had one child. For years she tried to get a job but failed because there were simply none available for an English teacher. She became frustrated and bitter, feeling that her life was passing her by. She felt that her household chores were wasting her skills and education. "How much creativity can you put into dusting?" she asked. When she compared herself to her husband she felt trapped. When asked what she did for a living, her apologetic, embarrassed response was, "I am just a housewife and a mother."

Terry dreaded the empty hours of her day. She took "uppers" to fight off depression and smoked, drank, and watched television to pass the time. She did not have sufficient energy to read a book or call a friend. She found it difficult to communicate with her son; she often lost her temper and became afraid that she would hurt him. She began to have fantasies of suicide. "If that's all that life is," she said, "it's not worth it."

Sara, in contrast, was happy with her life. She had worked for a number of years as a nurse but was very happy to leave her profession when she married. She had wanted to be a mother, a wife, and a homemaker in a beautiful house. Sara took care to be properly dressed and groomed. She spent time every day in exercise and beauty care. She took as much pride in her house and garden as she took in her appearance. Sara liked to spend time with her children and was involved with their school and after-school activities. The children liked to bring their friends home, and her house was always filled with people.

Sara had many friends who were housewives like herself. They provided a supportive social system for each other. She was active in a charity organization and in the PTA and worked in ceramics with great success. She perceived her life as meaningful and fulfilling.

There are some objective differences between Sara and Terry. Sara's husband had a higher income; her house was more luxurious; she could afford clothes, beauty salons, tennis lessons, and help with the house and the children. She could take time for herself. Sara appreciated the material benefits of her marriage because she came from a very poor family, but Terry felt disappointed with what life had done to her great potential.

Other differences between the two are more subjective and cannot be explained by economic realities or by fulfilled or failes aspirations. Sara was involved in a support system of other women like herself, but Terry felt isolated and lonely. Sara felt in control of her life, and her housework gave her variety and a sense of success and significance. Terry, however, felt very much out of control of her life. She was ashamed of her role as a housewife and derived neither meaning nor satisfaction from it. Sara was at the lowest end and Terry at the highest end of our tedium scale.

Two decades ago most American women worked only at home. Primary occupational roles were those of wife, mother, and homemaker. Occupational success was measured by cleanliness of the home, well-behaved children, and contented husbands. Like Sara, many women who chose to stay home felt very lucky, luckier than men in their freedom from work. They could do what they wanted while fulfilling their ambition: raising a happy family. They did not resent, as Terry did, being called "Mrs. John Watkins" or "David's mother." They were proud and secure in their roles.

Women's work in the United States has evolved since then. Most women in the paid labor force no longer work only to supplement the family income. Today more women work outside the home, choosing demanding professions in which they excel. But American culture still expects that the working woman will make marriage and motherhood her primary vocation. These expectations result in external situational stress and in internal emotional stress, both affecting the working woman's self-perception as a competent human being. Both kinds of stress lead to burnout and tedium.

Individuals can change their attitudes—with effort. Women who know they are going to be homemakers for several years can make the most out of this period by taking interest in the tasks homemaking entails. Getting involved in adult education classes or a hobby can also make this time more satisfying. Taking a day off is very important when a housewife feels under particular pressure: she can stay home and, when the family is away, have lunch with a friend or tour the city. Most important, she can arrange a support system of other homemakers who are dealing with similar issues. The availability of such a group can be the determining factor in a homemaker's coping with burnout and tedium.

The working women's work stress

Women in the human services

Sex-role stereotyping of occupations exists on all levels of the labor force. Women are believed to prefer work such as teaching, counseling, and nursing which represents an extension of their domestic roles and involves helping, nurturing, and socializing activities. Employment figures in industrial countries suggest this stereotyping of occupations. The bulk of women workers are in teaching and nursing.[11]

In a research investigating people's perceptions of a professional women,[12] we found that being "feminime" was highly correlated with being "sex-appropriate" and "better adjusted" and with being less "aggressive" and "active" and more "sensitive," "warm, " and "kind." The attributes that make women seek work in the human services and may make them more qualified for that work may be the same attributes that make them more vulnerable to the dangers of burnout.

The homemaker who is a service professional has the added stress of a job at home. She is expected to spend both her professional and personal life being empathic, understanding, and sensitive to the needs of others. In the chapter on burnout of professionals in the human services, we mentioned three antecedents of burnout: (1) working with people, (2) a self-selective sample, and (3) a client-centered orientation. These antecedents are particularly powerful for women, especially those who are carrying the double burden of a family and a profession:

1. Women are often drawn to occupations in which they work with people, especially in a helping role. Women are disproportionately represented in teaching, nursing, counseling, social work, and social welfare. These are professions that require contact with people in intense, painful, or emotionally demanding situations; women also are expected to provide this nurturance at home.
2. Sex-role stereotypes describe women as affectionate, caring, empathic, sensitive to the needs of others. If this is true for women in general it may be more true for women in the human services. Of the self-selected helpers, women are the most predetermined.
3. The professions that many women choose are often client-centered, and similarly the role of mother is child-oriented. Being child-oriented is an endless process: there is always more a "good" mother could do, and this societal norm is a source of guilt for many women.

If a woman is sensitive, the professional struggles can be more frustrating than if she is not. If she is empathic, the suffering and helplessness she sees are more painful. If she knew herself as a caring human being, the realization that she has become numb to others' needs is more devastating. Thus the problems of burnout have special relevance for professional women in the human services.

Three generations of professional women

A study involving 424 professional women in three generations explored similarities and differences in tedium and its antecedents.[13] The first generation consisted of preprofessional female students whose average age was 21, the second generation was professional women whose average age was 34, and the third generation was postprofessional retired women whose average age was 66. The women were questioned about tedium, daily activities, attitudes toward women's issues, and life and work satisfaction. The results of those surveys are summarized here.

THE MID-CAREER PROFESSIONAL WOMEN

Those career women/housewives-mothers who were the ones supposed to be the most overburdened by two full-time jobs were found to project the most positive picture of the three groups. Though they worked more than the others they had more satisfaction from their work, found their professional role more enjoyable and rewarding, and held more liberal attitudes toward working women and working women's issues. They felt they had more variety, more autonomy, and more complexity in their lives. Although they had less time for themselves, they were in better health and had more positive life attitudes than the younger and older women. In short, they revealed a very positive attitude toward both life and work.

THE PREPROFESSIONAL WOMEN

The young students reported the most tedium and the least satisfaction in their work and life. They felt overextended in commitments and social obligations and were conflicted about their school work and social life. They frequently reported being disturbed while studying by thoughts about romantic involvements, but while with their dates they were distressed by guilt and anxiety about neglecting their school work and the effect this neglect would have on their future. These women felt they had less autonomy than the two other groups and they enjoyed their professional role less. They spent more time than the other women in study and reading but they enjoyed these activities less. They had poorer relationships with people at school, probably as a result of academic competition.

The younger women, in summary, were experiencing more tedium than their dual-career counterparts. One possible explanation for these unexpected results is tedium's process of selection: those young women who are most distressed at college may drop out before they begin a professional career or shortly afterward. Another possible explanation for the positive picture of the career woman is self-rationalization: it is easier for some people, like the students, to acknowledge distress before choosing a career. Once the decision has been made and has been costly in training and the effect on marriage and home, it may be harder to admit difficulties.

THE POSTPROFESSIONAL WOMEN

The postprofessional women had the worst health, felt the least overextended, and had the fewest distractions and conflicts. They spent more time than the other groups watching television and in hobbies and community work; they also spent more time in housework and shopping, the traditional homemaker's activities. Although these women had been professionals at a time when careers were unusual for women, they agreed more than the younger women with statements such as "raising a child can keep most women satisfied," "children of working mothers tend to be maladjusted," and "the spouse's career is more important" than their own. These women spent the least time talking to friends and relatives and, though they rated highly their relationships with friends, they felt they had the least unconditional support when they needed it.

In summary, the main findings in three generations of professional women were the stressful environment of college for the preprofessionals and the isolation and the traditional attitudes of the post-professionals. The mid-career professionals had liberal attitudes toward women's issues, more satisfaction from their lives, and more satisfaction from their work. Although they carried the dual burden of home and career, they did not have more role conflict and did not express more tedium.

In the case study of Rose that was presented at the beginning of this chapter, we described role conflict as one of the major causes of stress for professional women. Yet it appears from the data presented above that dual-career women experienced less role conflict than did preprofessional college students. This contradiction is resolved when one considers that the mid-career women were compared not to men or to professional women without families but to students and retired women. The contradiction is further clarified when one looks at the mid-career women's perceived autonomy and variety. The professional women felt more in control of their lives than the other two samples and perceived their dual roles not as conflictual but as sources of greater variety. Role conflict is indeed a source of stress and a major antecedent of tedium as the data of the preprofessionals indicates.

Professional women and men: a comparison

The study of tedium among three generations of professional women found that women in mid-career who carry a double load of a job and a family had the most satisfaction from their lives and their work. Although they worked more and had less time for themselves, they had more variety, autonomy, and sense of significance. However, the picture of professional women changes when they are compared to professional men rather than professional women at other times in their careers. In a study of tedium and its antecedents and correlates in men and women, we found that women were at a disadvantage, especially in their work conditions.[14]

Professional women had slightly more tedium than professional men but had four times more of its most extreme level; they felt they had less freedom. autonomy, and influence in their work as well as less variety, less challange, and a less positive work environment. They reported having fewer opportunities for self-expression and self-actualization and felt less adequately rewarded for their work. These women also had more of such negative features as environmental pressures and overextension caused by the demands of other people. These findings, plus research that showed women suffer from discrimination and harrassment in male-dominated professions, support the findings of greater burnout and tedium among women.

One reason for the tedium-causing work environment of women is the occupations and roles most women choose. Another reason, according to Margaret Henning and Anne Jardim, is sex-role differences in work attitudes.[15] Henning and Jardim, who interviewed more than 100 women working as executives in business and industry, claim that women see a career as a source of personal growth and self-fulfillment and they seek in it the satisfaction of doing what one wants to do. These perceptions may cause women to have higher expectations of their careers than men. When these expectations are not met, women may burn out or develop tedium. In our study we found that the more self-actualized women were, and the more opportunities for self-expression they had, the less tedium they experienced. This was less true for men.[16]

Men may see a career as an upward progression of jobs with recognition and rewards, whereas women may be less concerned with advancement, seeing their work occupation as a series of jobs rather than a life career. In our study, low position and inadequate financial rewards were correlated with tedium for men but not for women. Although men look upon a particular job as part of a career, women separate the two. For them, a job involves the present and a career is in the future. Men concentrate on achieving long-range goals; women focus on short-term planning with little concern for long-term implications.

Men, claim Henning and Jardim, find it difficult to separate personal goals from career goals. They see each as dependent on the other and try to negotiate between them when they conflict. Women, however, try to keep their lives separate from their careers. In our study we found that the conflict between life and work was very stressful for both men and women, but women saw their life outside work as more important than men did.

Women were found to have more stressful work environments with significantly fewer positive features than men. In the sphere that women felt was most important, their homes, they had little variety. They worked at home more than men, felt more frequently overextended emotionally, and had more guilt and anxiety about not fulfilling their duties as completely as they wanted. As a result of their stressful work environment and the added emotional burden of their roles, women tended to have more extreme levels of tedium than men. The important support for women, more than for men, was their social systems.

Women's values may make ambition and competition secondary to good work relationships and good personal relationships at home. Good personal relationships were very highly correlated with tedium for women[17] (the better the relationship the less tedium); this was less true for men. Tedium was found to be lower for employees, especially women, who were involved in social networks and support systems. Women seem to have a higher sensitivity than men to the social aspects of their life and work; they have better personal relationships, more emotional assistance from their family, friends and coworkers, and more unconditional support in times of stress than men.

People's perceptions of a professional woman

At the beginning of this chapter we demonstrated the impact of role conflict in the case of Rose. Every career woman who wants to have a family faces Rose's dilemma. A critical issue for many career women is other people's perceptions of their double role. In one study we examined these perceptions.[18] The woman who served as the example in our study was struggling with a role conflict similar to Rose's and she wanted to examine people's perceptions of her as one way to sort the issues. For the purpose of the study we asked her to separate the two roles onto two videotapes. Both tapes started with the same interview in which she talked about her history, educational background, and interests. The tapes had two different endings in which she talked about her plans for the future. In one tape she presented only her career plans, saying she wanted to accept a university position, teach, and publish scientific articles. In the second tape she presented only her family plans, saying she intended to stay home with her child while he was young and work in the house and garden.

College students were shown only one of the two tapes and asked for their perceptions of the women in it, the "stimulus person." All the students saw the identical initial interview that established her abilities. Yet, after viewing the career tape, students described her more with adjectives traditionally ascribed to career-oriented males; aggressive, dominant, independent. In addition, she was perceived as more success-oriented and ambitious, attributes that are associated with the pursuit of a career. By contrast, in the family tape she was seen as less independent, less active, less aggressive, less ambitious, less dominant, less success-oriented and less able to withstand pressure. A woman's choice to have a family seemed to automatically decrease her perceived competence.

There was a difference in response between men and women who saw the tapes. The women perceived the "stimulus person" as more competent and attributed more positive characteristics to her when she described her career goals than when she described her family goals. For many of them her conflict was not an intellectual exercise but a real issue they must resolve for themselves. It seemed that the stimulus person was perceived more favorably by women when espousing career goals because of the role-conflict identification and because of the social desirability of the women's movement among college students.

In contrast, men had a more favorable impression of the stimulus person on the family tape. They found her to be more feminine, open-minded, sincere, intelligent, kind, well adjusted, sensitive, warm, and determined. They also liked her more in the family tape and said they would want to spend more time with her. There are several tentative explanations for these findings. It may be that career women are somewhat threatening for men, especially a women as competent and successful as this one. It may also be that she was perceived as potentially less able to provide for men because of her commitment to a career and thus was seen as less feminine and less desirable. A woman who decides to give up a career and stay at home is more understandable, better fitting the usual sex-role stereotypes, and possibly less threatening. Thus, the stimulus person was perceived by men both as a stereotyped woman (warm, sensitive, and kind) and as more open-minded, well adjusted, and similar to themselves.

One result seemed evident. Even for students, most of whom have been schooled in the negative effects of sex-role stereotypes and who are considered open-minded, the professional woman is still in a bind in which she is "doomed if she does and doomed if she does not." If she chooses career she will be seen, especially by men, as less feminine, less likable, and less desirable. If she chooses a family she will be seen as less competent.

The double bind of professional women
as a cause of burnout

With the changing roles of women and the growing influence of the women's movement, more women are choosing a career as an integral part of their life. This change is evident in the growing proportion of women who are entering the job market: the percentage of women in the United States labor force increased from 20 percent to 40 percent between 1920 and 1978.[19]

There is also a qualitative change in women's participation in the labor force. More women are choosing professional careers over occupations.[20] Occupations offer primarily financial gains and relatively few challenges. Careers involve continual learning and require high degrees of commitment. This change in work orientation has important consequences for women who regard their work as essential to their lives as a result of their increased commitment.

When they decide to have a family, many of these women feel conflicted about their two roles. Because of the career commitment, their roles at home and at work take on a new meaning. Sometimes this results in changed priorities, in which equal priority for home and work roles replaces the traditional preference for the home role. This conflict leads women to burnout and tedium[21] and, in extreme cases, to emotional breakdown and suicide; among professional groups such as physicians and psychologists, for example, women have higher suicide rates than men, though the reverse is true for the general population.

In order to avoid this conflict, increasing numbers of women are choosing not to have a family at all. Others resolve this dilemma by giving the family precedence over the career when they conflict. Other options, such as part-time positions and job sharing, are becoming more common and are making the choice of having both family and career more manageable.

Some professional women deal with their conflict by overadhering the sex-role stereotypes at home. These women do not see their jobs as a justification for doing less at home, as most men do. They therefore have high expectations of themselves that, when frustrated, cause them to feel guilt and anxiety about not fulfilling all of their responsibilities. These women believe that in addition to being "superprofessionals" they have to be "supermothers" and "superhomemakers."

It is the unfortunate reality that the woman still carries the burden of the conflict between career and family and she may pay the ultimate price of her choice—burnout and tedium—because this conflict promotes the physical, mental, and emotional stress characteristic of these syndromes.

Two full-time jobs: the reality

In addition to the occupational stress that they have in common with men, working women may have stresses that result from their womanhoood. These stresses can stem from external or internal social mores such as the belief that a woman can be either feminine (desirable) or competent and successful (unfeminine, undesirable). Thus the professional women often finds herself in a normative dilemma with little support from most of society.

Stress can be the result for women who combine a career and a home. A women who takes a job outside the home is taking on two full-time jobs: she has the duties of the job as well as the major responsibilities for housework and child care.[22] As a result, employed wives have the least time to spend on themselves. The career woman/housewife-mother had been described as frantically performing all her duties simultaneously.[23] She may be the first one up in the morning to prepare breakfast for the family. During lunch she takes care of the family's errands. She shops for groceries on the way home and often, while her husband and children relax, she prepares dinner. In the evenings and on weekends she cleans the house, does the laundry, and takes care of the emotional needs of her husband and children.

Women's daily routines also contain a higher proportion of domestic interruptions than do those of men.[24] It is usually the mother who takes the children to the doctor and stays home with them when they are sick. It is usually the mother who goes to "conference day" with the teacher and is called when there is a problem at school. She may have no choice but to do these tasks at the expense of her job.

Most of the difficulties professional women encounter are the result of social barriers to women's abilities to implement their personal skills in a career.[25] Some of these barriers are sex-related role and occupational stereotypes that lead to the career/home conflict. In research on women, we found that role conflict and the distractions at home and at work were highly correlated with tedium; the more conflict and the more distractions, the more tedium.[26] The mother employed in a full-time job is more likely the one who is overburdened, harrassed, and guilt-ridden. She is someone who cannot afford to get sick, take time for herself, or even collapse. She is also more likely than the professional man/father to be chronically exhausted and therefore is a likely candidate for burnout and tedium.

Shared antecedents of burnout and tedium for professional women and how to cope with them

In the study of three generations of professional women, the women showed similarities in their life satisfaction, their enjoyment of their roles as women, and the quality of their family relations. All of these are negatively correlated with tedium; the more satisfied a woman is with her life, the better her family relations and the more she enjoys her role as a woman—the less likely she is to develop tedium.

For all three groups we found that tedium increased as several variables increased. These variables were: being overextended in social obligations, having conflict between work and life outside of work, being distracted at work by thoughts about home problems, and being distracted at home by occupational obligations. These are sources of stress and thus antecedents of tedium for all professional women.

In the scientific literature, role conflict is perceived as a major sources of stress, and not only for women. Role conflict exists when any individual in a particular role is torn by conflicting demands. Most commonly this occurs when a person is caught between two or more groups who demand different behaviors. Role conflict has serious consequences for one's subjective experience of stress as well as for one's performance.[27] Previous research found that those who suffered more role conflict had lower job satisfaction and higher job-related tension.[28] It was also found that the greater the authority of the people "sending" the conflicting role messages, the more job dissatisfaction produced by the role conflict and the more physiological strain. Role conflict also tended to make women more likely to work less effectively and to leave the organization.[29] And we found that tedium increased as role conflict increased.[30]

In our research, we found that home pressures contributed as much to role conflict and stress of professional women as out-of-home pressures.[31] Other research has shown that the marriage role and the motherhood role are most likely, and the work role least likely, to be perceived as conflictual.[32] In another of our studies overlap between life and work stresses was found to be highly correlated with tedium.[33]

One recommendation for professional women is to separate home and work as much as possible, especially in regard to problems: when at work concentrate on the job and avoid thinking about home and home problems; try not to bring work home and avoid the intrusion of work problems into the home time. This is, of course, easier said than done. One way of implementing this strategy is to make a period of relaxation and "decompression" between work and home, allowing time to unwind from one set of stresses before facing another. One woman we interviewed said she went window shopping for decompression. Another just sat at the bus stop watching buses pass by. Others mentioned walking, jogging, listening to music, and meditating. Compartmentalization can help keep stresses limited in time and place and thus reduce conflict and tedium.

Although role conflict is a very important cause of tedium, the number of roles does not necessarily mean more conflict and more tedium. Various roles may be different routes to a women's self-actualization and self-expression and thus add to her life satisfaction rather than cause distress. Our recommendation is to use home and work activities as alternate sources of satisfaction. On days when a woman feels incompetent as a mother and a homemaker she can use her job to boost her self-esteem and sense of success. When things do not go well at work, her home can serve as an excuse. The happiest women are those who feel competent and successful in both roles. They derive a sense of variety and achievement from the different activities in their multiple roles. In each role they express a different part of their personality and their abilities. As a result they are likely to be busy but they may live a full and exciting life. Sylvia was an example of a dual-career woman who coped successfully with the demands of her home and work.

Sylvia was a social worker in a perinatal unit of a children's hospital. Instead of being overburdened by the emotional stress of working with premature babies and their mothers, her work provided her with a daily reminder of the value of life and health and her own good fortune. She knew she could not handle a full-time career while her child was young, so she worked only part-time. When at work she was involved totally, but when she left her work she avoided thinking about the tragedies her clients were dealing with. After working as a caseworker for two years, she decided to participate in a research project as a way to obtain some distance from her work. She needed to intellectualize several of the issues her clients were presenting because she felt too close to them. She was learning about research and felt it was a growth-producing experience. Syliva loved her work and felt very successful in it. She also felt good about herself as a mother and a wife. She was very aware of the dangers of burnout in her work and was very careful to avoid them.

"Everything is a given, and yet you have a choice"

There are burned-out homemakers and happy homemakers. There are overburdened and harrassed career women, and there are fulfilled and self-actualized career women. These are just two of the many contradictions of modern women. The ancient Hebrew scholars said that, although everything is a given, one still had the final choice. The choice that women have is their greatest advantage, and advantage many of them never realize.

A women can choose to have or not to have a family. She can also choose to have or not to have a career. It is crucial for these decisions to be made in full awareness of their possible consequences. Each decision should be based on the woman's needs, desires, and abilities and be minimally influenced by social pressures. Each decision has almost irreversible consequences. It is difficult for a career woman to decide at age 45 that she would like to have four children. It is equally hard for a homemaker to decide at age 45 to venture into a brilliant scientific career. These far-reaching consequences make the initial choice facing women complex.

Thus this decision must be made in full awareness and, once made, be accepted without daily regrets. With either decision a woman may face powerful social pressures, and she must weigh her ability to withstand or accommodate such stress. She must be aware that she will face daily struggles for priorities of her time and energy. The home/career woman must define her goals in each of her different roles and distribute her mental, physical, and emotional energy accordingly. A decision to combine family and career means making compromises. The woman herself must decide how these compromises will be made, both between and within her roles.

The conscious and continual allocation of resources among a woman's various roles will reduce conflict and stress. This allocation may go beyond preventing burnout and tedium to bring about personal growth, if it takes into account the woman's own needs.

Notes

1. R. D. Arvey and R. H. Gross, "Satisfaction Levels and Correlates of Satisfaction in the Homemaker Job," *Journal of Vocational Behavior* 10 (1977): 13–24.
2. Ibid.
3. M. Marx Ferree, "The Confused American Housewife," *Psychology Today* 10, no. 4 (1976): 76–80.
4. Ibid., p. 76
5. Ibid.
6. Jessie Bernard, a research scholar at the Department of Sociology, Pennsylvania State University, is the author of *The Future of Marriage, The Future of Motherhood*, and several other books on sex roles, marriage, and the family.
7. A. Oakley, *The Sociology of Housework* (New York: Pantheon, 1975).
8. Arvey and Gross, "Satisfaction Levels."
9. Reported by Carol Tavris in "Women's Work Isn't Always the Answer," *Psychology Today* 10, no. 4 (1976): 78.
10. Among our various research samples we had a group of thirty-two homemakers. We also worked with homemakers in our burnout workshops.
11. Oakley, *Sociology of Housework*.
12. The study was done in collaboration with Joy Stapp and Trudy Solomon and was described in detail in the following publications: A. Pines, "The Influence of Goals on People's Perceptions of a Competent Woman," *Sex Roles* 5, no. 1 (1979): 71–76; A. Pines and T. Solomon, "The Social Psychological Double Bind of the Competent Woman," *Research in Education*, February 1979; J. Stapp and A. Pines, "Who Likes Competent Women?" *Human Behavior* 5, no. 1 (1975): 49–50.
13. For a detailed description of the study, see A. Pines and D. Kafry, "The Experience of Life Tedium in Three Generations of Professional Women," *Sex Roles*, in press.
14. For a detailed description of the study, see A. Pines and D. Kafry, "Tedium in the Life and Work of Professional Women as Compared with Men," *Sex Roles*, in press.
15. M. Henning and A. Jardim, *The Managerial Woman* (New York: Doubleday, 1976).
16. The correlation between tedium and self-actualization for men was $r = -.18$, for women $r = -.29$. Only for women was the correlation statis-

tically significant ($p < .05$). The correlation between tedium and self-expression for men was $r = -.01$, for women $r = -.42$. Only for women was the correlation statistically significant ($p < .05$). The correlation between tedium and personal relations was $r = -.42$ for women and $r = -.21$ for men.

17. See note 16.

18. See note 12.

19. R. J. Schiffler, "Demographic and Social Factors in Women's Work," in *Emerging Women Career Analysis and Outlook*, ed. S. H. Osipow (Columbus, Ohio: Charles E. Merrill, 1975).

20. R. Rapoport, and R. N. Rapoport, "Further Considerations on the Dual Career Family," *Human Relations* 24 (1971): 519–533.

21. We investigated the conflict between life and work as a tedium correlate in eight of our samples. The correlations ranged from .24 to .38 and all were statistically significant.

22. Tavris, "Women's Work."

23. Oakley, *Sociology of Housework*.

24. Ibid.

25. S. H. Osipow, "Concepts in Considering Women's Careers," in *Emerging Women: Career Analysis and Outlook*, ed. S. H. Osipow (Columbis, Ohio: Charles E. Merrill, 1975).

26. The work has been described in detail in the following publications: A. Pines, "Burnout and Life Tedium in Three Generations of Professional Women." Paper presented at the American Psychological Association Convention, San Francisco, California, August 26–30, 1977; Pines and Kafry, "The Experience of Life Tedium"; Pines and Kafry, "Tedium in the Life and Work of Pressional Women."

27. C. L. Cooper, and J. Marshal, "Occupational Sources of Stress: A Review of the Literature Relating to Coronary Heart Disease and Mental Ill Health," *Journal of Occupational Psychology* 49, (1976): 11–28.

28. R. L. Kahn, D. M. Wolfe, R. P. Quinn, J. D. Snoek, and R. A. Rosenthal, *Organizational Stress* (New York: Wiley, 1964).

29. D. T. Hall, "Pressures from Work, Self and Home in the Life Stages of Married Women," *Journal of Vocational Behavior* 6, (1975): 121–132.

30. In the study involving 424 women, cited earlier in the chapter, the correlation between tedium and life/work conflict was $r = .34$, $p < .001$.

31. The correlation between tedium and distractions at work was $r = .36$, tedium and distractions at home $r = .35$; both are significiant at the .001 level.

32. Hall, "Pressures from Work, Self and Home."

33. The study involved 563 subjects and was done in collaboration with Steve Weinberg and the Management Training Program at the University of Alabama. The correlation between life/work overlap in terms of stresses and tedium was $r = 42$, $p < .01$.

part three

What to do about burnout and tedium

6

Organizational
coping strategies

The first research on burnout examined precipitants of staff burnout in day-care centers. The study involved eighty-three staff members from twelve child-care facilities.[1] It was found that: (1) large child-staff ratios resulted in cognitive, sensory, and emotional overload for staff members; (2) those facilities that required the longest working hours with children produced the most stress and negative attitudes in the staff; (3) loosely structured programs took an emotional toll on the staff members; (4) those facilities that had the lowest rates of burnout and the greatest job satisfaction were those with frequent staff meetings where staff could socialize, provide support and advice, clarify goals, and influence the policies of the center.

Various changes occurred at the day-care centers as a consequence of this research. Staff members were asked to complete a burnout questionnaire in which they were asked about their work characteristics, attitudes, and stresses. After considering these issues, some staff members reevaluated their jobs and changed their approaches to their work with children. In one day-care center the staff organized a series of meetings around the findings of the research and made structural changes in the operation of the center. Six months later, a follow-up evaluation of these changes was conducted by observing the daily program and interviewing the staff members.[2] We will present what happened at this particular day-care center as a case study in one organization's practical application of research findings and as a demonstration of what an organization can do to combat burnout.

A case study of organizational changes

The day-care center prior to change

The day-care center was located in a housing complex for married students and served these students almost exclusively. It had a permissive and nondirective educational philosophy. There was no formal structure to the program. Staff members were available to provide play materials, read stories, organize games, and handle problems but they rarely directed the children's activities.

The center was a parent-cooperative drop-in center; Each parent was expected to contribute three hours a week as a teacher-helper; children could be dropped off at the center at any time between 8:00 A.M. and 5:00 P.M. The center accommodated a total of sixty-one children: eight pretoddlers (18 months to 2 years), eighteen toddlers (2 to 3 years), twenty-seven preschoolers (3 to 5 years), and eight kindergarteners (5 to 6 years). However, children arrived at different hours so that the maximum at any one time was forty-five. The center was at full capacity between 10:00 A.M. and 3:00 P.M., with a reduced number of children in the early morning and late afternoon.

The center was housed in a garagelike building with high ceilings that amplified sounds. The building was divided by child-high walls into three rooms for children, a staff lounge, a kitchen, and a large play area. Adjoining the main building was a small indoor gym, a children's bathroom, a changing room, and a nap room. Outside there was a yard with climbing structures, swings, a sandbox, and various outdoor toys. The three children's rooms were roughly divided into a babies' room, a toddlers' room, and a "big-kids" room. In each room there were a head teacher and a few other teachers under his or her supervision, for a total of twelve teachers. In spite of this room division, children were free to use any room, and all teachers shared coverage of all parts of the center, no matter how many children were there. In addition to parents and teachers, the center used student volunteers who worked as teacher-helpers in return for university course credits. With the addition of parents and volunteers, the adult-child ratio was 1 to 3.

The day-care center was characterized by a lack of structure, a constant flow of people, and high levels of noise and aggression. Although the philosopy was one of permissiveness, the operation of this center cannot be viewed as a good model of this approach. Indeed, one might argue that it represented a poor level of child-care practice. On the surface, flexibility may seem advantageous. But there were some serious negative consequences to this loose structure. For example, one result of the loose arrangement was that there was a commotion in the center during all hours of the day. Parents came and went, delivering and retrieving their children as well as serving their parent hours; children arrived and departed at different times; student volunteers dropped in during their free time. One teacher calculated that he had to communicate with about one hundred people daily; including all of the children, all of the parents, all of the volunteers, and the administrators. Because of the great number of people and the irregular schedules of the children, activities had to be flexible and spontaneous. It was difficult for teachers to carry out any regular educational program. Because children were coming and going all day, no one knew whom to expect and when. A teacher planning a project had to be prepared for all or none of the children taking part in it. One teacher might have children from 2 to 6 years old participating in an activity while another teacher might be taking care of only one baby. In addition, because of the mingling of age groups the teachers were constantly alert to protect the younger or weaker children. Just as there was no structured program, there was no structured space in the center. In addition to the three main rooms, there was a large, empty area in which children were allowed to run and play aggressively in order to "let out their energy." As a result they felt free to use, and sometimes abuse, other rooms and toys.

Although teachers in this center liked children, were affectionate with them, and were committed to their work in child care, they were exhausted after work and were increasingly negative about children and about their jobs. They frequently took vacations in which they engaged in solitary activities, needing to get away from people, especially children. One teacher who had wanted to have eight children of her own decided she was not sure she wanted any children at all. Teachers felt they were subjected to tremendous stresses and were dissatisfied with work.

Changes instituted in the day-care center

After taking part in the study and reviewing the research report, the staff of the day-care center decided to institute modifications in their program. The changes centered around two of the factors that were identified as contributing to burnout: the ratio of staff to children and the degree of structure in the program. The finding that emotional exhaustion was correlated with nonstructured programs was especially surprising to this group of teachers. Although they recognized their own physical, mental, and emotional exhaustion, they had not associated it with their center's permissive and nondirective philosophy. Indeed they considered these characteristics to be virtues and they were proud of this arrangement.

The staff decided on and implemented two major changes: a new division of the center's physical space and a division of the staff's teaching responsibilities. The staff apportioned six rooms in the center: one for babies, two for toddlers, two for "big kids," and one for kindergarteners. A team of two teachers was assigned to each room, as was a specific group of children. Each staff member had responsibility for only his or her group of children. As a result, the teachers could spend more time with each of their children and could prepare specific activities for the group. This change was augmented by several structural changes in the program. Each child was scheduled for a specific period of time at the center, rather than being allowed to arrive and depart at any time. Similarly, volunteers and parents were assigned to work at specific times and in specific rooms, each with its own staff, children, toys, and play materials.

A short-term evaluation of the changes

Six months after these changes were instituted, interviews were conducted with almost all of the teachers who had been working at the center before and after the changes were made. The interviews focused on the teachers' assessment of the effectiveness of the changes for the children and for themselves and on their feelings about their child-care work. According to the staff, the changes in the day-care center had a great impact on the children. Because of the new groupings, the children now knew their own room, teachers, and classmates. Children no longer got "lost in the shuffle" because they now had a place in a particular group. This group identity gave the children a new sense of security and belonging. The toys and games in each room were now available only when a child wanted to play with them, resulting in less abuse of these materials. The children's play was more constructive, which the teachers felt produced a greater sense of personal accomplishment. In the small groups, individual children received more attention. Negative behavior, such as bullying or clowning, decreased. The staff agreed that the children seemed happier and more relaxed with each other and with the staff.

The teachers commented that close relationships were developing between children who had never interacted before and that the new groupings reduced the amount of fighting among the children. Separated by age, each group of children had its activities that were appropriate to their interests and abilities.

Because the teachers now worked with fewer children, they were able to develop a deeper relationship with them. They now knew the location, activity, and feelings of each child. The teachers therefore felt less scattered, confused, and drained. Many reported that only now did they feel they were dealing effectively with the emotional development of each child and only now did they have the time to attend to each child's personal needs.

The interaction between staff and parents also changed for the better. Because each teacher was now working with fewer children, he or she was in contact with fewer parents and could get to know them better, both in parent conferences and during parent service hours. The teachers began to understand the children in the framework of their families and they felt more at ease talking about them with the parents.

The teachers agreed that the changes in the center had had an impact on their work and on their feelings about the job. Since they had been given a specific group of children and a defined space, the teachers felt a stronger sense of order, security, and belonging. A routine was established with fewer unscheduled interruptions, so teachers could now plan and carry out projects. They felt more responsible for the materials in their rooms and kept better track of toys, books, and games; as a result, less time was wasted cleaning up at the end of the day. Because of these changes many teachers felt more able to realize their potential as teachers.

The teachers also described their relationships with each other as greatly improved. Teams of teachers worked together in planning and carrying out activities. The communication between coworkers was more open; they felt more willing to give each other help, emotional support, and companionship. All the staff members became involved in discussions at staff meetings. The teachers felt that these discussions helped them deal with disagreements, find solutions to problems, plan educational strategy, and focus attention when necessary on particular children.

An additional reason for the improved staff relationships was that they had been able to share and effectively deal with their feelings of burnout. This participatory experience alone helped develop better communication among staff members and increased their identification as a group. However, the teachers attributed much of the improvement to the changes they made in teacher-child ratio and program structure because these changes directly altered their interaction with each other.

New problems

Although the teachers were enthusiastic about the changes in the day-care center, they did note a few negative consequences. Some of the teachers expressed sorrow at being cut off from the other children with whom they had previously had close relationships. The greater degree of structure also imposed some additional demands on the teachers. Because they were now responsible for the program of their group, they were challenged to make it "work." They had to be clearer about their goals, more organized, and better prepared than before. The most negative consequence of the changes, according to some teachers, was the potential for interstaff rivalry. The division of the day-care center into six independent units could have resulted in conflicts of interest between different teams of teachers.

Several things can be recommended to prevent such staff rivalry from occurring. One of these is to arrange some center-wide activities, such as movies or nature trips. Holidays can also be celebrated as all-center activities. As this center had many foreign children, several international holidays were included for greater fun, camaraderie, and unity. For the staff members, meetings, parties, and continuing education programs were encouraged. Such opportunities for interaction allow staff to emphasize their mutual goals as educators and to discuss any concerns about staff divisiveness. Furthermore, they provide staff members with a broad system of social support and intellectual stimulation.

Conclusion and a brief case analysis

In summary, the staff's reactions to the changes were very positive. They felt that the organizational changes instituted to combat burnout had greatly improved the center's program and had made their work easier, pleasant, and exciting. Although the job still involved some emotional stress, it was considerably reduced. As one teacher put it, "The changes have made an incredible difference. I

could not have gone through another year like the last one."
According to another teacher, "I used to get totally drained, but now I
enjoy coming to work. Everything is better, and I feel really
optimistic." After the changes had been in effect for some time, the
staff members all voted to continue the new system; no one wanted to
return to the previous routine.

In terms of coping with burnout and tedium, the case of this
child-care center demonstrates the impact organizational changes can
have on the psychological well-being of staff members. It is significant
that the changes were initiated and carried out by the staff. We are
convinced that the staff's active participation in the decision-making
process increased their sense of autonomy and control and improved
communication patterns. Focusing on goals for themselves, for the
children, and for the center helped increase the staff's sense of
meaning; planning and executing their own educational programs
increased their sense of challenge and self-actualization. All these
procedures reduce the stress and increase the rewards of any job,
thereby reducing the incidence of burnout.

Organizational remedies for tedium and burnout

Burnout and tedium are more likely to occur in certain organizational settings than in others. Even organizations that are similar in
goals, structure, and operation can have different rates of turnover
and levels of staff morale and other indices of burnout and tedium. In
one of our studies, which involved 724 workers in fourteen mental
retardation facilities in eleven states of the United States, we found
significant differences in mean tedium between the various facilities.[3]

In another study[4] involving 137 Israeli nurses in six different
departments, it was found even though the departments were all in
the same hospital they varied tremendously in terms of their features
as correlates of burnout. For example, variety was a negative correlate
of burnout (the more variety, the less burnout) in the heart operations
department but not in the department of internal medicine, while
complexity was a significant correlate of burnout in the intensive care
unit but not in geriatrics. It is difficult in the absence of detailed
observational analysis to know exactly why these different patterns
emerge. The main point here is that there is a great deal of variability
in the causes and effects of burnout within different segments of the
same organization.

Our work pointed to several factors in the work situation that influence whether staff will burn out or will cope successfully with the stresses inherent in their work: the ratio of the staff to clients, the availability of "time out" in periods of stress, the amount of time spent in stressful situations, the severity of the problems presented by clients, organizational flexibility, training, positive work conditions, and work significance. We will discuss each of these factors at some length.

Reduced ratio

The quality of interactions in human service professions is affected by the number of people for whom the professional is providing care. As this number increases so does the cognitive, sensory, and emotional overload of the professional. In the research on child-care centers[5] twelve centers, which varied in the ratio of staff to children from 1 to 4 to 1 to 12, were studied. The staff from the latter high-ratio centers worked a greater number of hours in direct contact with children and had fewer breaks during work. One consequence was that staff were more approving of techniques to quiet children, such as compulsory naps and tranquilizers for hyperactive children. They felt little control over what they did on the job and in general liked their jobs less than did the staff in the low-ratio centers.

In the research on mental health settings, mental health institutions were studied that varied in size as well as staff-to-patient ratio.[6] It was found that the larger the ratio of patients to staff, the less staff members liked their work and the more they tried to separate it from the rest of their lives. In settings with these larger patient-to-staff ratios, staff said they would change their jobs if given a chance. They did not seek self-fulfillment or social interaction in their jobs; they felt the best aspect of their work was the money they received for doing it. In contrast, when the ratio is low, a staff member has fewer people to provide care for and can give more attention to each. There is more time to focus on the positive, nonproblematic aspects of the patient's life and less need to concentrate on immediate problems or symptoms.

Unfortunately, in most human service organizations, there is a tendency to impose large ratios of service recipients of staff members, as a result of cost/benefit calculations or insufficient staffing. We emphasize that organizations must include the cost of burnout in these calculations. Work overload in general and large ratios in particular may save money for the organization in the short run, but they are extremely costly for everyone in the long run.[7]

Availability of "times out"

Opportunities for individuals to withdraw from a stressful situation are important when they are under mental strain; these opportunities are of critical importance with *emotional* strain. The concept of "time out" is relevant for any work that involves high degrees of emotional, mental, or physical stress. Times out were repeatedly found to be correlated with low levels of tedium.[8]

"Times out" can be particularly beneficial to people who serve other people. In the research of child-care workers[9] and mental health workers,[10] a factor in preventing burnout was the opportunity to withdraw from direct contact with children and patients when feeling strained and under pressure. "Times out," which are the most positive form of withdrawal that we observed, are not merely short breaks from work such as rest periods or coffee breaks. Rather, they are opportunities for the staff members to choose some less stressful work while other staff take over their more stressful responsibilities. This alternative work is usually characterized by lack of direct interaction with people, such as paper work, cleaning, or food preparation. Thus, staff on time out are serving the organization and replenishing themselves simultaneously.

In the child-care study, times out were often available in centers that had sufficient staff, shared responsibilities, flexible work policies, and, most important, a variety of tasks for each staff member. In centers where times out were not available, work relations were poorer and the staff reported being impatient, irritable, and psychologically distant. In the menal health study, staff who took times out showed more favorable attitudes toward patients and were more optimistic about their patients' chances to be cured than staff who did not have this option available.

This form of withdrawal is more positive than other techniques professionals often use to protect themselves, because good patient care can be maintained while the employee is taking an emotional breather. When times out are not available, professionals are more likely to feel trapped by their responsibility to their clients; they cannot withdraw temporarily without feeling guilty. The withdrawal then is often an escape at the expense of the clients because there is no one else to take over. Thus it is important that institutional policies allow for voluntary times out. Such temporary withdrawals from direct contact when used for noncontact work will not be at the expense of the service recipient if the structure of the organization allows other staff to cover.

Limited hours of stressful work

The number of hours a person works is likely to be related to that person's sense of fatigue, overload, boredom, and stress. Consequently one might suspect that long working hours would result in a higher incidence of burnout and tedium. In human service professionals, longer work hours were found to be correlated with stress and negative feelings on the part of the staff member.[11] The more hours a day they worked, the less they liked the job, the less responsible they felt for clients, and the less control they felt they had. Yet it is not the number of hours per se that has the most impact on staff but the number of hours in direct contact with service recipients. In the child-care study,[12] longer working hours were associated with more stress and negative attitudes in the staff, primarily when the longer hours involved more work with children. When the longer hours involved administrative work, this negative response and burnout were less likely to occur. Staff members who worked longer hours with children developed more negative attitudes toward children; on vacation they wanted to get away from children and child-related activities; after work they reported feeling less tolerant, less satisfied with their performance, less creative, and more moody than staff who worked shorter hours with children. Both the organization and the individual can be aware of the limit to the number of hours one can work and still be productive. The psychoanalyst Herbert Freudenberger described the common practices of double shifts and frequent overnight work as emotionally suicidal practices that can result in entire organizations burning out.[13]

The negative effect of prolonged direct contact with clients is increased by the severity of the clients' problems. Long hours of direct contact with severely ill or emotionally disturbed children is many times more stressful than contact with healthy, well-adjusted children. In mental health settings, it was found that the higher the percentage of schizophrenics in the patient population, the more burned out the staff.[14] These staff members were also less aware of their goals, spent more time in administrative duties, felt less job satisfaction, and were more interested in leaving their jobs. In a study of occupational tedium in one social service organization, we found that dealing full-time with difficult clients was the most stressful task associated with the highest levels of tedium.[15] Other studies have shown that crisis intervention and emergency room work are particularly demanding if done exclusively.

Such work can be limited in duration. When workers begin jobs that are known to be stressful, their stay on the jobs could be limited to a certain period of time. Rotation of stressful jobs can prevent the individual's guilt and sense of failure and can reduce the costs of burnout for the organization. For example, priests who worked in certain community-based programs for a maximum of five years were less likely to burn out than those who did not set such a limit for themselves. Rather than succumbing to the stresses of such work, these priests left the programs feeling they had done their best and were ready for a change. Teachers in inner city schools who felt unable to cope but were denied transfers had psychophysiological and psychological complaints that increased until many became disabled.[16] When stressful work is limited in time, employees can devote themselves to it with the knowledge that they will not have to do it forever.[17]

The stressful effect of long hours of direct client contact in the human services is similar to the effect of long hours in peak-stress situations in non-human-service jobs. The recommendations to combat the resultant tedium are also similar. The organization must take into account the effects of stressful tasks on the employee and limit the work time in such surroundings. One way to do this is to create shorter work shifts, more breaks, special leaves, or part-time positions. Jobs can balance stressful and nonstressful tasks. Organizations can reduce the number of years that employees are involved in stressful work by job rotation, lateral job changes, and tapered retirement. They can institute shared part-time positions and shared work. Rotation and sharing take some pressure off the individual staff member and make the job more varied, interesting, and stimulating. Research indicates that with more work sharing, jobs are less personally stressful and staff attitudes are more positive.[18]

Organizational flexibility

Organizational structures can be made flexible enough to accommodate the individual rather than the individual accommodating the organization. To do this attention must be given to the individual differences among workers. Some workers are interested in policy making, others in community contact, and yet others in serving clients. Enabling workers to select tasks they like will reduce burnout and tedium and will improve the functioning of the organization and the quality of its services. In one social service department we met a young woman who liked working with cases of incest and was very effective in her interventions, but she disliked working with alcoholics and felt she could not be helpful to them. Organizational flexibility in her department made it possible for her to see all the cases of incest. Within a short time she became an expert on the problem and was invited to give talks and train others. She was also spared the frustration of working with people she felt could be more effectively served by other staff members.

Obviously, not all organizations will accommodate their employees' needs. For example, an anesthesiologist who had difficulty working with babies in the operating room was required by the hospital to continue anesthetizing babies. In her distress she had frequent nightmares and periods of depression following operations on children. She went through a severe crisis of burnout and quit her job for a year. When she returned to work, the rule was still in effect: employees must treat the patients to whom they are assigned. The organization would not change to accommodate her.

These two cases exemplify the impact organizational flexibility can have on the ease or discomfort of the individual's functioning. In terms of cost/benefit to the organization, we feel flexibility is much more beneficial as an organizational policy because it minimizes employee tedium. Organizational flexibility beyond all implies awareness and concern about the needs of the individual. It means giving individual workers some freedom to choose their clients or tasks. It also means giving them as much autonomy as possible to work on their own schedules in their own styles. The organization stands to gain by allowing employees to work under their most productive circumstances.

An organization can also be flexible enough to allow growth and change in their workers. If an employee shows signs of tedium on a particular job, he can be given something different to do. In contrast, many organizations ask people who do something well once to do that job "forever." Even if a worker enjoyed his work initially, routinization can result in burnout and tedium. (Johnny Carson, the host of one of television's most successful programs, told the network he wanted to leave the show. "I am no longer able to bring to the show everything I would like to. After 17 years I am mentally and emotionally tired," said Carson.) Instead of repeatedly assigning the same workers to certain jobs, organizations can rotate functions among different workers. Currently organizations tend to burn out their staff by assigning difficult tasks to the "only" person who can handle them and imposing deadlines on the "only" person, invariably the busiest, who can be trusted to complete tasks on time. Variety in these routines can provide relief from stress.

Some industrial psychologists investigating occupational stress have emphasized the importance of selection as a preventive measure, even though the means of selection for complex jobs are not exact and interviews have not been successful as a selection device.[19] We have often been asked by heads of personnel departments how they can know during their initial interview how likely are different prospective employees to burn out and if we could provide them with some written test that would predict who will burn out and when. The idea, of course, is to select people who will not burn out or develop tedium. Our answer is that even if there were such a test we would recommend against using it. The reason should be clear to the reader. As we mentioned previously, those individuals who are potentially the most valuable resources in an organization because of their idealism and concern are precisely those who are most apt to burn out. Accordingly, such a screening device would deprive the organization of its most valuable potential employees. If we were in charge of an organization we would choose as our employees the most idealistic, caring, and concerned individuals we could find, and then we would work to create an environment that minimizes burnout. An indirect support to this contention is the fact that most of the turnover that is the result of burnout is voluntary (i.e.,the employee quitting), while poor selection would result in involuntary turnover (i.e., the employee being fired).[20] Because burnout and tedium are largely an inevitable function of system characteristics, it is more practical to focus on organizations than on selecting individuals.

Training

Formal education for a career can include training designed to minimize burnout and tedium. For staff members with higher education the original reason for choosing their work is often a search for "self-fulfillment." They begin their careers with very high expectations of themselves and their work and within a short time they burn out. Advanced education, especially in the human services, tends to create these high expectations in students, emphasizing the need for self-expression and authenticity. It also emphasizes the value of the experimental, the new, and the exciting. These great expectations are frustrated when professionals find themselves to be small parts of a bureaucratic machine or in an uneventful career. In training for human service careers we feel it is crucial to prepare students for the stresses that they will encounter in their work and to provide them with a more realistic and balanced view of the professional-client relationship. Students should be able to recognize danger signs of impending burnout in themselves and in people around them and know how to take care of themselves when under stress. It is also important to include training on how to work in a bureaucracy.

Similarly, other professionals need training for handling mental and physical stress. When such training is not included in higher education it becomes the responsibility of the employee's organization. Training for new employees could include familiarization with the job stresses, the danger signs of burnout and tedium, and coping strategies. In such training the requirements of the job can be made clear so that those who find that they cannot fulfill them will be free to leave.

Continuing education on the job can also be helpful. Staff retreats, conferences, and workshops reduce tedium and burnout. Such education provides workers with an opportunity to get away from their work, examine their work pressures, clarify their goals, and consider available but unused coping strategies.

Staff training can give workers the opportunity to develop skills directly related to their work. These may be clerical skills, computer skills, computer-related skills, or diagnostic and interviewing skills. Effective training programs and supportive supervision are two methods the organization can supply for skill acquisition and improvement.

Positive work conditions

Environmental pressures such as noise, uncomfortable work settings, pollution, and extreme temperatures are highly correlated with tedium; the more environmental pressures, the more tedium.[21] Comfortable physical environments that are pleasant and designed to meet workers tastes, needs, and preferences were found to produce far less tedium than unpleasant environments. Trying to concentrate, interview, and do therapy in inadequate or noisy offices was a source of frustration for many employees. Private, quiet, and tasteful environments were specifically mentioned as positive work features and considered indicative of organizational concern for the psychological well-being of employees. Albert Mahrabian, professor of psychology at the University of California Los Angeles, emphasized that the same kind of environment is not good for eveyone.[22] Just as you don't make people wear the same shoe size, you shouldn't make them live and work in the same kind of environment. Working and living spaces should accommodate as much as possible the individual's needs and preferences and be as personalized as possible.

Work conditions also include the degree of bureaucratic interference, such as the extent to which administration interferes with the goal achievement of individual workers, and administrative annoyances, such as paper work, red tape, and communication problems. Both bureaucratic interference and administrative annoyances were found to be highly correlated with tedium.[23] Organizations can attempt to reduce environmental pressures and make the physical work environment as pleasant as possible. This might include dividers to increase privacy and reduce noise, pleasant colors, plants, indirect lighting, or workers' freedom to decorate their own offices. Organizations can also combat tedium by simplifying such bureaucratic hurdles as complex forms, tangled communication channels, and unnecessarily complicated work precedures.

Work significance

When people do not see completion in their work, they may not believe they have significant impact. Human service professionals who do only intake interviews are at a disadvantage to those who do brief therapy and can see changes in their clients. Industrial workers who put the front fender on cars are at a disadvantage to those who work as a team and put a whole car together. A sense of completion is unfortunately lacking in many industrial assembly-line jobs, as well as in human service jobs involving chronically sick or needy people.

In such jobs it is particularly important for the organization to provide employees with some sense of completion. R. E. Walton, who wrote about innovation in the work place to avoid workers alienation, mentioned innovative and successful management techniques at General Foods in Topeka, Kansas.[24] Autonomous work groups at the plant were given collective responsibility for large segments of the production process, so that workers shared a variety of tasks and enriched their job.

One way to provide a sense of completion is to set clear, achievable organizational objectives and to review periodically individual and organizational success in achieving these objectives. Objectives can include both internal organizational goals and more general goals such as providing the best service to the public and attaining professional excellence.

Feedback is another organizational tool for increasing an employee's sense of significance at work. Feedback and constructive criticism provided by supervisors should be specific and directly related to attainable improvements. Such feedback enables individual workers to improve their performance and enhances their feelings of meaning and success; it also improves the morale of the whole organization.

The rewards provided by the organization can increase a worker's sense of significance. Rewards include pay; extrinsic advantages such as benefits, security, and promotional opportunities; and intrinsic advantages such as appreciation and recognition. Lack of rewards has been found to be a significant correlate of tedium.[25] Organizational psychologists emphasized job enrichment as a tool to increase workers' motivation and sense of significance and to provide them with opportunities for psychological growth.[26]

Organizations must recognize the needs for completion, rewards, appreciation, and meaning. When these needs are satisfied, they serve as powerful buffers against tedium and burnout.

Notes

1. C. Maslach and A. Pines, "The Burnout Syndrome in the Day Care Setting," *Child Care Quarterly* 6, no. 2 (Summer 1977): 100–113.
2. A detailed description of this case study is presented in A. Pines, and C. Maslach, "Combatting Staff Burnout in a Day Care Center: A Case Study," *Child Care Quarterly* 9, no. 1 (1980): 5–16.
3. The study was done in collaboration with Steve Weinberg and the Management Training Program at the University of Alabama. Mean tedium score ranged from $\bar{x} = 2.9$ to $\bar{x} = 3.4$, $p < .0004$.
4. E., Eldar "Burnout in Hospital Nurses and Its Association with Objective Measures of Departments Characteristics." Thesis for M.Sc. degree in Management Sciences, Organizational Behavior, submitted to the faculty of Management, Tel Aviv University, Isreal. One of the goals of the study was to provide a detailed observational analysis that will explain these different patterns.
5. Maslach and Pines, "Burnout Syndrome."
6. A. Pines and D. Maslach "Characteristics of Staff Burnout in Mental Health Settings," *Hospital and Community Psychiatry* 29, no. 4 (1978) 233–237.
7. For example, Mitzi Duxbury, professor of nursing at the University of Minnesota, has documented the relationship between burnout and turnover in perinatal units all over the United States. John W. Jones, a psychologist at De Paul University, Chicago, Illinois, found that burnout was significantly correlated with measures of job turnover, absenteeism, tardiness, discipline, and alcohol use.
8. In a study involving 205 professionals, the correlation between tedium and the availability of time out was $r = -.18$, $p < .05$. For eighty-five students the correlation was $r = -.35$, $p < .05$.

9. Maslach and Pines, "Burnout Syndrome."

10. Pines and Maslach, "Characteristics of Staff Burnout."

11. Ibid.; Maslach and Pines, "Burnout Syndrome."

12. Maslach and Pines, "Burnout Syndrome."

13. H. J. Freudenberger, "The Staff Burnout Syndrome in Alternative Institutions," *Psychotherapy: Therapy Research and Practice* 12 II (Spring 1975): 73–82.

14. Pines and Maslach, "Characteristics of Staff Burnout."

15. A. Pines and D. Kafry, "Occupational Tedium in a Social Service Organization " (Research report, Berkeley. Calif. 1979). The mean tedium for dealing with problem cases was 5.1, for providing information to the public 3.1, for examining evidence 3.1, for providing technical guidance 2.7, for clerical tasks 2.2.

16. A. M. Block "Combat Neurosis in Inner City Schools." Paper presented at the 130th Annual Meeting of the American Psychiatric Association, May 1977.

17. E. Walster, and E. Aronson "The Effect of Expectancy of Task Duration on the Experience of Fatigue," *Journal of Experimental Social Psychology* 3 (1967): 41–46.

18. Maslach and Pines, "Burnout Syndrome"; Pines and Maslach, "Characteristics of Staff Burnout."

19. For example, R. Kahn, "Job Burnout, Prevention and Remedies," *Public Welfare*, Spring 1978, pp. 61–63.

20. Personal communication, Mitzi Duxbury, School of Nursing, University of Minnesota. R. Van Der Merwe and S. Miller, "The Measurement of Turnover," in *Labor Turnover and Retention,* ed. B. O. Pettman (New York: Wiley, 1975), pp. 3–30.

21. For example, in a study involving 205 professionals, the correlation between tedium and environmental pressures at work was $r = .27, p < .001$, while that between tedium and comfortable physical environment was $r = -.29, p < .001$.

22. A. Mehrabian, *Public Spaces Private Places.* (New York: Basic Books, 1976).

23. For example, in the study involving 205 professionals, both the correlation between tedium and bureaucratic interference and the correlation between tedium and administrative hassles were $r = .20, p < .05$.

24. R. E. Walton, "Alienation and Innovation in the Work Place," in *Work and the Quality of Life,* ed. J. O'Toole (Cambridge, Mass.: MIT Press, 1974), pp. 227–245.

25. In the study involving 205 professionals, the correlation between tedium and adequate rewards at work was $r = -.33, p < .001$.

26. F. Herzberg, *Work and the Nature of Man* (Cleveland: World Publishing 1966).

7

Social support systems

"No man is an island, entire of itself; every man is a piece of the continent," said John Donne, the sixteenth-century poet. Poets as well as psychologists have recognized for a long time the fact that human beings are social animals, that their need for intimacy and their interdependence on one another are a vital aspect of being human. We all know that the human infant could not survive for very long without being cared for and nurtured by that part of a social system known as the family. What is equally true is that adults as well are dependent on membership in an elaborate social system without which survival as a human being would be extremely unlikely. Social factors play a primary role as both causes and cures of burnout and tedium. The role of social factors in burnout is the focus of this chapter.

Social systems

Kurt Lewin, one of the founding fathers of social psychology, emphasized the importance of social factors such as group membership on almost every type of behavior: the goals that people set for themselves are influenced by the social standards of the groups to which they belong and wish to belong.[1] According to Kurt Lewin, the individual is usually a member of many overlapping groups. One might be a member of a professional group, a political party, and a hobby club. Different groups influence an individual's behavior to different degrees. For one person business may be more important than politics; for another, the political party may be the most influential. The influence of different groups varies at different times; when one is at home, for example, the influence of one's family is generally greater than when one is at work. The group to which a person belongs is one of the most important constituents of the "ground on which he stands": "The speed and determination with which a person proceeds, his determinants to fight or to submit, and other important characteristics of his behavior, depend upon the firmness of the ground on which he stands."[2]

Marc Pilisuk, the University of California scholar, wrote that "for most of the history of humankind, the particular web in which an individual was enmeshed consisted of a group of perhaps 15 to 150 individuals, spanning the life cycle."[3]

Most people belong to one family in which they are children and to another family in which they are spouses and parents. People also belong to extended families in which they are grandchildren, grandparents, inlaws, aunts, uncles, nieces, and nephews. During their lives, people develop networks of friends. Some maintain very special relationships with childhood friends throughout their adult lives. Others change friends frequently and develop relationships with people they live near to or with whom they share interests. Some neighbors and group members become intimate friends; others remain at the level of acquaintances. In addition to the social systems of family, friends, and community, people belong to social systems at work. These social systems include supervisors, subordinates, coworkers, and clients. They also include colleagues in other settings and professional groups.

Each of the systems one belongs to involves demands that are built into the role played in that system. For example, there are certain things expected of a "father," a "wife," or a "business partner." If one violates these demands one can be ridiculed or criticized. In extreme cases of rule violations one may be divorced, fired, or punished by law. Each one of the systems involves some common and some unique stresses and rewards.

Given the fundamental importance of this elaborate network of social systems with their concommitant benefits and demands, it should not be surprising to learn that: (1) conflictual demands from various systems, or the ambiguity of such demands are a major source of burnout, and (2) the efficient and creative use of a social support system is among the most effective ways of coping with burnout.

Identifying pressures imposed by one's social systems

We have found it to be very valuable for individuals to clarify the extent to which various social systems place demands on their time. In our workshops we asked people to make a list of the social systems that are most salient to them (such as nuclear family, extended family, and work) and under each heading to make a list of the demands that each of these systems places on the individual. For example, Philip teaches biology at the University. He is 34 years old and has three young children. For Phil, the most demanding aspect of his life is his job. His list of demands includes:

1. doing a lot of individual research
2. publishing that research
3. training graduate students to do research
4. being a stimulating and entertaining lecturer in a large undergraduate class
5. advising dozens of students about courses, their career, etc.
6. being a helpful resource to his colleagues
7. serving on a great number of university committees (and impressing the other committee members with his brilliance)
8. being the "life of the party" at social gatherings organized by the chairman of his department
9. "casually" dropping references to poetry and literature during conversation with his older colleagues as a way of letting them know that he is not "narrow"

When one lists the demands in this manner and then examines this list, one is in a better position to ascertain the extent to which the demands are essential, current, legitimate, and reasonable. For example, Philip feels that all of these things are important and that he must exert a great deal of energy meeting these demands if he is to be promoted to tenure in his department, which is his paramount concern.

Compared to this, the demands imposed by his nuclear family are extremely light. Naturally he must earn a living to support his wife and young children; he also stays home and babysits one afternoon a week so that his wife can take a pottery course. And he helps discipline the children, occasionally tells them bedtime stories, occasionally takes them on a weekend outing, and so forth.

Interestingly enough, Philip felt more resentment at the relatively small demands placed on him by his family than he did at the huge lists of demands that he saw as emanating from his job. Moreover, he considered his family much-more important to him than his job. What Philip learned from making this list was that he was shortchanging his family. In addition, by scrutinizing his list in a careful and honest manner, he came to realize that many of the demands he listed as emanating from his university job were more self-imposed than system-imposed. In other words, under close inspection he gained insight into the fact that he was making demands on *himself* as a teacher, researcher, and colleague far in access of what his university expected of him, and these demands were usurping time and energy that could perhaps be spent more productively in other systems that, according to his own values, were more important to him.

We would recommend that the readers make their own lists and do their own scrutinizing. As was mentioned above, it is of great importance to clarify any ambiguity that exists between a real demand imposed by a particular system and one's own self-demand. For example, David's mother might like him to call her occasionally, but he puts the demand on himself to call her three times a week. After a while he may act as if the "three times a week" dictum emanated from her—and under close examination he will realize that this was his own. One must separate actual requirements from one's interpretation of them and from the requirements one imposes on one's self. Occasionally one can even test this—thus Philip could take on fewer advisees and serve on fewer committees, David could cut back to one phone call a week and see if there were any serious repercusions.

In addition to making demands, social systems are a source of some of our most important rewards. One of the main rewards provided by people, and a major function of a social system, is support.

Social support systems

Social support was defined by Sidney Cobb, M.D., of Brown University, as *information* leading subjects to believe that they are cared for and loved, esteemed, and valued, and that they belong to a network of communication and mutual obligation.[4] Dr. Cobb reviewed an extensive body of literature documenting that supportive interactions among people are protective against the health consequences of life stress. From his review it appears that social support can protect people in crisis from a wide variety of pathological states: from low birth weight to death, from arthritis through tuberculosis to depression, alcoholism, and social breakdown. Furthermore, social support may reduce the amount of medication required and accelerate recovery. Strong evidence over a variety of transitions in the life cycle from birth to death documents that social support is protective.

Social support systems have been defined by Gerald Caplan, who studied them extensively, as *enduring interpersonal ties* to groups of people who can be relied upon to provide emotional sustenance, assistance, and resources in times of need, who provide feedback, and who share standards and values.[5] The practical definition of a support system is the people who support an individual through crises and calm and with whom feelings can be shared without fear of condemnation. By providing emotional sustenance, supportive others help individuals master their own emotional problems by mobilizing their psychological resources. Additionally, by providing these people with tangible aid, resources, information, and cognitive guidance, the supporters further enhance the individuals' ability to cope with stressful situations. Ideally, according to Caplan, one belongs to several supportive groups at home and at work, in church and in recreational or avocational sites. Social support systems serve as buffers for the individual; they help maintain the psychological and physical well-being of the individual over time.

In our work we have found that the creative use of social support systems provides an effective prevention mechanism against burnout and tedium. We have also found that most people do not make adequate use of potential social support systems; rather, they squander this valuable resource out of a lack of understanding of the importance of social support systems, their various functions, and how to best utilize them.

The functions of a social support system

Social support systems serve a multitude of functions. We have found it useful to organize these various functions into six basic categories: listening, technical support, technical challenge, emotional support, emotional challenge, and the providing of social reality. When individuals encounter people in their environment who fulfill all these functions they are well protected against burnout and go a long way toward reducing stress in life and work.

It is extremely important for individuals to learn to discriminate among the different social support functions. People in a situation that tends to produce a great deal of burnout often have the vague feeling that they are not getting enough social support. This often results in a general feeling of disappointment in those people who are closest to them (e.g., a wife or a husband) for not providing enough support *even when the specific support needed is far beyond the scope of their usual role.* To be disappointed in a person for not supplying the kind of support that could not reasonably be expected from him or her is, of course, terribly unfair. The nature of this unfairness will be clear in a moment, when we describe the various functions of a social support system. For now, let it suffice to say that our listing six functions is not simply an academic exercise, not simply a way of conceptualizing a problem. It has immediate, practical application because individuals must learn to discriminate among these functions, so that they can be aware of which functions are being fulfilled and which are not. Moreover, once individuals have learned to discriminate among the various functions, they can make a realistic assessment of which individuals in the environment would be most appropriate to fulfill those functions that have been left uncovered.

Listening

Everyone has occasions when they need one or more people who will *actively* listen to them, without giving advice or making judgments. They need someone with whom they can share the joys of success as well as the pain and frustration of failure. They need someone with whom they can share conflicts as well as trivial everyday incidents. People working in a stressful occupation occasionally need to let off steam, A good active listener listens with understanding and sympathy. A poor listener can blunder in several different ways. For example, suppose a ninth grade teacher working in a very difficult ghetto school has just had a difficult time with a student and comes into the teachers' lounge complaining about the intractability and aggressiveness of that student. What the teacher needs is someone who will pay attention and who will indicate interest, understanding, and perhaps even sympathy for the situation. What the teacher *doesn't* need is someone who will immediately give free advice or someone who will play "Can you top this?" (i.e., who will say in effect, "You think *that's* bad, let me tell you about one of *my* students"). Another thing the teacher *doesn't* need is someone who seems insensitive to the fact that the teacher is simply letting off steam and who will decide the teacher doesn't really care or understand students. It should be clear that finding a good active listener (and being one for other people) is not as easy as it seems; indeed most people in our environment are quick to give advice or make judgment rather than simply listen. And giving advice, making judgment, or playing "Can you top this?" usually increases burnout.

Technical appreciation

All individuals need technical appreciation for the work they do; when they do a good piece of work, they need to have it acknowledged. In order to provide individuals with technical appreciation and affirmation of competence, a person must meet two important criteria: he or she must be an expert in their field and must be someone whose honesty and integrity they trust. In other words, this person must understand the complexities of the job they do and be courageous enough to provide honest feedback. If those requirements are met, individuals can accept support as genuine. A moment's reflection should reveal that, for most people, their mother is not an ideal person to fulfill this function: for most people, their mothers are not technical experts; moreover, their mothers are not objective enough to provide them with "trustworthy" positive statements. Mothers, spouses, or nonexpert friends *can* provide us with general encouragement, but it may not be as meaningful as if it came from someone who can appreciate the technical intricacies of the job situation. The ability to provide technical appreciation is especially powerful and useful when it comes from knowledgeable supervisors.

Technical challenge

It can be comforting to be in an environment where one is the expert and no one challenges that expertise. This comfort might be especially useful and welcome when under stress. Unfortunately, too much comfort of this sort can produce burnout; that is, if we are not challenged we run the long-term risk of stagnation and boredom. A comedian may go from nightclub to nightclub telling exactly the same jokes. As long as the audience changes at each nightclub he can get away with doing the same routine. Chances are that within a year he will begin to burn out. If the comedian has a weekly television show, he is forced to change his act, because the audience is the same from week to week. While this is more difficult, it prevents him from stagnating. Television presents him with a technical challenge that forces him to develop new routines continually, and the challenge produces growth.

Contact with colleagues who know as much or more about the job keeps workers from stale or superficial efforts. Critical colleagues can challenge workers' ways of thinking; stretch them; encourage them to attain greater heights; and lead them to greater creativity, excitement, and involvement in the job. People who fill this role of challenger must have two characteristics: they must be good enough at the job to be able to identify what could be improved and they must be trustworthy—that is, workers must know that the colleagues' criticism is not intended as humiliation or to enhance their own ego at the workers' expense. The best of colleagues can trust each other both in appreciation and in challenge functions.

Emotional support

An important function of an effective support system is emotional support or appreciation. By emotional support we mean that people are willing to be on an individual's side in a difficult situation even if they are not in total agreement with what the person is doing. Most individuals need someone who is willing to provide unconditional support at least occasionally. This can be vital in a stressful job. It is enough to have one person who is in one's corner; it is marvelous to have this kind of support from *four* or *five* people. If this is not present or possible at work, it is essential to have it at home. Unlike technical support and technical challenge, for which the supporter must be an expert in the individual's field, emotional support is something that people at home—parents, spouse, and friends—can do. Emotional support does not require any kind of technical expertise; what it does require is someone who cares more about the individual as a human being than about the particular position the person is espousing at the moment, the particular piece of work just completed (which may not be among his or her best), or even about the bad mood the person might be in at the moment. Especially when under stress, individuals appreciate the people at work and at home who support them win or lose.

Emotional challenge

People can delude themselves into thinking they are doing their best when they are not. It is comforting for them to convince themselves that all avenues have been explored when they have not. Occasionally it is easy to blame someone else rather than take responsibility for problems or crises. These defense mechanisms occasionally are useful because they keep people from putting excessive emotional pressures on themselves, but their continual use can block emotional growth and impede the most efficient employment of their energies. At that point friends can help by questioning their excuses.

To serve in this stretching function, friends can challenge the individuals, questioning if they are really doing their best to fulfill their goals and overcome the obstacles. Emotional challenge is different from technical challenge. Friends do not have to be expert in a particular area of expertise in order to offer the opportunity to grow emotionally. Friends merely have to say, "Are you sure you are doing enough?" But trust is still a prerequisite for this function.

In other cases individuals may be so emotionally caught up in a situation that they cannot think rationally or logically, and yet they have a problem that needs a rational solution. The rational solution may be right in front of them, but their emotionality prevents them from seeing it. An emotional challenge in this situation does not require specific expertise but rather requires the use of logic as a way of helping the individuals cut through their own emotionality in order to arrive at a rational solution. An example will clarify.

A friend of ours whom we will call Joshua reports an incident where his old college roommate visited him in a state of obvious distress. His roommate was facing a serious crisis in his marriage and needed advice. He was upset and confused and couldn't make up his mind as to whether or not to seek a divorce. Joshua was in a difficult position. While he cared a great deal about his old college roommate, he had seen him only on a few occasions during the past ten years, hardly knew his wife at all, and certainly did not qualify as as expert on his friend's marital situation. Yet he was able to function as an excellent emotional challenger. As he listened to his friend, it became clear that what was most upsetting to the latter was a certain set of behaviors that his wife persisted in performing and that he found unacceptable. Joshua asked two questions: first, is there any likelihood that she will change those behaviors? His friends's answer was a definite no. Second, is there any way that he can learn to tolerate those behaviors? The answer to that question was again no. Joshua paused and looked at his friend. At that moment his course of action became clear to him. Joshua did not have to give him any technical advice. All he had to do is help his friend see the logical conclusion he derived from the basic characteristics of the situation.

Sharing social reality

The sixth function is that of social reality testing and sharing: a social reality touchstone. There are two kinds of reality in the world:

physical reality and social reality. An example of physical reality is the rain that makes one use an umbrella or a raincoat. Social reality is vague; a friend can help one interpret this reality and decide on reasonable action. One example of this function can happen when people think they are losing the ability to evaluate what is happening around them. They may be sitting in a meeting and hear someone saying what seems like nonsense. They may believe everyone else is listening intently and may think, "My God, I must be going crazy! I'm the only one who's not fascinated." But if there is one person in that room whose judgment they trust, they need only to meet that person's eye and exchange annoyed looks. Then they can relax, realizing that this speaker is indeed talking nonsense and that although everyone else may agree with that nonsense or may go along with it for reasons of their own, They need not question their own perceptions. All it usually takes is one other person, not a majority of the people present.

In times of stress or confusion when one needs sound advice, a person with similar priorities, values, and views can be very helpful. A person with a shared social reality is most likely to give useful advice.

It should be clear that one person can fulfill several of these functions, but it is extraordinarily unlikely that one person can fulfill them all. Different people are needed to fulfill different functions: the function of active listening anyone can fulfill, whether they know the individual and the subject at hand or not. For the functions of emotional support and challenge, individuals need someone who knows them and someone they trust, but that person doesn't have to be an expert on the topic of discussion. For the functions of technical support and challenge they need a person who knows the subject matter, but this person doesn't necessarily have to be someone they know intimately. A person needs to have a similar world view and similar values to be a truly effective social reality touchstone.

Differentiating support functions

We have presented the six basic functions of a social support system, There may be variations on these functions, but we believe that these six are essential. As mentioned previously, it is important to discriminate one function from another, to be able to think of social support not in a global sense but as separate functions. Some people in our environment may be able to fulfill some of these functions but not others. Without realizing it, individuals may expect their best

friends or their spouses to fulfill all of these functions, and almost no
one can do that. Unfortunately, most people, especially when under
stress, do not make the effort to discriminate the various functions that
a social support system can play and are then left feeling that they are
not getting what they need. Frequently this sense of disappointment is
not verbalized but becomes associated with home life. The atmosphere of regret and disappointment may begin to erode the marriage
and family; the result is burnout at home.

It is useful to realize how many of the six functions of support
different people are expected to fulfill and to consider which of the
functions are appropriate for these people. One way to do this is to list
two or three people at home and work who either do or could fulfill
one of these functions (see Table 7.1). If there is someone who could
fulfill a function but one is reluctant to get into a relationship with that
person, note the source of reluctance. For example, a coworker might
be a superb technical critic, but an individual is reluctant to approach
that person to request critical feedback on his or her ideas. The
individual should be specific about what is preventing him or her from
approaching that person. Only then can the individual develop ways
to overcome these blocks.

To the extent that social support functions are not completely
covered, burnout can occur. To the extent that hardly any of them are
covered, burnout is almost inevitable in a stressful situation. It is
primarily important to deal with those areas in which support is
lacking, the functions of support that are *not* well covered.

We have all seen organizations in which the social environment is
terribly nonsupportive. People aren't listening to each other, they are
not expressing much technical appreciation for each others' work, and
rather than offering technical challenge they offer criticisms that are
destructive or wounding both in intent and effect. Occasionally we
have seen work environments where the social support systems are
functioning beautifully, where people are listening to each other,
where a great deal of *sincere* appreciation for work well done is
expressed, and where people are challenging each other in useful and
productive ways.

How can one turn a nonsupportive work environment into a
supportive one? Sometimes this can happen only if two or three
people take the lead in offering appreciation and challenge to those
around them. Since such behavior feels good, it tends to be contagious. Occasionally, however, individuals are deeply in need of
appreciation or challenge but are timid to ask for it and are so caught

TABLE 7.1. Social support functions

The following questions are aimed at helping you discriminate among the six functions of a social support system and examine what people in your environment are fulfilling, or may potentially fulfill, those functions for you.

How important are these functions of a support system for you personally? Please use the following scale to rate all six of the functions:

1	2	3	4	5	6	7
not at all important			somewhat important			extremely important

1. Listing_____ 2. Technical support_____ 3. Technical challenge_____
2. Emotional support_____ 5. Emotional challenge_____ 6. Sharing social reality_____

For each function write down who the person is (or the people are) who fulfill(s) it for you. Indicate what your relation is to the person whose name you have written (i.e., wife, friend, colleague), and to what extent the person fulfills that function for you, on the following scale:

1	2	3	4	5	6	7
fulfills minimally			fulfills to a certain degree			fulfills completely

1. Listening:

2. Technical support:

3. Technical challenge:

4. Emotional support:

5. Emotional challenge:

6. Sharing social reality:

up in their own needs that they are unaware of the fact that others in their environment could benefit from praise and challenge they themselves might offer.

In an earlier chapter we discussed an organization where many individuals were experiencing tedium, in part because of a strong need for appreciation from supervising personnel high up in the hierarchy. Such appreciation would have been almost impossible to arrange without a major reorganization. As the reader will recall, our intervention in that organization involved training people to value and respect the technical appreciation and challenge that could be forthcoming from their peers and to train them to offer such appreciation and challenge to one another.

While it would be presumptuous for us to offer advice on details of how to establish a social support system (since we don't know the details of everyone's work and life sphere), what we can do is suggest finding ways to ask for support from relevant colleagues and to give support where it seems appropriate. It is conceivable that anyone may become the one person who is instrumental in changing a nonsupportive work environment to a supportive one.

Social support systems as buffers against tedium: research findings

We examined social systems as buffers against tedium in a study involving 290 students and 241 professionas. These 531 subjects, between 17 and 87 years old, were asked to describe their social relationships including family, work, friends, coworkers, and acquaintances. Results indicated that all of the social relations were negatively and significantly correlated with life tedium, i.e., the better the social relationships a person had, the less tedium there was. The highest correlations were for coworkers and friends.[6] Subjects were also asked if when having a difficulty at home or work they could confer with someone to get advice and support. The availability of support in times of need was negatively and significantly correlated with tedium (the more support, the less tedium).[7] The respondents were asked, "How often do you feel lonely?" The frequency of loneliness was very highly correlated with tedium, with poor social relations (especially with friends), and with lack of support in times of need.[8]

Social support systems can be seen as mediating variables that act as buffers and supports to individuals in their social environment; these mediating variables reduce the effects of stressful environmental conditions and thus slow the tedium cycle.

One social system that merits special discussion is *work relations*. The nature of the relationship with one's boss, subordinates, and colleagues can be a major source of stress at work; good work relations between members of a group is a central factor in individual and organizational health.[9] Social contacts are almost always a key cause of job satisfaction.[10] A trusting and caring environment is important to the functioning of organizations and an effective support system is essential in combating burnout. Yet workers tend to get so caught up in the daily routine of work that they neglect each other. They do not often enough or caringly enough compliment, support, and acknowledge each other's efforts.[11]

Burnout was found in several studies to be reduced for individuals who had effective social networks or support systems at work.[12] When work relations were good, professionals experiencing stress often turned to others for advice, comfort, tension reduction, help in achieving distance from the situation or in intellectualizing it, and a sense of shared responsibility. Burnout was less severe in those institutions that allowed staff to express their feelings, get feedback and support from others, and develop new goals for their clients than in those institutions that did not allow it.

In one study involving seventy-six mental health professionals[13] it was found that work relationships were related to staff members' attitudes toward their work, the institutions, and the patients. When relationships between staff members were good, staff members were more likely to confer with each other when having problems, express more positive attitudes toward the institution, enjoy their work, and feel successful in it, than when relationships between staff members were poor. When work relationships were good, staff members reported many "good days" and few "bad days."

The quality of the relationships between staff and patients was also correlated positively with staff members' perceptions of the institution, other staff members, the work, and the patients. When the interaction was good, staff members liked their work, felt successful at it, and found self-fulfillment in it. They appreciated other staff members more and conferred with them more often than when staff-patient relationships were poor. They also rated the institution more highly, described patients positively, and felt involved with both the institution and the patients.

A surprising set of findings in this study was that a high frequency of staff meetings was correlated with negative attitudes toward the patients. Staff members who often participated in staff meetings gave more weight to information about a patient that came from the patient's family or the psychiatric interview than they did to information coming directly from the patient. They saw less chance of curing patients and tended to have job-oriented goals in their work, rather than self- or patient-oriented goals. These staff members spent time with their coworkers in order to detach themselves from patients, rather than give each other support and advice about problems with patients. Such staff socialization, to avoid contact with patients, was a reliable indication of burnout.

In the other health and social service professions, staff meetings served several important functions.[14] They enabled the staff to socialize informally, to give each other support, to confer about problems to clarify their goals, and to exert direct influence on the politics of their institution. In those professions, frequency of staff meetings was negatively correlated to burnout (i.e., the more meetings, the less burnout). In psychiatric institutions, on the other hand, the frequency of staff meetings was positively correlated with burnout (i.e., the more meetings, the more burnout).

We believe that the reason for this outcome was that most staff meetings centered around case presentations. In these meetings a staff member would describe a patient in terms of his mental illness, using professional terminology that identified the patient with a disease and served to distance the staff from the patient. The meetings very rarely focused on the problems of the staff.

Staff meetings as support systems

Staff meetings can be effective organizational buffers against burnout and tedium if they fulfill several functions. They should provide the staff with opportunities to express themselves and to influence the institution's policies. This would allow staff to exert some control over their work and would give them a greater sense of commitment to the institution. Furthermore, staff meetings should have a balance between time for discussion of clients' problems and time for staff to confer about their work stress. In this way the meetings can be divided between task focus and emotional support for the staff; when the work-based emotional needs of staff members are fulfilled, staff meetings can become a tool for stopping the cycle of burnout.

Meetings are also a place where workers can discuss staff problems. Staff complaints are best dealt with when they are eventually stated as positive recommendations. One approach can be that every complaint must be followed by a recommended solution. An alternate approach, suggested by industrial psychologist Norman Maier, is to have several steps in the process leading from a complaint to a recommended solution.[15] In the first step, staff just complain and let off steam in a gripe session; staff should be allowed to express all their feelings of hurt and anger without inhibition. The second step is the problem definition; this step requires a different mode of thinking.

Every solution should be allowed to be presented without criticism, judgment, or mockery. The last step is choosing the best solution among the different alternatives.

Another function of professional support systems that can best be achieved through staff meetings is power. In these meetings employees can see where they can exercise more autonomy and gain more control over their organization. A staff meeting can reframe individual complaints into a staff problem and unite to solve it; employees can identify areas of stress and develop ways to ease pressure. In organization there is power, control, and autonomy, and these three are negative correlates of burnout and tedium. Staff meetings are one setting in which staff can attempt to increase them.

Staff meetings can periodically devote time to evaluating staff skills and deficiencies. skill acquisition and other opportunities for personal and professional growth will increase mutual support in the office and will reduce burnout.

Relationships with supervisors—when growth-enhancing—can also be a buffer against burnout. Supervisors who give direct, specific, and encouraging feedback provide employees with a sense of significance, success, and challenge. Supervisors can reduce the impact of job stress if they are involved with workers on a regular, rather than crisis, basis; communicate concern rather than suspicion; and mediate between the individual and the organization. Supervisors can also make the staff aware of long-term and short-term goals of the organization and can share financial or political problems with the staff. This increases the staff's knowledge of and commitment to the organization. Such supervisory skills require training, but their benefits to the organization are great enough to warrant the extra expense.

Obstacles to the creation of social support systems

Cary Cherniss, a professor of psychology at the university of Michigan, describes six obstacles to the creation of social support networks within human service organizations.[16]

1. Different theoretical orientations and personal values may cause problems. For example, friction can be created when some staff members in a mental health clinic share a psychoanalytic orientation, while others are committed to a behavioristic approach.
2. Differences in resources, status, and power often contribute to conflict. Competition may exist between older staff members and younger ones, between men and women, black and white, and so forth. The competition can be on who gets the larger office, the approval of the supervisor, or anything else.

3. The role structure itself sometimes hinders the development of support networks. For example, when most of the work is done in the field, and the professional does not see much of the other workers, there are not enough opportunities for social and professional interactions. Another example is overload, which can be an obstacle to social interaction when it is so overwhelming that it forces the workers to work on their own, trying to catch up, both at work and after work hours.

4. Outside interests, involvement in family, friends, politics, and hobbies can limit the time and emotional energy that people are willing to invest in the social aspects of their work, especially when they demand involvement after work hours. We take an exception with Professor Cherniss on this point, because we recommend the very thing that he sees as an obstacle. We recommend that professionals compartmentalize between their work and home life and get involved in outside activities and interests as a way to prevent burnout.

5. Informal norms can limit interaction among various groups in an organization that can potentially become support networks. Such norms can also inhibit serious discussions between professionals that could be challenging and growth-producing.

6. High staff turnover rates, which are a common phenomenon in many human service organizations, prevent the development of cohesion and group feelings. Since everyone seems to be quitting, staff members are reluctant to invest energy in each other.

Cary Cherniss's suggestions for dealing with these obstacles when attempting to develop social support networks include: assessment of the situation, identifying which of the six obstacles are present, and direct confrontation of the obstacles when they have been identified. In new places, he recommends building mechanisms that will avoid the development of these problems; for example, role structures and work settings that enhance interaction between workers.

A support system in private practice

As we have indicated throughout this chapter, many people in the helping professions burn out because they give in their work more than they receive: they give more effort and energy in helping their clients than they receive in appreciation. This problem is reduced for people who have effective support systems that provide them with feedback, appreciation, and challenge. The problem is amplified for people in private practice who may not have such a support system.

Dentists, to use the example presented in Chapter 1, usually work in offices without other dentists to provide either technical appreciation or technical challenge. The dentists cannot get significant feedback or appreciation from their patients because patients do not see what they do, are not expert enough to evaluate it, and often are uncomfortable and want to leave the office quickly. Patients usually report to dentists only when something goes wrong; it is expected that they will do things right. This bias toward negative feedback is built into most service professions but is particularly painful for private practitioners who do not have a group of colleagues with whom to share their feelings of success and failure.

Our recommendation for private practitioners is to establish a social support system with other colleagues in private practice. This is also applicable to supervisors and directors of organizations. Some people at the top of organizations may have a romantic notion of self-sufficiency. Although this "lone wolf" image may be attractive, it does not prevent burnout; "if the Lone Ranger were still riding around, heigh-hoing Silver today, he'd be one burned out cowboy. . . ."[17]

For people in private practice, and for heads of organizations, the best resource for a support group are those people who do the same work in a different setting. Motivated by impending burnout, professionals can find out who holds the same position in similar organizations and contact them. Such contact can generate new resources and innovative ideas about ways to grow on the job. A support system of fellow professionals can provide a place to share triumphs and difficulties and to give and receive feedback, solace, appreciation, and understanding.

Men and women: differences in social supports

In a study involving 96 professional men and 95 professional women, sex differences in the experience of tedium and its antecedents and correlates were investigated.[18] It was found that work relationships, as well as other support systems, were more important influences on tedium for women. For example, women's relationships with supervisors, subordinates and coworkers were negatively and significiantly correlated with tedium (i.e., the better the relationship, the less tedium). For men, the relationships with supervisors and subordinates was not correlated with tedium, and the relationship with coworkers, though significant, was much less so than for women. For women the relationship with spouse, family, and friends was also negatively and significantly correlated with tedium, but for men only relationships with friends and spouse were significantly correlated with tedium and, again, less so than for women.

Women's sensitivity to the social aspects of their life and work may account for the finding that women considered "people" a greater source of stress in their work than did men. Another explanation is the disproportionate representation of women in the human service professions which have more "people" stresses. Women felt more overextended emotionally than men both at work and outside of work. But women also received more support from people; they shared more with others in their work and outside of work and felt they received more unconditional support in times of need.

In another study that investigated coping strategies, the same sex differences were found.[19] Women reported using social support systems for coping with tedium more than men, and women reported the social strategies to be more effective than did men. Women seemed better able than men to share work stresses by discussing their sources of stress and talking openly about their doubts, problems, and failures.

How to avoid sabotaging your own social support system

As we have said over and over again in this chapter, establishing a viable support system is one of the most effective ways of avoiding or diminishing burnout. Yet few people have an adequate social support system, There are several reasons for this; in the following pages we will discuss two powerful forces that help prevent people from making full use of a social support system.

Misattributions

It seems to be part of human nature to seek the causes of events; that is, virtually every time we see something happen we attribute a cause to it. If one is watching one's favorite football team and the tight end drops a very easy pass in the end zone, one could come up with several reasons. It may be that the player is untalented. Another possibility is that he was out drinking the night before; Or perhaps his child is sick and he is distracted with worry. Yet another possibility is that he bet on the other team and wanted to lose the game intentionally; there are any number of possibilities. How one feels about that person depends on what one attributes his behavior to; that is, one is going to feel differently about that football player if one attributes his dropping the pass to his concern about his child than if one attributes it to the fact that he bet on the other team.

There are two categories of attributions: one is dispositional and the other is situational. We make dispositional attributions when we attribute the cause of an event to the personality of the person. We make situational attributions when we attribute the cause to something in the situation. Research done on attributions has shown that people tend to explain their own behavior in situational terms and the behavior of others in dispositional terms. For example,

> when a student who is doing poorly in school discusses his problem with a faculty adviser, there is often a fundamental difference of opinion between the two. The student, in attempting to understand and explain his inadequate performance, is usually able to point to environmental obstacles such as a particularly onerous course load, to temporary emotional stress such as worry about his draft status, or to a transitory confusion about life goals that is now resolved. The faculty adviser may nod and may wish to believe, but in his heart of hearts he usually disagrees. The adviser is convinced that the poor performance is due neither to the student's environment nor to transient emotional states. He believes instead that the failure is due to enduring qualities of the student—to lack of ability, to irremediable laziness, to neurotic ineptitude.[20]

This difference in attributions can have a great effect on interpersonal relations, particularly because there are usually few opportunities to correct wrong attributions once they have been made. For example, an individual may have a colleague who is an expert in her area and has a finely tuned critical ability. She may be reluctant to make use of him, however, because on one or two occasions she saw him behave in an aggressive manner, and she concluded that he was an aggressive person. Once she has attributed the cause of his behavior to his personality, she believes that she has a good reason to avoid him. But suppose that he is not really an "aggressive person"; rather, she happened to see him when he was particularly irritable because of sleeplessness, problems in the family, or budgetary concerns. In short, he is not *really* an aggressive *person*. He is a person who behaves aggressively when he is under certain kinds of situational stress.

Because of the importance of social support systems, it is essential for individuals to periodically reassess their early judgments of their colleagues and acquaintances in order to avoid dismissing erroneously valuable human resources.

Indeed, interpreting people's behavior in situational rather than dispositional terms has general utility. By making a dispositional attribution, one renders oneself powerless to affect the interaction. A situational attribution, however, offers the possibility of changing the situation. That sense of power is extremely useful in combating burnout even if the options for change are limited. The belief that the environment is malleable is important in itself.

Self-fulfilling prophecies

Most individuals have within them the capability of behaving intelligently or stupidly, gracefully or clumsily, gently or harshly. All other things being equal, if the people around them treat them as a graceful person, it will bring out more of their graceful behavior than their clumsy behavior. This proposition was demonstrated brilliantly in an experiment by Mark Snyder, a social psychologist at the University of Minnesota; we will describe the experimental procedures of one study in some detail.[21]

In this study students participated in what they thought was an investigation of the processes by which people become acquainted with each other. Pairs of unacquainted males and females were told that they would engage in a telephone conversation. All male subjects received a snapshot of what they believed was the female member of their dyad. Actually the snapshots were not of the female subjects but were pictures chosen previously for receiving high or low attractiveness ratings. Male subjects were randomly assigned pictures of very attractive or very unattractive women. Female subjects did not get snapshots and knew nothing about them being given to the men. Each dyad then engaged in ten minutes of unstructured conversation by means of microphones and headphones connected through a tape recorder that recorded each participants voice on a separate channel of the tape. Raters listened *only* to the track of the tapes containing the women's voices and rated them on dimensions such as animation, enthusiasm, intimacy, and friendliness.

The data revealed that those women who were perceived as attractive came to behave in a friendly and likable manner in comparison with those who spoke with men who thought them to be unattractive.

Similarly in everyday life, if one thinks a certain person to be cold or aloof, one will behave in a way that will bring out that person's coldness and aloofness. The same person can be warm and friendly in another social encounter. It is important to avoid writing people off unless the evidence against them is overwhelming.

Notes

1. K. Lewin, *Resolving Social Conflicts. Selected Papers on Group Dynamics*, (New York: Humpe and Brothers, 1945), pp. 94, 95.
2. Ibid.
3. M. Pilisuk and S. Hillier Parks, *Networks of Social Support: A Review*. Unpublished manuscript, University of California–Davis, 1980.
4. S. Cobb, "Social Support As a Moderator of Life Stress," *Psychosomatic Medicine* 5, no. 38: 300–314.
5. G. Caplan, *Support Systems and Community Mental Health* (New York: *Behavorial Publications*, 1974).
6. The correlation between life tedium and various social support systems was as follows: family $r = -.18$, work $r = -.22$, friends $r = -.23$, coworkers $r = -.25$, acquaintances $r = -.17$. All p value are equal to or smaller than .001.
7. The correlation between unconditional support and tedium was $r = -.21, p < .001$.
8. The correlation between the frequency of being lonely and life tedium was $r = .47$, and family relations $r = -.23$, and work relations $r = -.26$, and relations with friends $r = -.32$, and relations with coworkers $r = -.26$, and relations with acquaintances $r = -.28$, and unconditional support $r = -.33$. All p values are equal to or smaller than .001.
9. C. L. Cooper and J. Marshall, "Occupational Sources of Stress: A Review of the Literature Relating to Coronary Heart Disease and Mental Heatlh," *Journal of Occupational Psychology* 49 (1976): 11–28.
10. M. Marx Ferree, "The Confused American Housewife," *Psychology Today* 10 (April 1976): 76–80.
11. H. J. Freudenberg, "The Staff Burnout Syndrome," *Alternative Institutions Psychotherapy: Theory Research and Practice* 12, no. 1 (1975): 72–72.
12. See, for example, C. Maslach and A. Pines, "Burnout: The Loss of Human Caring," in A. Pines and C. Maslach, *Experiencing Social Psychology* (New York: Random House, 1979), pp. 245–252.
13. A. Pines and C. Maslach, "Charateristics of Staff Burnout in Mental Health Settings," *Hospital and Community Psychiatry* 4, no. 29 (1978): 233–237.
14. Maslach and Pines, "Burnout."
15. N. R. F. Maier, *Problem Solving Behavior vs. Frustration Behavior, Psychology in Industrial Organizations* (Boston: Houghton Mifflin 1973).
16. C. Cherniss, "Social Support Networks," in *Burnout in the Helping Professions*, ed. K. Reid (Kalamazoo: Western Michigan University Press, 1980).
17. From the motion picture *Burnout*, MTI Teleprograms Inc., 4825 North Scott Street, Schiller Park, Ill.

18. A. Pines and D. Kafry, "Tedium in the Life and Work of Professional Women as Compared with Men," *Sex Roles,* in press.
19. D. Kafry and A. Pines, "Coping Strategies and the Experience of Tedium," Paper presented at the Annual Meeting of the American Psychological Association, Toronto, Canada, August 1978.
20. E. E. Jones and R. E. Nisbet, "The Actor and the Observer: Divergent Perceptions of the Causes of Behavior," in *Attribution: Perceiving the Causes of Behavior,* ed. E. E. Jones et al. (Morristown, N.J.: General Learning Press, 1971), pp. 79-94.
21. M. Snyder, E. D. Tanke, and E. Berscheid, "Social Perception and Interpersonal Behavior: On the Self-Fulfilling Nature of Social Stereotypes," *Journal of Personality and Social Psychology* 35 (1977): 656–666.

8

Intrapersonal
coping strategies

In the early chapters of this book we showed that human service professionals burn out as a result of working with people over long periods of time in situations that are emotionally demanding. Bureaucrats develop tedium as a result of working within complex organizations characterized by excessive overload, lack of autonomy, and lack of support and appreciation. Professional women who are also homemakers are prone to experience burnout and tedium as a result of their role conflicts. Burnout and tedium are not caused by bad or incompetent people but rather by stressful situations.

Positive environmental variables

Just as there are stressful conditions that induce burnout and tedium, there are positive environmental conditions that ameliorate and prevent them. These positive features in the environment promote certain tendencies in the individual that work against tendencies toward burnout. For example, an environment that is conducive to learning or an environment that promotes the feeling in the individuals that their work is meaningful and significant will reduce the likelihood of burnout and increase the likelihood of personal growth. We have identified six such variables that we will discuss in this chapter: (1) learning, (2) meaning and significance, (3) success and achievement, (4) variety, (5) flow experiences, and (6) self-actualization.

Learning

The world offers a variety of experiences that can enrich existence. Learning and understanding are basic motivators for human action. Humans are born with a quest for learning and exploration which is frequently referred to as "curiosity," Curiosity about the world is a major factor even in animal behavior. For example, it is well known that animals will go through difficult or unpleasant behaviors in order to obtain food. That is not surprising. What is surprising are the results of experiments by the well-known animal psychologist Robert A. Butler that show monkeys will go through difficult or unpleasant behaviors for no other "reward" but the privilege of satisfying their curiosity by looking out of a small window![1] Similarly, curiosity among young children is a universal characteristic casually observed by all parents. Some adults are blessed with a childlike curiosity. For example, Albert Einstein once commented, "My scientific work is motivated by an irresistible longing to understand the secrets of nature and by no other feelings." Yet most of us somehow become immersed in the trivia of everyday living and do not allow ourselves to exercise our curiosity, thereby neglecting our own learning and development.

Some organizations provide opportunities for the expansion of learning and awareness by continuing education, conventions, or in-service classes. Unfortunately not all organizations provide this and, even where it is available, many employees do not take advantage of the opportunities available to them. Interviews with professionals showed that people's use of the resources for growth at work and outside of work can affect their level of tedium. A learning environment can be somewhat subjective. Even in the same environment, different people can see different opportunities for learning. A simple example will demonstrate this point. We encountered two people who held the same job in a bookstore in a small university town. One of them developed tedium: "My job is so boring that I cannot take it anymore. All I do is sell books or help people find them, which I can't do efficiently since I don't know where most of the books are anyway. Sometimes there are no people in the store and all I do is sit and wait for the day to end." A different picture was presented by the other person: "I make it a point to know about most of the new books that come into the store. I read their covers, try to read some of them at home or at the store when there are no customers. I feel that I'm constantly learning about books and about people. I sometimes exchange opinions with customers and like to note what kinds of books each person buys. I am busy all the time and I don't have one moment of boredom."

These two people are in the same external environment but their internal environment differs markedly: one has made himself open to new experiences and the other has not done so. Individuals in a variety of professions seem to vary in their need for learning and the chances they take for its enhancement. Those for whom the need is most important tend to seek environments that facilitate it and to use every opportunity for intellectual development.

The point we want to make should be obvious by this time. Learning and development need not involve formal institutions; openness to new experience leads to constant acquisition of information. For people who are interested in other people, every train ride, museum visit, or stroll can be exciting. Those who are interested in natural phenomena or technological developments can also be exposed to new ideas almost incessantly. When we decide to be more open to learning, and make ourselves aware of the fact that the world is full of new experiences, that's when we all become less likely candidates for tedium.

Meaning and significance

Challenging the meaning of one's life sets human beings apart from animals. This thesis is the basic belief of Viktor Frankl, the leading proponent of existential analysis.[2] While the urgent questioning of the meaning of life is most apt to occur during adolescence, it may also come later, usually precipitated by some shaking experience. Spiritual distress, the existential crises of a mature person struggling to find content for his life, have nothing pathological about them—however, a negative resolution to the quest for meaning produces a sense of ennui or "tedium vitae." In other words, if people cannot find meaning in their work or outside of their work, they become apathetic. This concept of Frankl's is very similar to the mental or spiritual aspect of tedium that we have described. Our research has shown that the loss of sense of meaning and significance in life is a major contributor to tedium and burnout, and one of the ways in which it is manifested is apathy.[3]

Closely allied to mental exhaustion is "existential neurosis." Salvatore Maddi, a psychologist at the University of Chicago, defined existential neurosis as the belief that one's life is meaningless and dominated by apathy, boredom, and alienation from self and from society.[4] Maddi's example of an existential neurotic is Meursault in Albert Camus' *The Stranger*. Meursault believes that his life is meaningless and arbitrary, and he feels only boredom and apathy. The major event of the novel is Meursault's murder of an Arab while walking on the beach. One would expect the commission of such an act of violence on the part of a middle-class bureaucrat like Meursault to be a major emotional trauma. And yet what is so strange about this act of murder is that it is committed in an apathetic, almost matter of fact, manner. Meursault murders in apathy, without provocation or reaction, as part of his random behavior. His life is a psychological death, a state of nonbeing. The novel ends with Meursault, on his way to his execution, uttering that "nothing matters."

Meursault may be perceived as an extreme case of tedium; in more moderate tedium there is still some emotion, albeit the emotions tend to be the least pleasant ones: annoyance, anxiety, sadness, and so forth. People who feel total apathy, in extreme burnout and tedium, have very little energy. In their state of apathy, the work situation feels hopeless and there is no chance that anything will change it. When offered the opportunity to attempt to reverse these symptoms they are too apathetic to seize it. For example, when we offer workshops designed to help people cope with burnout the most extreme cases frequently do not attend out of apathy and hopelessness.

The Israeli sociologist Aaron Antonovsky proposed a new approach to "health, stress, and coping."[5] Central to his approach is what he calls "the sense of coherence"—a general attitude characteristic of those who consistently enjoy good health—that the world is comprehensible; that one's own life is meaningful, orderly, and reasonably predictable; and that one participates in the shaping of one's destiny.

As mentioned earlier, one can develop tedium because of the lack of meaning in one's life or work. The need for meaning may be especially acute in those jobs where the employee does not have a sense of completion or effectiveness. This is a problem for professionals who deal with a client for brief periods of time without being able to follow through or when a person produces a small part of some product and does not see the product in its completed form.[6]

Certain activities are inherently more meaningful than others. For example, working as a brain surgeon is almost certainly more meaningful than working as a salesman of used cars. And yet it is possible for some brain surgeons to become apathetic, believing that their work is meaningless; and it is possible for some car salesmen to derive a sense of meaning from their work. Like the two salesmen in the bookstore, one can either introduce meaning into one's work activities or turn one's back on the inherent meaning in those activities. Even though there is no universal list of significant life and work values and even though meaningful things differ for different people, the way to change "tedium vitae" into "delirium vitae" (the passion for life) is universal.

Success and achievement

Achievement and success are important in human societies, enhancing economic development, cultural growth, and individual well-being. David C. McClelland, a Harvard psychologist who studied achievement motivation, showed that men with high needs to achieve are more successful, especially in the business world, than those with low achievement needs.[7] McClelland's achievement syndrome includes moderate risk-taking strategies; that is, high achievers are neither too risky nor too cautious. Similarly, people with higher achievement motivation show energetic instrumental activity to attain goals, a willingness to take personal responsibility for actions, a desire for knowledge about the results of their actions, and a tendency for long-range planning. Our own work suggests that people who employ these strategies in their work, especially with bureaucratic organizations, are less likely to experience tedium.

Our studies also showed that a sense of success and achievement is negatively correlated with burnout and tedium.[8] Successful professionals tend to see themselves more positively and to develop less tedium; those who have the frustration of failure are more likely to experience tedium. The negative correlation between success and burnout does not imply causality. It could be that failure causes burnout; it could be that burnout causes a feeling of failure; it could also be that certain qualities in an individual or a situation promote both burnout *and* a sense of failure.

Success and failure are not always judged by objective absolute terms. Individuals' perceptions of their achievements occasionally have very little to do with absolute objective reality. For example, if a college student got 92 percent correct answers on an exam, we might consider that very successful. But if his three best friends got 97 percent on the same exam, he might consider himself a failure. Some people may be successful by others' standards and yet view themselves as failures because they are comparing themselves to someone above them in ability or achievements. It is unfortunate that, for these people, the positive effect of a real success is emotionally lost, since each success can serve as a powerful buffer against burnout and tedium. Accordingly, it is important for individuals to learn to acknowledge and indeed bask in their own success before pushing on to other challenges. But there are pressures that subvert this needed experience of success. Competition is an example of such a pressure.

As the example of the college student has shown, people who are caught up in a highly competitive game do not judge their accomplishments relative to their skill or effort but relative to other people's success. They do not evaluate their achievements relative to their previous achievements or to their expectations but relative to the achievement of others. For example, a successful lawyer told us, "This year I made 20% more than last year, but my partners still made a lot more than me." A research psychologist said, "I have a nice list of publications and a good prospect of getting tenure in the department, but a friend who graduated with me already has an international scientific reputation. I'll never be as good as he is." Such comparisons can be self-destructive: the achievement is not enjoyed to its fullest because its importance is diminished relative to others who achieve more. The obsession with competition is a stress that some people never overcome. If the achievement of money, fame, or professional excellence is compared not to one's own aspirations and needs but to those of others, no level of success will suffice. This can only add to the pressures that produce burnout.

The drive for achievement can also be self-destructive when it dominates a person's life, as witness this statement by a middle-aged, ulcerated executive:

> For years I have been completely immersed in my career. I worked days and nights, weekends and holidays, to establish and develop my private business and to make more money. Almost all of a sudden I realized that I do not know my wife and my children. I don't have any real friends because our social activities were always targeted around potential clients or business partners. I feel as if life passed me by, when I was too busy with the wrong things.

This preoccupation causes a double pressure: the push for more achievement and the absence of the other rewards in life.

When people are extremely achievement-oriented or future-oriented, attaining success is usually not associated with happiness but rather with disappointment. For example, we once encountered a scientist who worked hard to reach his prominent position and who made a discovery that brought him sudden recognition; he then became severely depressed. In effect, he seemed to be saying to himself: "Is that it? Is that what I have worked all these years for?" In a life dominated by the future, success satisfies only for a moment, and this moment is painful because it makes the price of success evident.

To sum up this section, success and achievement are positive aspects of life that can alleviate tedium and provide the person with a sense of fulfillment. But they are subjective experiences and do not necessarily reflect reality. When the drive for success becomes all-encompassing, it can be a source of stress and an antecedent of tedium. In order to turn success into a positive rather than a negative outcome, people must learn to take some time to relax and enjoy successful accomplishments and to make that experience part of themselves before moving on to meet the next challenge.

Variety

Most people spend part of their time performing routine activities; most routine activities, repetitive and brief, are sources of stress when performed exclusively for long periods of time. But people may prefer them to nonroutine activities when they break long periods of overload. The same police officer or nurse who developed overload during the day can feel underload on a tranquil night shift. Routine, however, results from both the number of activities performed, and the types of activities. If one performs a large number of repetitive activities, one may suffer both from boredom and from overload.

Our studies have shown that people who perform monotonous activities tend to experience tedium; people who perform a variety of activities that enable them to use their capabilities rarely experience tedium.[9] This was true for both work and nonwork situations. For many people, boredom with their daily routines is a part of life. But these routines can be used to add variety to life. One can enjoy a creative, stimulating activity and then relax in a routine activity. The sense of variety and interest is not necessarily a mattter of outside stimulation; rather, it originates largely from within the person.

Several theoretical frameworks may account for the effects of variety on behavior and happiness. One of these involves the physiological activation or arousal system.[10] People function at their best at an optimal activation level. Extremely high activation levels create anxiety and strain and extremely low levels create boredom and anger. Studies of sensory deprivation, in which people were put in situations where visual, auditory, and tactile stimulation were severely restricted, documented reduced cognitive and motor capabilities, irritation, emotional regression, and even hallucinations.[11] Similarly, after eighteen months in solitary confinement as a suspected spy in France, Christopher Burney wrote, "I soon learned that variety is not the spice; it is the very stuff of life."[12]

The variety of stimulation, as well as the level of stimulation, affect people's reactions. There seems to be a certain level of stimulation needed to satisfy the psychological complexity level of the organism.[13] When this level is not met, either because of overstimulation or understimulation, the individual tends to react negatively. When stimulation is too novel and variable, the individual will attempt either to narrow attention or to integrate it in large units of processing. When the amount of novelty and variety is too low, individuals will either become bored or will attempt to change their environment by seeking new events in their physical environment, their social environment, or their own thoughts.

No matter how initially exciting one's work may be, over time, boredom with the task and the monotony of the problems can wear anyone down. One way of circumventing these debilitating reactions is to have employees change tasks periodically. Our recommendation is that people add variety and challenge to their life and work rather than simply repeating what they are good at. One can give oneself permission to be less than perfect as one experiments with new ideas, abilities, and approaches.

There are jobs in which there is little room for innovation; here, the people themselves can provide increased interest because people, in their uniqueness, can be a great source of variety. This can be a positive rather than negative characteristic of work, particularly for individuals in the human services who tend to choose their profession in order to work with people. The reader will recall that one of the recommendations we made to dentists (see Chapter 1) was to spend more time getting to know their patients: dentists can get bored drilling and filling innumerable teeth. Teeth can be boring. But dentists are working primarily with people—not teeth. When they begin to recognize that every person they deal with is different and needs a different kind of reassurance, treatment, and conversation, then each appointment can become a unique experience. One's interest and sense of variety can be continually freshened by humanizing each situation, differentiating each person, and offering each a different part of one's self.

One alternative available for increasing variety in certain settings is lateral job change. Another solution is more drastic job change—i.e., getting out of the profession. Before making a radical change, workers should be certain that they are using all the resources for variety and lateral change that are available on the job. When radical job change in unavoidable, it is most productive to go "toward" new challenges rather than "away from" problems. Such positive career changes at mid-life, described as "starting over in midstream," were the subject of a study by Sol Landau, a Miami rabbi.[14] Landau interviewed individuals who switched to a new career during their middle years, ages 35 to 54. His interviewees represented a wide educational and socioeconomic background, but all of them were financially success-ful in their first careers. "I wanted to interview people who were making midlife changes because of their internal needs," he said, "not because they had been unsuccessful in their first career." Landau found most of the participants in his study "secure" and "self-reliant." "They are not habitual or complusive changers," he learned. Theirs was a "quest for self-renewal," an escape from the dull routine that their day-to-day work had become. Landau found that among those he interviewed the most satisfying second careers were those most dissimilar to the first ones. Such switches included a mattress dis-tributor who became a stockbroker, a military pilot-turned-physician, an executive who became a hypnotist-counselor, and a photographer who became a sociologist.

Expressing one's range of interests and skills is a crucial factor in allievating burnout and tedium. In the words of Bertrand Russell, "The secret of happiness is this: Let your interests be as wide as possible, and let your reactions to the things and persons that interest you be as far as possible friendly rather than hostile."[15]

Flow experiences

It is customary to think that people who are involved in creative work experience less tedium than others. In a recent book, Mikaly Csikszentmikalyi describes such people: people who have "peak ex-periences," who are internally motivated, and who are involved in play as well as in work activities including chess players, rock climbers, dancers, surgeons, composers, and basketball players.[16] He looked for similarities in their experiences, motivation, and in the situations that produced enjoyment in them. What he found was that these people engage, more than others, in "autotelic" activities which are performed for their own sake and not for the purpose of receiving tangible rewards. These activities are an exploration of the limits of one's abilities and an attempt to expand them. Most people studied described their autotelic experience as involving creative exploration; it is an experience that lies at the optimal place between boredom and anxiety. The feeling during these autotelic activities was described as a "flow experience," a complete involvement with little distinction between the self and the environment and between past, present, and future.

Such "flow" is found most readily in activities such as chess and sports. It can also be found in art, in sciences, and in religious activities. Csikszentmikalyi reported that this variety of experiences has a similar inner flow where the activity is all, a state so enjoyable that people are willing to foresake a comfortable life for its sake. In his opinion, the clearest sign of "flow" is the merging of action and awareness; the person is aware of the action but not of the awareness. The awareness is centered around the activity and not around performance. Another characteristic of the flow experience is the centering of attention on the activity alone, ignoring other stimuli in the environment. Nikolai Krogius, the Russian chess grandmaster, reported an incident that occurred during a chess tournament: a water jug fell to the floor with a resounding crash; almost everybody looked up except the English master Burn, who continued gazing at the chess board and later reported not hearing anything.[17] Other characteristics of flow are the loss of ego or self-forgetfulness, without losing touch with one's own physical reality; the control of actions without an active awareness of control and without worry about lack of control; coherent, noncontradictory demands for action with clear feedback on the actions; and no need for external goals or rewards.

Mikaly Csikszentmikalyi also describes "microflow" activities that occur in everyday life. When people were asked to report enjoyable events but not necessarily those that they do during a normal day, two sets of activities accounted for over half of the events reported: the first included patterns of body movements (e.g., touching, rubbing, fiddling with objects, walking, running); the second included forms of social interaction (e.g., talking and joking with other people, partying, hugging, kissing, and making love). The findings represent two approaches to experience; people who reported the first were less frequently engaged in the second and vice versa. These findings suggest that people enjoy different activities, just as they find meaning in different things and have different needs for learning and variety.

Flow experiences constitute some of the happiest moments in people's lives, and remembrance of these experiences can be a major determinant in people's perceived happiness. "The peaks decide the meaningfulness of life, and a single moment can retroactively flood an entire life with meaning. Let us ask a mountain climber who has beheld the Alpine sunset and is so moved by the splendor of nature that he feels cold shudders running down his spine—let us ask him whether after such an experience his life can ever again seem wholly meaningless.[18]

The experience of flow seems to be the opposite of tedium. And, indeed, preliminary findings indicate that people who are involved in activities to the point of "flow" are reporting less tedium.[19] All individuals can identify flow experiences in their own life. A person can determine their frequency and consciously attempt to increase it. This seems easier said than done, and yet a person can make a start by exploring the conditions required to have such experiences and arranging to produce those conditions both at work or outside of work. As Csikszentmikalyi has indicated, there are certain kinds of activities where the likelihood of a flow experience is greater than others. If such an activity is part of people's vocation, they are indeed fortunate. If it is not, there are two things they can try to do: one is to try and make them part of their avocation (e.g., they could think back to the kinds of things that they do, such as hiking, dancing, or painting, that make them experience a "flowlike" feeling and try to increase the frequency of these activities). But most people spend almost half of their waking lives at work. Accordingly, it should be of great importance if they could find some aspect of their job that lends itself to a flow experience—that is to say, while very few people play chess or paint as an occupation, it is also the case that there are very few occupations that are so barren as to not include some possibility for the creative individual to find a way to flow, at least some of the time, on the job.

Self-actualization

Several psychological theories of personality postulate a need for self-fulfillment and growth as a basic motivation for human endeavor.[20] One of these theories, posited by Abraham Maslow, has become quite popular over the last decade.[21] Maslow maintained that a central tendency of personality is people's drive toward actualization of their human potentialities. Maslow called this tendency the self-actualizing tendency. The self-actualizing tendency promotes expression of people's unique characteristics and results in a rich and meaningful life.

Maslow viewed self-actualization as the highest need in a human's hierarchy of needs; that is, self-actualization can be satisfied only after the satisfaction of lower-order needs. Maslow's hierarchy includes five levels of basic needs. At the bottom of his hierarchy are physiological needs such as food, water, air, and sleep. Once these physiological needs are satisfied, people attempt to satisfy the next level of needs—the safety needs. They achieve this by attempting to create a secure environment, free form threats and danger. On the next level are the love needs, which involve interpersonal dynamics such as the need to be loved and accepted by others. Next in the hierarchy are the esteem needs—the need to be respected and valued. Finally, at the top of the hierarcy is the need for self-actualization.

The actualization of the self is also a major theme in the writings of Carl Rogers.[22] "There is in every organism, including man, an underlying flow of movement toward constructive fulfillment of its inherent possibilities, a natural tendency toward growth. It can be thwarted but not destroyed without destroying the whole organism." Self-actualization involves acting in concert with one's inherited nature in the enhancement of life. It is the fulfillment of desires stemming from one's character. Self-actualization involves continual pressures to act and develop and to experience oneself in accordance with one's conscious view of oneself. Hence, self-actualization is the integration of the various aspects of the self; it is the congruence between self and society; it is the expression of one's potential; it involves changes and growth; it is openness to new experiences; it is active and creative life.

It would seem obvious that a low degree of burnout would occur among those people whose work and whose life outside of work allowed them to feel challenged and to feel that they were living up to their potential, and indeed there is data that corroborated this expectation. For most professionals who participated in our studies, self-actualization was a highly desired quality. The lack of a real opportunity for self-actualization in work and home life was significantly related to tedium and burnout (i.e., the less self-actualization, the more tedium).[23] Professionals who spend many years in training for a certain occupation often have expectations that their career will provide them with both continual challenge and opportunities for self-actualization. When these expectations do not materialize, when work does not allow for the expression of talents and acquired skills, they suffer severe frustration, tedium, and burnout.

Perhaps the best way to sum up what we have been saying in the last several pages is by focusing our attention on the two young people working as salesmen in the bookstore. The reader will recall that, although they were working at the same job, one of them found it to be an occupation that was full of opportunities for learning, while the other found it boring and stagnating. It would be tempting to explain the differences in their experiences in terms of their personalities: Sam is a more curious, sunny person; Harry is closed and sullen. Needless to say, people do differ from one another; at the same time it would be a grevious error to assume that vast differences in behavior are solely the result of rigid and unchangeable traits. In our work we have learned time and time again that individuals can change their own behavior and their own orientation to the world without the necessity of long-term psychotherapy or deep-seated personality change. What people need is the opportunity to become aware of the causes of their own stress, the drive to take some responsibility for change, the opportunity to gain cognitive clarity over what aspects of their environment (including the internal environment) can be changed, and the development of certain basic skills. Thus, with some effort, Harry could learn to treat the bookstore as a place where he could learn a lot and could also see his occupation as one that is meaningful, For example, working in a bookstore can be envisioned as providing people with a service and instilling in them an excitement about books, some of which might change their lives. Similarly, both Sam and Harry, with the proper orientation, would be able to make proper use of whatever success they were able to achieve. As we indicated earlier, success can be a cause of burnout, if it is simply viewed as a step on a never-ending ladder toward some mythical goal or as a means of comparison to someone who is apparently more successful. With a little thought and care Harry could learn to take the time to enjoy and appreciate his own accomplishments before moving on to the next challenge. Let us look at variety. We have already indicated that Sam saw the bookstore as a place of infinite variety: different kinds of books, different kinds of customers, and so forth. There is no reason why Harry could not become aware of the same aspects of the bookstore with a little bit of effort and a little bit of trying. By the same token, while we would not presume to tell Sam, Harry, or those who read this book precisely what activities in their life would produce flow experiences or would help them actualize more of their potential, we do believe that the active examination of their day-to-day life, and the search for increasing these experiences, are reasonable first steps toward this realization.

Coping: what to do about burnout and tedium

In the overview to this book (Chapter 1) we presented four major strategies for dealing with burnout: (1) being aware of the problem,

(2) taking responsibility for doing something about it, (3) achieving some degree of cognitive clarity, and (4) developing new tools for coping and improving the range and quality of old tools. In subsequent chapters we recommended that people who work in the human services change their client-centered orientation to a more balanced relationship between themselves and their clients; we specifically recommended developing and maintaining a "detached concern." For people in bureaucratic organizations, we recommended learning how to become "good bureaucrats." We have suggested to professional women that some of their conflicts are a result of a social-psychological double bind and recommended that they make their life choices without succumbing to pressures from the outside, without guilt and without regrets. To move beyond burnout and tedium we suggested in the present chapter that the individual become involved in the active pursuit of learning, variety, a sense of meaning and success, flow experiences, and self-actualization.

Although we can make generalized recommendations about strategies for coping with burnout and tedium, people obviously vary in their individual coping styles, and those coping styles differ in their effectiveness. Coping refers to *efforts* to master conditions of harm, threat, or challenge when an automatic response is not readily available.[24] Coping in itself does not imply *success* but *effort*. It is the link between stress and adaptation. This formal definition of coping was used in stress research and in our own studies. Stress studies focused mainly on coping at times of severe stress, such as injuries, the death of a child, imminent death, natural disaster, and job loss. In spite of the clinical and theoretical importance of coping with everyday life, there is very little research on this topic. Thus, our own work focused on coping with chronic stresses inherent in everyday life, rather than with dramatic life events.[25] We believe that it is the chronic nature of the stresses and their mundane meaningless character that makes them so difficult to endure.

Four coping strategies

Richard Lazarus, a leader in the field of stress research, suggested two general types of coping: (1) direct action, in which the person tries to master the stressful transaction with the environment and (2) palliation, in which the person attempts to reduce the distrubances when unable to manage the environment or when action is too costly for the individual.[26] Direct coping, or direct action, is a strategy applied externally to the environmental source of stress, and indirect coping, or palliation, is a strategy applied internally to one's behaviors and emotions. In our own work, in addition to the direct/indirect dimensions of coping, we found an inactive/active dimension.[27] Active ("approach") coping strategy involves confronting or attempting to change the source of stress or oneself, while inactive ("avoidance" or "withdrawal") coping strategy involves avoidance or denial of the stress by cognitive or physical means. These two dimensions, direct/indirect and active/inactive, generate four types of coping strategies, each of them represented by three actions (see accompanying illustration of coping grid).

1. Direct-active: changing the source of stress, confronting the source of stress, finding positive aspects in the situation
2. Direct-inactive: ignoring the source of stress, avoiding the source of stress, leaving the stressful situation
3. Indirect-active: talking about the stress, changing oneself to adapt to the source of stress, getting involved in other activities
4. Indirect-inactive: drinking or using drugs, getting ill, collapsing

Coping Grid

	ACTIVE	INACTIVE
DIRECT	• Changing the source of the stress • Confronting source • Adopting a positive attitude	• Ignoring source of the stress • Avoiding source • Leaving
INDIRECT	• Talking about the source of stress • Changing self • Getting involved in other activities	• Alcohol or drugs • Getting ill • Collapsing

In one study involving 147 subjects, we asked what their major life and work stresses were, and then asked them to describe how they coped with these stresses. Twenty percent of the respondents reported that they confronted the source of their stress as a coping technique. Twenty percent indicated that they avoided the sources of stress (18 percent) or did nothing about them (2 percent). Forty-nine percent used a variety of indirect-active techniques: talking about the stress (20 percent), thinking about it (12 percent), studying (9 percent), getting involved in other activities (7 percent), physical activities, religious activities, and relaxation (1 percent); 11 percent reported a variety of indirect-inactive coping styles: worrying and crying (4 percent), drinking, eating, and smoking (1 percent), accepting the situation (4 percent), nothing (2 percent).

In a second study involving eighty-four subjects, we provided a list of the four categories of coping strategies and asked them to indicate how often they used each coping strategy and how successful they subjectively perceived the coping to be. The results of this study indicated that active strategies were used most often to cope with tedium and were reported the most successful. Inactive strategies were used less frequently and were reported least successful: the more frequent the use of active strategies, the less tedium; the more frequent the use of inactive strategies, the more tedium. An exception to this pattern was the direct-inactive action of ignoring the source; this action was found more similar to the active strategies than to the passive ones. It is important to make the distinction between ignoring and avoidance on the one hand and denial on the other hand. Ignoring the stress is a conscious decision that an individual perceives as directed at the problem. Denying the stress implies that the problem is still present, and its denial can be emotionally taxing to the individual. Indirect-inactive strategies seem to be symptoms of high levels of tedium; hence individuals who use them frequently also report high levels of tedium. It is not clear whether burnout causes an individual to drink, smoke, or take medication to excess or whether these excesses make one burn out, but clearly there is a relationship between them.[28] Indirect-inactive strategies are at best ineffective, inasmuch as they do not reduce stress but ultimately weaken individuals so that they become less capable of functioning adequately. In fact, it might be argued that a coping mechanism that involves drinking alcohol to excess, depending upon sleeping pills, and so forth, is not a coping strategy at all but simply a way of attaining very temporary relief from anxiety.

People who use active strategies successfully find they alleviate tedium, because active strategies are likely to change the source of stress. Professionals who attack the source of their stress directly, for example, by confronting their boss; professionals who avoid the stress, for example, by ignoring the outburst of a client; and professionals who deal with the stress indirectly, for example, by talking about it with a friend are all going to experience less tedium than the professionals who drink to forget the stress.

Even though people can indicate which is the common coping strategy they tend to use, it is important that they do not label themselves as such copers exclusively, i.e., "I am a direct-active" coper. A comparison between men and women, for instance, revealed that women tended to use more frequently indirect methods of coping, such as talking about the stress, getting ill, and collapsing. Men tended to use the direct strategies of changing the source of stress and ignoring the source of stress more often, Women also reported talking about the stress to be a more successful coping strategy and ignoring it less successful than did men. Even if one uses one strategy successfully in certain situations, that does not mean one has to use that particular strategy exclusively. We encountered men who labeled themselves direct-active copers and who found themselves paralyzed when they had to be in a situation where a direct-active approach would be disfunctional. For example, suppose the major source of stress for one person is a result of gruff and threatening behavior on the part of his supervisor, and he knows that if he confronts him directly on the issue the supervisor will respond in a gruff and threatening manner. If he has labeled himself a "direct-active" person, and if somehow that is tied up with his self-image as a "man," what he has succeeded in doing is paralyzing himself—that is, if by his own definition it would be "unmanly" to try to cope indirectly with the stress, and since he is convinced that the "manly" approach would be a disaster in this situation, he has doomed himself to live with that stress. The best coper is a person who is capable of mastering conditions of harm, threat, and challenge in a variety of ways, and who uses in each situation the best, most effective strategy for that particular situation.

Stress situations and response effectiveness

Under what circumstances is each coping category (or response cluster) appropriate or likely to be effective? Dov Eden, a business administration scholar at Tel-Aviv University, attempted to answer this question.[29] According to Professor Eden, stressful situations can be classified according to two independent dimensions, which combine to make the different responses to stress more or less feasible or effective. The first dimension is mutability. The situation may be immutable, such as a hazard built into the task itself which threatens the individual's well-being, for example, a test pilot. He can't remove potential dangers from his job; one of his tasks is to reveal these dangers by exposing himself to them before they have been discovered. The situation may be mutable, as in the case of a subordinate caught between the conflicting demands of two superiors. By informing them of the conflict, or by meeting with both together, or by using the good services of a third party, the stressful conflict can be in principle, and often is in practive, reduced or eliminated. So the first step in diagnosing a stressful situation is to determine its degree of mutability.

The second dimension is continuousness or intermittency. Some stresses are continuous, that is, constantly pose a threat to the individual. Others are intermittent. Intermittent stresses have different periodicities. Tax consultants have a period of stressful overload building up gradually for several months and peaking in April. Stress periodicity is predictable for many jobs, such as urban taxi drivers (rush hour), school teachers (beginning and end of school year), and preventive maintenance crews (during prescheduled shutdowns). Periodicity may be variable and unpredictable, such as emergency crew call-ups, hospital emergency room staffs, military units in wartime, negotiations during wildcat strikes, and fire-fighting crews. The combination of dichotomized mutability and intermittency produces four categories of stress situations.

The best coping with a mutable and continuous situational stress is direct-active coping. Mutable stress can be changed, and, since it is continuous, it is probably worth investing the effort to alter the source. When the source is mutable but the stress is intermittent, direct-active coping is still possible, but, depending on periodicity, how severe the stress is, and how much effort is required to change the source of stress, the individual might prefer to leave or ignore it.

When the source is immutable and the stress is intermittent, people cannot use direct-active coping. They can seek relief, temporary (catharsis or diversion) or permanent (change self), and thus adjust to an unalterable situation. The suggestion here is that people need intermittent relief from intermittent stress. They do not need the adjustment responses when the stress is "off" but do when it is "on." Adjustment can aid them in getting through peak periods of stress.

Immutable stress that is continuous is the most difficult situation for individuals. They cannot cope because it is immutable. The situation offers no relief, for the stress is continuous. If the individuals can use indirect-active coping, they will generate their own relief. If, however, they cannot change themselves enought to narrow the gap between the environmental demands and their own capacity, or if the temporary relief achieved through catharsis and diversion is insufficient to enable them to continue functioning in the situation, their only alternative to burnout may be to escape stress by leaving the situation.

Recommendations for intrapersonal coping

The general strategies for dealing with burnout that were presented in the previous chapters, and the classes of responses to stress presented in the previous paragraphs, can be viewed as general approaches that can be effective against burnout. The rest of this chapter will be devoted to more specific and concrete recommendations for coping on the level of the individual. Some of them have been mentioned earlier but we feel that they should be emphasized even at the risk of redundancy.

Examining individual coping

Keeping a log of daily stresses, coping strategies, and success or failure in coping can be a first step in becoming aware and in reducing burnout and tedium. At the end of each day (for a period of one week to one month) people can list and describe the day's stresses and joys. People who have kept such a log claimed that it was important to start with the list of joys, since starting with stresses can be so depressing that by the time they were finished they could hardly remember any joyous experiences at all. Each stress and joy can be evaluated on the following intensity scale:

1	2	3	4	5	6	7
not at all intense			moderately intense			extremely intense

Each stress should be described in terms of the coping effort it generated. For example, if the stress was a nasty comment by an individual's supervisor, what was the individual's response? Did he confront his supervisor actively and directly and tell her how her comments made him feel? Did he avoid her for the rest of the afternoon (direct-inactive)? Did he call up his best friend and cry on his shoulder (indirect-active)? Or did he sneak out of the office to get a drink at a nearby bar (indirect-inactive)? For each one of these responses the individual should also indicate how successful it was (from 1 = not at all to 7 = extremely). At the end of a week or a month people can go over their log and try to identify patterns in their stresses and in their attempts to master them. Some people find their stress generated primarily by work, others by their home life, still others by certain people or activities. Some people also identify in such a log patterns of coping behavior that they find effective. Others realize that they are locked into very ineffective coping strategies. Most people find that they use a rather limited vocabulary of coping strategies and that they should try to broaden their response repertory.

Goal setting

The stresses that are likely to be the hardest to cope with are those generated by frustrated hopes. All of us remember why we chose our line of work; periodically we can explore to what extent our original hopes and expectations are being fulfilled. Burnout and tedium are usually associated with the lost awareness of hopes and ambitions. It is not clear whether losing the awareness of goals is the cause or the result of burnout, but their coexistence implies a recommendation: we strongly suggest that individuals continually reappraise both their long-term and short-term goals. It is important that these goals and hopes be realistic both for themselves and for those with whom they deal. For example, it may be worthwhile for therapists to develop their diagnostic skills so they know what to expect realistically of themselves and of their clients. In this regard we mention a self-destructive experience shared by many such professionals: when starting a career, professionals attempt to do things simply because they do not know that these things are impossible. They may devote themselves to a case and perform a "miracle." But forever after these professionals feel guilty doing less than that first effort, knowing they once were capable of that maximum. Such goals are unrealistic and self-destructive.

Before setting goals it is important for individuals to clarify priorities. One way of doing this that we have used successfully in our workshops is fantasizing stripping off roles. When people think about the roles they play in life, what is important in those roles, and the relative importance of each one, they should try to get in touch with the feeling of what life would be like without that role: what it would be like without being a "loving father," a "beloved wife," a "sexy woman," or a "successful professional." In order to become aware people can imagine peeling off these roles as one peels off layers of clothing. Getting in touch with the feeling of what it is like to peel off each one of these roles forces reconsideration and a rewriting of priorities in a way that simply thinking about priorities doesn't.

Focusing on reevaluation and reassessment enables consideration of what changes individuals may want to make in the way they live their day-to-day lives and exactly how much power and how many options they have in making these changes. There are some changes that could be extraordinarily difficult to make; there are some that would be easier than they think.

When setting and clarifying goals, it is important to distinguish between problems that can and cannot be changed. The two most common mistakes are: giving up too early and hanging on too long. Individuals can both see how to solve a problem and distinguish the problems that can be solved from those that cannot. Some people have a dysfunctional tendency of focusing on fifty things that cannot be changed and thus either frustrating or depressing themselves. One can be most effective by focusing on the few things that can be changed.

Acknowledging time

It is always easy for people to put off making changes by convincing themselves that, for one reason or another, "the time isn't right." This occurs primarily because the anticipation of change almost always produces some anxiety. At the same time it is important for them to realize that if they have decided that the change is an important one to make, it is unlikely that there will be a better time than now. A friend of ours who never went to college projected herself as graduating from college five years in the future. But then she said, "But my God, I am forty-eight years old. If I started college today, I will be fifty-two by the time I am finished." "And how old will you be in four years if you don't go to college?" we asked. It is helpful when planning for the future to project life five years from now in terms of such things as house, car, spouse, job, and so forth. The greater the difference between the future projection and current reality, the sooner the change must start. It is important to recognize time as a precious and limited resource.

Acknowledging vulnerabilities

There is a limit to everybody's energy. Everyone must be aware of self-imposed stresses and of danger signs of burnout and tedium, and be willing to nurture themselves. Our emotional, mental, and physical energy supplies are not endless. After a certain point, the longer and the harder we work, the less we are probably accomplishing.

If people are feeling fatigued, resentful, disenchanted, and discouraged, or experiencing even more severe symptoms of burnout and tedium, it may be wise for them to take some time off work. Time off can be a long weekend, a week, a couple of weeks, a month, or even more if possible. During this "time off" they can analyze what is happening and why it is happening. Such analysis will probably also suggest better coping strategies.

People should not wait for a crisis to take time off. They must limit the number of hours on a given job and regularly take time off on evenings, weekends, and vacations. This is especially important if they work and live in the same place; if they do, then they can work four weeks and take the fifth week off, work three months and take the fourth month off, and so on. All people must have an outside life that is separate from the work sphere, have some space of their own even in a live-in situation. This is true for homemakers as well as for professionals. It is essential to beware of workaholism, of working overtime regularly and letting work get introduced into your home. When the job becomes overwhelming, the worker must stop and examine priorities.

Compartmentalization

It is important to keep a balance between energy invested in the work sphere and the energy invested in life outside of work. It is also important to compartmentalize life and work, being at work completely, and then leaving completely. This compartmentalization enables people to be involved in each one of the roles they play and yet to limit the stresses inherent in those roles to their time and place. Overlap between life and work stresses was found to be highly correlated with tedium. It is important, for example, not to bring work problems home. Discussing a work crisis with friends or spouse will recreate the traumatic experience; presenting one's own side of the situation is not likely to provide any new understanding or any new resources for coping.

It is useful to have a period of "decompression" after work, time to be quiet, meditate, exercise, or relax. Such a period of decompression will help get away from the problem at work and will make homecoming less stressful, especially for dual-career women. In our work we found a variety of decompression techniques people use, including listening to operas on the long drive home, sitting at a bus stop and watching the buses pass by, siting in a jacuzzi, jogging, swimming, sleeping, and window shopping.

Providing one's own reinforcements

Committed workers tend to burn out because they take on too much for too long and too intensely. They need to develop safeguards that will help them cope more effectively. The safeguards include being aware of work stresses, recognizing the danger signs of burnout and tedium, acknowledging vulnerabilities, putting reasonable limits on their work, and setting realistic goals. Most important for people in the human services is to be willing to provide for themselves as well as for their clients by changing the client-centered orientation to a more balanced client-provider relationship. They can learn to treat themselves as if they were their own client. They should make time to do the things they love but do not do often enough and acknowledge themselves as people who have legitimate needs. In order to be of help to others people must have a nourishing life of their own. Overinvolvement at work can be a sign that workers have given up trying to find meaningful outside activities and relationships. People can become so immersed in the organization that they have no time left for themselves and their own lives.

One technique to avoid overinvolvement is to list the three things they enjoy but seldom do and the three things they hate but do too often. A need to reorder priorities may be apparent. For example, if their work life is primarily cerebral, verbal, future-oriented, or emotionally demanding, they may need to add more physical things that are nonverbal and are present-oriented. One of the most consistent findings in our studies is the high correlation between burnout or tedium and poor physical health.[30] Being in good physical shape enables one to withstand better whatever stresses one encounters.

One can provide one's own reinforcements. This means building one's self-esteem so that if people at work have difficulty appreciating one's skill, one can provide that appreciation and that respect for oneself. Specifically, at the end of each day, or at least at the end of each week, people can ask themselves what they did this day or week that was good. They can allow themselves the luxury of real appreciation for the skill and hard work that go into their day-to-day life. They can be their own best audience. This is easier if they set their own short-term goals and are willing to acknowledge achieving them.

Changing dispositional self-attributes

Burnout is the result of a social-psychological interaction between a person and an environment. People need to learn to see themselves in situational rather than dispositional terms. For examples, it is not helpful for them to think of themselves as "shy" people.[31] It is much more useful for them to cut through the labeling and examine the situations that induce them to pull back and not assert themselves and thereby fail to get what they want. Once they examine this it may become clear that with a little extra effort they can behave in ways that are more productive and personally satisfying.

Positive attitude

Some things that look serious at the time they happen can appear funny a week or a month later. If people can learn to laugh at themselves thirty minutes later rather than a month later, they can ease their stress. They can rank difficult experiences on a 1 to 10 stress scale, remembering to save the extreme negative end of the scale for the real tragedies of life and bringing their evaluation of everyday stresses down the scale *when* they are happening. They must keep their sense of humor. Although professionals must take their work seriously, they must not take themselves seriously all the time. They must be prepared to laugh at their own foibles and at some of the difficult but often hilarious things that happen in their work and life.

The list of intrapersonal coping strategies is not all-inclusive. It represents the best of our knowledge about buffers against burnout and tedium and about those experiences that can transcend prevention to enhance personal growth.

In the struggle to go beyond burnout and tedium, having faith that one can do something often provides its own verification. There is a class of events where the belief that something can be done helps get the task finished. But even when the task does not get finished, or does not get done well, having faith in one's ability makes performing the task more interesting, more exciting, more fun. Reality demands a certain degree of compromise, but the concessions made should not be too large. A belief in the power to shape one's life and a merging of reality and imagination are important for a sense of happiness. One has to believe in the alliance between one's actions and needs, one's lifestyle and wills, one's dreams and daily living.

Achieving this alliance is not simple. Past paths promise the security of the known; new avenues provoke the anxiety of the uncertain and the risk of failure and regret. But this anxiety is an integral part of life that involves change and growth. Choosing new paths requires courage and the recognition of one's power over one's life. It also requires a sense of control over one's actions in selecting among existing alternatives and generating new ones. If one wants to go beyond preventing burnout and tedium, if one wants to achieve an alliance between dreams and reality, one has continually to seek alternatives for actions and to create new options.

Although burnout can be a traumatic and depressing experience, it can also be the beginning of greater understanding and increased awareness in an individual's life. Such growth can be likened to the martial arts in which one uses the momentum of the opponent to defeat him or her. So it can be with burnout and tedium: if people are provided with adequate tools for coping with stress, they often emerge wiser, stronger, and more insightful than if they had not burned out in the first place.

Notes

1. R. A. Butler, "Curiosity in Monkeys," *Scientific American*, 190 (1954): 79–95.
2. V. E. Frankl, *The Doctor and the Soul* (New York: Bantam Books, 1967).
3. In one study involving 205 professionals, significance in life was correlated $r = -.22, p < .05$ with tedium. For a sample of 84 students, the correlation was $r = -.33, p < .05$.
4. S. R. Maddi, "The Existential Neurosis," *Journal of Abnormal Psychology* 72 (1967): 311–325.
5. A. Antonovsky, *Health, Stress and Coping* San Francisco: Jossey-Bass, 1979.
6. R. Walton, in his article "Alienation and Innovation in the Work Place" in *Work and the Quality of Life*, ed. J. O'Toole (Cambridge, Mass.: MIT Press, 1974), pp. 227–245), writes about innovative management techniques where autonomous work groups were given collective responsibility for the large segments of the production process so that jobs were enriched and employees had more variety, autonomy, and a sense of significance.
7. D. C. McClelland, *The Achieving Society* (New York: Van Nostrand, 1961).
8. For example, success in life was correlated with tedium $r = -.48, p < .001$, for a sample of 205 professionals; and $r = -.58, p < .001$, for a sample of 84 students.

9. For example, in a study involving 205 professionals, variety in life was correlated with tedium $r = -.23, p < .01$; for 84 students the correlation was $r = -.44, p < .001$.

10. E. Duffy, *Activation and Behavior* (New York: Wiley, 1962).

11. J. P. Zubeck, *Sensory Deprivation: Fifteen Years of Research* (New York: Appleton-Century-Crofts, 1969).

12. Christopher Burney, *Solitary Confinement* (New York: Coward-McCann, 1952).

13. Duffy, *Activation and Behavior*.

14. Reported by Manson Syndicate in the *San Francisco Chronicle*, May 9, 1979.

15. B. Russell, *The Conquest of Happiness* (New York: Liveright, 1930).

16. M. Csikszentmikalyi, *Beyond Boredom and Anxiety: The Experience of Play in Work and Games* (San Francisco: Jossey-Bass, 1975).

17. N. Krogius, *Psychology in Chess* (Albertson, N.Y.: RHM Press, 1976).

18. V. E. Frankl, *The Doctor and the Soul* (New York: Bantam Books, 1967), p. 35

19. A pilot study involving 29 professionals indicated that frequency of reporting complete concentration, feeling of harmony with the environment, control of self-demand for action were negatively correlated with tedium.

20. For a review, see S. R. Maddi, *Personality Theories: A Cognitive Analysis* (Homwood, Ill.: Dorsey Press, 1976).

21. A. Maslow, *Toward a Psychology of Being* (New York: Van Nostrand, 1962.

22. C. R. Rogers, *On Becoming a Person* (Boston: Houghton Mifflin, 1961).

23. For example, in one study involving 205 professionals, the correlation between tedium and self-actualization was $r = -.27, p < .01$. In another study involving 84 students, the correlation was $r = -.26, p < .01$.

24. A. Monat and R. S. Lazarus, *Stress and Coping* (New York, Columbia University Press, 1977).

25. D. Kafry and A. Pines, "Coping Strategies and the Experience of Tedium." Paper presented at the American Psychological Association Convention, Toronto, August, 1978.

26. R. S. Lazarus, "Phychological Stress and Coping in Adaptation to Illness," *International Journal of Psychiatry in Medicine*, 5 (1974): 321–332.

27. Kafrey and Pines, "Coping Strategies."

28. Ibid.

29. Dov Eden, "Toward an Analysis of Stress Situation and Response Effectiveness," private communication, Tel Aviv University, Israel.

30. The correlation between tedium and physical health in different studies ranged between $-.20$ and $-.46$, all correlations statistically significant.

31. P. G. Zimbardo, *Shyness: What It Is, What to Do about It* (Reading, Mass.: Addison-Wesley, 1977).

9

Postscript: Burnout and tedium outside of work

This entire book has been oriented toward occupational burnout and tedium. It would be misleading to leave the reader with the impression that burnout is merely an *occupational hazard*; rather, burnout can occur in all aspects of life. One can be a burned out husband, a burned out wife, and a burned out parent. One can experience tedium as a student or simply as a function of the aging process. Burnout can also be affected by cultural mores and societal expectations. Accordingly, the present chapter will address burnout in three rather different spheres: burnout in the life cycle, burnout in family life, and burnout within a cross-cultural perspective.

Burnout in the life cycle

In Western thinking the dominant image of human life is a line that starts at one end and stops at the other. Accordingly, psychologists have treated human development until recently as a lifeline, emphazing childhood and largely ignoring the later stages in life.

Other cultures, however, see human development differently. Taking their metaphors from the natural world, they see life's course as cyclical rather than linear. There are natural seasons to a person's life, each of them equally essential to the development of full humanness: childhood, adolescence, adulthood, middle age, and old age. Socialization never stops: humans change, develop, and experience similar crises in any particular stage.

Burnout and tedium can occur at any stage of the life cycle. It is not an indication of maladjustment or immaturity but rather a reflection of a lifelong quest for growth. In some stages burnout seems to result more from external environmental stresses; in other stages it seems to result more from stresses inherent to that developmental stage.

In this chapter we discuss tedium in two age groups: young adult students and mid-life professionals. In addition to environmental stresses, both groups deal with issues inherent in their life stage; for students the issue is entrance into the adult world and for middle-aged professionals the issue is passing through mid-life and into old age. Despite these similarities the two groups represent extremes in the continuum between phase-specific stresses and environmental pressures: for students the major stresses are in their college environment, and for middle-aged professionals the major stresses are frequently the result of mid-life crises they may go through.

Young adulthood: tedium in college

Young adulthood is probably the life cycle's most glorified period, with the notion of youth, romance, and freedom. It comes after the painful adolescence and before being tied down by responsibilities to a family and a career in adulthood. It is an age in which people are particularly vulnerable to powerful feelings, an age in which they experience the heights of idealism, hopes, and dreams. And if these romantic views of young adulthood are true in general, they are even more true for university students. There are about ten million young people attending colleges and universities in the United States.[1] These young people are viewed by many as having the fantastic privilege and luxury of spending their time in learning and growth. And yet numerous indicators suggest that the college years are a period of tremendous stress for young adults. One of the most dramatic of these is the phenomenon of student suicide. Self-destruction by a young person is tragic and a source of great concern. Richard Seiden, a University of California scholar, has documented that college students run a greater risk of suicide than their noncollege peers; students have a significantly higher number of successful suicides and they attempt suicide far more often than they succeed.[2]

Another phenomenon attesting to the stress of college years is dropout. Research of college students' attrition dates back at least forty years. A recent review of this research literature concluded that only 55 to 80 percent of the students who enter American universities receive degrees within seven to ten years after their initial enrollment.[3]

In many colleges there are psychiatric services to assist students in their adjustment to university life. Students seeking help at college mental health facilities comprise from 2 to 25 percent of the college population, with 5 to 10 percent being the usual range. Figures for those thought to need help vary depending on the criterion used but commonly are said to be about twice the number of those who seek help.[4]

It is easy for the scientific community to dismiss these findings by suggesting that the researchers are not dealing with the typical college student but rather are generalizing from information about suicidal students, dropouts, and students visiting mental health clinics. If one attributes the research findings to those selective samples, one can still cling to the belief that most students do enjoy college; our own work attempted to go beyond these selective samples to obtain information about the typical students.

We investigated the extent to which students might be experiencing tedium and their ways of coping with it. Our expectation was that they would show less tedium than other professional groups. Young adults, we reasoned, do not encounter the variety of pressures and stresses experienced by working adults, and whatever stresses they do encounter are limited to their time in college and could not be perceived by them to be chronic. So like others we adopted a romantic image of young adults and attributed additional charm to the college experience, where they are supposedly free to learn, read, and grow in the presence of interesting people and stimulating activities. If college in general in thus positively perceived, the campus of the University of California in Berkeley is truly among the best college environments. It is considered one of the top universities in the country, located in the San Francisco Bay area, one of the most beautiful places in the world, where the climate is perfect year-round and people are famous for their friendliness. Seemingly students are the most unlikely group, and Berkeley the most unlikely place, in which to study tedium, precisely why we chose to study tedium there.

Eighty-four Berkeley students in a typical class and 205 professionals from the San Francisco Bay area participated in the study. The main goals of the study were to compare the students and the professionals in terms of their tedium and the features in their environments that are tedium correlates. We were very surprised to discover that the students' level of tedium was higher than that in any of the professional groups, including business people, scientists, human service workers, and artists. [5] Students perceived their school life as having few of the features stereotypically attributed to them: they perceived themselves as having less variety and their work as being less significant and less innovative than did the professionals. Students also perceived themselves as having less freedom than the professionals and less influence on decisions that affected their lives. Despite the notion of freedom of expression, students felt they had fewer opportunities for self-expression than did most professionals. Students perceived more demands to prove themselves in competitive situations than did the professionals. Competition is among the most stressful characteristics of college and is frequently the cause of students' isolation from each other, loneliness, and superficial relationships. Students in this research described their interpersonal relations as worse than those described by most professionals. They were particularly aware of comparison, competitiveness, and lack of sharing, especially in academic performance.[6]

All of these findings were replicated in a second study that involved 294 students. This study examined how students perceived their school life and their outside life. It was found that the students saw in their school a preponderance of negative features, such as bureauratic interference and administrative hassles and conflicts. They saw life outside of school as positive, offering more than did school: variety, autonomy, significance, feedback, self-expression, self-actualization, personal influence, rewards, appreciation, support, sharing, emotional reciprocity, and good personal relations.[7]

In a third study, 147 students were asked to list their major pressures and joys.[8] A total of 61 percent of these pressures fell into two categories: school pressures, including grades, tests, competition, and overload of assignments; and interpersonal relations, including romantic relationships, friends, family and roommates. Other problems mentioned concerned finances, health, work, career planning, the meaning of life, self-actualization, loneliness, and boredom. Of the joys mentioned by students, 40 percent were related to interpersonal relations and 13 percent were related to their school work. Others had to do with hobbies, sports, nature, traveling, music, relaxation, reading, eating, sleeping, and self-actualization.

The obvious conclusion from these results was that school-related activities were a source of pressure more frequently than a source of joy. An analysis of the results showed an interesting relationship between pressures, joys, and tedium: as the number of joys increased, tedium decreased, but, although tedium was very highly correlated with the intensity of pressures, the correlation between tedium and the number of pressures was not significant. We concluded that it was not the number of pressures but their perceived intensity that most influences tedium.

In addition to these environmental pressures are the developmental tasks that late adolescents must master. These tasks include developing roles and relationships in which adult identity can be realized and enhanced.[9] These are tasks that intensify issues of competence. As a result, at this age one's self-image is closely tied to a sense of how well one is doing. And indeed we found that students experienced more demands to prove themselves in competitive situations than did professionals. They also experienced more pressures of decision making and more conflict between their work and life outside of work. These are additional stresses that contribute to the high levels of tedium reported by students.[10]

Middle age and the mid-career crisis

One phase of adult development that has attracted much interest recently is the mid-life crisis and its correlate, the mid-career crisis.[11] Between the ages of 40 and 50, people who may be successful in their professions frequently begin to question the value of their lives. This is a period of reassessment of one's self, one's life, and one's career. It often happens to people who started their careers with great enthusiasm and conviction, believing they would make major contributions to society. By mid-career, they have begun to realize that their contribution may be far smaller than they had dreamed.

According to William Bridges, who has worked extensively with people at mid-life, the trigger for a mid-career crisis may be a failure of some timetable, a critical event on which all hopes were dependent, such as realizing one will never make it to the top of one's profession or never manage to save enough money to buy one's dream house. The triggering situation may also be a long-standing difficulty, perhaps with one's health, spouse, colleague, or patient, that finally must be faced. The trigger may also be the death of a friend or a life-threatening illness of one's own. In all cases, the precipitating event makes what seemed to be a substantial world look fragile and unreal.

During the mid-life crisis the difference between obtaining or not obtaining one's dream seems less important than the difference between the dream itself and reality. Bridges writes:

> When the dream has been gained, the vice-presidency, the book, the three kids and the handsome home—there is the moment of realization: "O.K., I've got it, now what?" and even "*Is this it? Is this* the destination that I've sacrificed everything for?" The discrepancy between public image and private awareness can be excruciating at this point in life. And what of the person who didn't make it? The denied dream is the other gateway to reality. There one is faced with the nevers. "I guess I have to face the fact that I'm *never* going to be the head of the company . . . *never* going to be a famous writer . . . *never* going to be the parent of four, happy, well-adjusted children." And with that acknowledgment comes the strange sense that one has been chasing a carrot on a stick, that the sunset into which one was riding was painted on the other end of the train car.[12]

Associated with mid-life crisis and mid-career crisis are feelings of emptiness, disillusionment, and deep despair. There is a painful awareness of one's mortality and the passage of time, time remaining and time passed.

In our experience people in mid-life crisis and mid-career crisis report symptoms similar to those of burnout and tedium. Burnout appears to be a mid-career crisis that can happen at any age: we saw professionals in top management positions who have been work-aholics for years, who have sacrificed their home life and every out-side interest to an all-consuming ambition. We saw them experience tedium in mid-career and start questioning the value of their life, recognizing the high price they paid for their success (if indeed they were successful). For some of them the realization was so painful that in order to justify their great sacrifices they tried to convince them-selves that their work was very important. In order to bolster this belief, they intensified the extent to which they threw themselves into their work at the further expense of their families. But, as indicated earlier, such behavior is not limited to people in their mid-life. The insidious thing about burnout is that the symptoms have all the trappings of a mid-life crisis, but they can occur even among young people near the beginning of their career.

Students and mid-career professionals have to face stresses in their environment—stresses that are antecedents of burnout and tedium for them as well as for everyone else. In addition to the antecedents of burnout and tedium in their environment, both students and mid-career professionals face problems specific to their life stages: students need to master a unique set of developmental tasks in their move toward adulthood. Mid-career professionals must face the physical, emotional, and mental reamifications of the aging process. But, as the previous discussion indicated, for students the major stresses and antecedents of tedium are external, in the college environment; for many mid-career professionals the major antecedents are inherent to their life stage. Thus the two groups represent the two poles in the continuum between phase-specific stresses and environmental pressures in people's continual struggle with burnout and tedium.

Implications for action

One of the major undercurrents of this book is our belief in the importance of being open to change. A close friend of ours was once invited to lead an encounter group for individuals who had terminal cancer. At first he was reluctant to do it, fearing it would be depressing. But it became one of the most exciting groups he had ever worked with, because he felt that some of the members were more open to change than any he had met. Realizing that they had only a few months to live, these group members were asking themselves, "What aspects of my life are gratifying? What aspects are neither essential nor gratifying but just automatic?" Many individuals make a serious attempt to reorder their priorities in life. But people living "under the gun" are more likely to rise to that most difficult of challenges.

> One of the most important learnings as leader of that group was the realization that we are all "terminal"; most of us have a good deal longer to live than the members of the group but we do not know how long. With that in mind each person can and should take stock and reorganize priorities: what is effective, what is gratifying, what is pleasurable; in effect what is the purpose of your life. Once you have done that you make your own decisions about what to change, how to operate, and how to organize your life.

Work and life outside of work as antecedents of burnout and tedium

If one were asked "What is more important to you, your work or your life outside of work?" what would the answer be? For the hundreds of subjects who were asked that question, "life outside of work" was almost always the answer.[13] This response is rather surprising given the great importance attributed to work by laymen and social scientists. In another study we asked 384 subjects what their favorite day of the week was. Twenty-nine percent said Saturday, 17 percent said Sunday (getting close to the work week), and 26 percent said Friday (the weekend is approaching). From this data it is clear that weekends are preferred to workdays for most people surveyed. We also found, in different samples, that the more satisfaction from life one experiences, the less tedium;[14] this is also true for satisfaction from work (but the correlations with life satisfaction tend to be higher). National surveys showed that only a small percentage of people ranked work as the central factor in their lives.[15] Family life was consistently mentioned as more important than work on most people's lists of important life factors.

In a study that compared work and life features as tedium correlates, several differences emerged.[16] Life outside of work was perceived as more important, more satisfying, and less pressured than work. Respondents felt that away from work they had more autonomy and more opportunities for self-expression, self-actualization, and personal growth. In their lives, in contrast to work, they felt they had more influence on decision making; they felt they received more adequate rewards, appreciation, and recognition; and they felt more support and emotional reciprocity.

Work stresses

In their work, more than in their life outside of work, respondents felt that bureaucracy, administration, and organization interfered with their goal achievement; they had more administrative problems, such as paperwork, red tape, and communication problems; they had more environmental pressures. At work respondents perceived more demands to prove themselves in competitive situations and more difficulty in decision making because of lack of information, lack of time, and lack of skill. At work the negative consequences of their errors were more stressful because of their potential effect on people and property.

Yet when pressures build at work, the home and the family often suffer first. People frequently bring work, work pressures, and work problems home but tend not to bring home the joys and rewards their work provides. In a study involving 714 subjects, we found that the more overlap of stresses between work and life outside of work, the more tedium, but not so with overlap of pleasures.[17] But even the sharing of joys beyound a certain point can increase tension in the family in a similar way to the sharing of stresses and frustrations. The family expects attention rather than continual and intensive involvement in work problems or successes. The implication is that one needs to compartmentalize work and home, especially with regard to problems. And one needs to spend with the family "clean" family time. What we mean by "clean" time is quality time, that is, time that is spent without disturbances, where the parents are able to focus their full attention on the children, and where the activities and conversations are directed solely and totally toward mutual enjoyment and satisfaction. This can be contrasted with a situation in which the parents believe that all meals must be taken with the family, but where the mealtimes arc frequently interrupted by phone calls from friends or business associates, where the conversation is frequently about financial planning or shop talking in which the children have no interest. An example of clean family time is the "love hour" in the Israeli kibbutzim. These are the afternoon hours, which kibbutz parents devote exclusively to their children. Even though the children live in separate dwellings with their age peers, they spend more quality time with their parents than do children of most American professionals who can never get away completely from their work.

When under pressure at work, some people develop the expectation that the spouse will be particularly supportive and understanding, much more so than their bosses, their clients, or their colleagues. As stress continues to increase, the expectations of support from the family, and especially the spouse, are often unrealistic; the demands exceedingly high; and the pressures unbearable. The family is simply not equipped to provide the support often demanded by the worker. Many cases of divorce are the result of burnout at work that destroyed family relations. In those cases the relationships could not withstand the excessive demands and the absence of positive experiences.

Home stresses

Although homelife apart from work is perceived as having more joys and fewer stresses than work, it still has many stresses of its own. Some stresses can be the result of poor health, some can be the result of a financial problem, but most stresses have to do with other people in one's home. Burnout in the life sphere occurs most in two roles: the marital role and the parental role, attesting again to the emotional stresses inherent in long-term involvement with people. Burnout at home can be more painful than burnout at work because it is more difficult to leave the home "battlefield."

BURNOUT IN PARENTHOOD

The joys of parenthood are a major theme in literature and in the popular media. However, as every parent knows, parenthood is far from being a state of eternal bliss. Some of the stresses inherent in the role of parents are a result of the physical requirements of raising children: feeding them, dressing them, spending time with them, and taking care of them when they are sick. Other stresses are the result of the demand to give all of oneself without expecting reciprocity. Another stress is that there is no way out of the role: one cannot quit being a parent or ask for a change of child.

Under these stresses some parents do burn out. This happens especially to those who had high expectations of parenthood or to those who are isolated and lacking in social support, and it occurs particularly during difficult periods in the child's life. One of our group participants, the mother of an adolescent boy who was an only child, started drinking to excess as a result of continual harrassment by her son. The adolescent stage of a child's development, which is a difficult period for most parents, was especially difficult because of her high expectations of herself. She told us:

> My relationship with my son is the most important thing in my life. But I don't understand him. He is constantly attacking me, blaming me for all of his problems and I don't know how to avoid him. I started going to the bar because that was the only place where I could calm my nerves with a drink and be sure I was not going to bump into any adolescent young-sters. I thank God for my work, It's the only thing that helps keep my sanity. I am emotionally and physically drained. There is a constant war between us and I am losing the battle.

In a study involving seventy-three mothers, we found a significant correlation between the implusivity of their school-age children and burnout.[18] In the same study we found a significant correlation, for both fathers and mothers, between burnout as a parent and the physical, emotional, and mental exhaustion of tedium.[19]

BURNOUT AND CHILD ABUSE

One of the most tragic expressions of burnout in parenthood is child abuse.[20] It is estimated that there are two million cases of child abuse yearly in this country, two thousand of which result in the death of a child.[21] Some professionals who work in "parental stress" agencies feel that burnout is one of the fundamental causes of child abuse. Parents calling on the "hot lines" and in therapy often say they have reached their limits: "I can't take it any more," "My child is driving me crazy," "I am falling apart," "I can't cope."

The triggers of abuse are rarely dramatic events. They are most often mundane daily problems of child raising, especially with children from birth to age 5. Abusive parents usually have low self-esteem and a sense of failure as a parent. They are ignorant of what to expect of a child at a given age and are often socially isolated and guilt-ridden. Abusive parents who are exhausted physically, emotionally, and mentally are unable to look for help or use positive coping techniques.

Children are more at risk for abuse until age 5 than later in life. These are ages in which the abusive parent is most likely to feel hopelessly trapped in the house, helpless in the face of all that is required to take care of a young child. There are other stressful periods when abuse is likely to occur. Holidays, especially Christmas, are times when parental stress agencies receive frequent distress calls. It is during family holidays that the incredible discrepancy between the image of the "happy family," as it is portrayed in the mass media, and the cruel reality of their own family life is most painful. Distress calls are also more likely to occur at the end of a day, when a parent runs out of energy, loses emotional balance, and is ready to explode at the slightest provocation. One of the most effective ways these agencies deal with abusive parents is to give them "time off." They may arrange to place the children with foster parents or baby-sitters so the parents can get away for a day or even a few hours. Other agency techniques involve teaching coping skills and acquainting the parents with community resources that reduce social isolation.[22]

In a pilot study we interviewed twelve abusive parents.[23] The level of burnout of the parents were extremely high, higher than any other group we studied. Most of these parents suffered from financial hardships, poor family relations, and a lack of support from spouse or friends. They expressed an inability to cope with their emotional and economic problems. They had few skills to help them face the demands of parenthood, and they resorted to violence to deal with their children's normal behaviors.

Parents, even those who are highly skilled professionally, are not trained to deal with children and most are ill-prepared for the stresses inherent in the parental role. Unrealistic expectations of themselves and their children, daily stresses and pressures without time for recuperation, and a child-centered orientation invariably result in burnout and, in particularly extreme cases, in child abuse.

An important part in avoiding burnout in parenthood, and especially child abuse during the early years of a child's life, is anticipatory training. For example, mothers of newly born babies should be told even before they leave the hospital that sometimes babies will go on crying even if their mothers have done everything possible to comfort them. Thus, when a baby cannot be comforted even after being fed, changed, and rocked, the mother will do her best to put on ear phones and listen to music for fifteen to twenty minutes. Mothers of young children should also be taught to recognize their own limits and know that it is crucial for them not to carry on with their housework to the point of physical collapse, because the emotional and mental fatigue of burnout will soon follow.

BURNOUT IN MARRIAGE

Burnout in marriage and family life is as common as tedium at work. It usually starts with a growing awareness that things aren't quite as good as they used to be or the spouse not quite as exciting as he or she used to be. It may lead to divorce, extramarital relationships, or dead, listless marriages. Several times in the previous chapters we alluded to the fact that burnout in marriage often results from a burnout on the job that spilled over to effect the family life. Now we would like to discuss burnout that is indigenous to permanent relationships involving two or more people.

Social psychologists studied interpersonal attraction and theorized about why people liked each other. One of these theories emphasized the impact of gain and loss of esteem on attraction. The gain-loss theory suggests that

> increases in positive rewarding behavior from another person have more impact on an individual, than constant invariant reward from that person. Thus, if we take being liked as a reward, a person whose liking for us increases over time will be liked better than one who has always liked us. This would be true even if the *number* of rewards were greater from the latter person. Similarly, losses in rewarding behavior have more impact than constant punitive behavior from another person. Thus, a person whose esteem for us decreases over time will be disliked more than someone who has always disliked us, even if the number of punishments were greater from the latter person. Once we have grown certain of the rewarding behavior of a person, that person may become less potent as a source of reward than a stranger. An example may help to clarify the

point. After fifteen years of marriage, a doting husband and his wife are getting dressed to attend a formal dinner party. He compliments her on her appearance—"Gee, honey, you look great." She hears his words, but they do not fill her with delight. She already knows that her husband thinks she's attractive; she will not turn cartwheels at hearing about it for the thousandth time. On the other hand, if the doting husband (who in the past was always full of compliments) were to tell his wife that he had decided that she was losing her looks and that he found her quite unattractive, this would cause her a great deal of pain, because it represents a distinct loss of esteem.[24]

Because people learned to expect love, favors, and praise from their spouses' such behavior is not likely to represent a gain in the spouses' esteem for them. By the same token, husbands or wives have a great potential as punishers—the closer the spouse and the greater the past history of invariant esteem and reward, the more devastating is the withdrawal of this esteem. In effect then, after a long relationship, one has the power to hurt the people one loves but very little power to reward them. A vivid description of this process appeared in Marilyn French's book, *The Women's Room:* "Marriage accustomed one to the good things, so one came to take them for granted, but magnified the bad things, so they came to feel as painful as a grain in one's eye. An opened window, a forgotten quart of milk, a T.V. left blaring, socks on the bathroom floor, could become occasions for incredible rage." [25]

The experience of burnout in marriage can become unbearably painful. Dina, who burned out after fourteen years of marriage, described her feelings:

> I feel hollow in this relationship. There is nothing between us: no bond, no communication, no sharing, no contact, no feelings, nothing. We have no plans together, no interests together. The tensions are making me tired and sad. There is no hope for us. There is nothing that he does to enhance my life in any way, either emotionally, intellectually, or physically. I don't feel like a couple, I feel emotionally deprived. I feel resentful and irritated. I have to close myself off emotionally to stop feeling that way. I can't give myself sexually or emotionally to him any more. I don't believe life has anything to give me. I would do anything to be free of him. I have no feelings for him except for irritation and sometimes pity. When I come home and he is there I get all uptight. I wouldn't stay with him for anything.

The pressures and stresses that are built into the process of two or more people sharing a life together are enormous. It is almost inevi-

table that these stresses will become intense and at times even unbearable, often resulting in a divorce or a dull and deadening plateau
of burnout punctuated by emotional traumas. Unlike the popular
romantic conception, when boy marries girl, they don't live happily
ever after unless they consciously or unconsciously take specific steps
to avoid or reduce the process of affectional erosion. That does not
mean that people have to know about burnout to have a happy
marriage, rather to have a successful marriage requires work and the
kind of work that is involved is akin to successful coping strategies
against burnout.

When we think about a marriage breaking up it is tempting to try
to seize upon concrete traumatic and dramatic events: the husband is
running around with other women; the husband gets drunk, beats the
wife, and screams at the children; the wife insults the husband's
integrity or manhood in front of their friends and colleagues causing
him intense humiliation. These are concrete events and they sometimes occur and occasionally lead to the break-up of a marriage. But
these are not the most common causes of marital burnout. Just as with
job burnout, marriages burn out most commonly by a gradual erosion, a gradual increase in boredom, a gradual build-up of petty
annoyances and minor dissatisfactions such that no one of them could
be singled out as a precipitating cause of stress. The law recognizing
this state of affairs has come up with the concept of incompatibility, as
if two people suddenly discovered that they were not made for each
other. What we are saying is that it is unlikely that, without a good
deal of hard work, any two people could continue to share a life with
each other for a great length of time that was harmonious, exciting,
mutually supportive, and productive. The gradual erosion of caring is
mitigated in trivial incidents: "he would slam the door loudly" or "she
would clear away my things."

People often complain about the large number of divorces; we are
not surprised at the large number of divorces or the even larger
number of marriages that hang together even without a good deal of
productive coping—quite the opposite. In view of all these erosive
tendencies, we marvel at the fact that a great many marriages are
exciting and mutually supportive. For two people to live together,
productively, in a mutually supportive way, requires not only love and
an earnest desire to accommodate each other but a great deal of hard
work and the skill, wisdom, and ability to communicate openly and to
work the minor and major annoyances as they arise. In short, just as
individuals need to learn certain skills in order to cope effectively with

their potential burnout in a job, so too do they need to acquire skills to effectively cope with the potential burnout of a marriage. Those skills mentioned in the previous three chapters can be adapted to the individual marriage situation.

Major life events and the experience of tedium

The research on major life events and research on stress in general has been greatly influenced by the work of Hans Selye.[26] Selye defined stress as the rate of all wear-and-tear on the body caused by life. He found that in response to stress a cluster of physiological changes occurs, which he termed the General Adaptation Syndrome. The syndrome develops in three stages: (1) the alarm reaction, (2) the stage of resistance, and (3) the stage of exhaustion. The stage of exhaustion occurs when exposure to stress is continual; tedium and burnout occur at this stage.

Most life events such as illness, death of a family member, job change, marriage, or divorce were assumed by psychologists to be stressful events that affect emotional and physical processes. Thomas H. Holmes and his colleagues at the University of Washington School of Medicine developed a list of forty-three life events, both desirable, such as marriage or an outstanding achievement, and undesirable, such as injury or illness.[27] They claimed that both kinds of events require some adaptive or coping behaviors in order to readjust to the event. Change, whether it is considered "good" or "bad," is stressful to the biological organism and makes it more susceptible to the onslaught of dysfunction. The intensity and duration of the readjustment vary with the type of life event. All events in their studies were arbitrarily compared to marriage, which was assigned the value of 50. Analysis of the values assigned to events showed that the greatest readjustment was needed for the death of a spouse, which received a value of 100, and for divorce, which received a value of 73. The lowest readjustment scores were assigned to minor violations of the law (12) and to Christmas (11). A person who experienced more than 150 life-change units in one year was defined as having a life crisis.[28] Life crises often preceded the onset of dysfunctions, ranging from heart attacks to emotional and behavioral disturbances.

In our own research we created a list of positive and negative life events in physical health, mental health, finances, family relations, work, recreation, and "peak experiences."[29] The list was presented to 322 professionals who were asked to indicate the events they had experienced during the previous six-month period. Respondents also completed the tedium measure.[30] Results showed that people who had negative experiences in physical health, mental health, family relations, and work had a higher level of tedium than those who did not report such events. In addition, people who had positive life experiences in work and recreation had lower tedium scores than those who did not report such events.[31]

These results indicate that, though many kinds of life events may require readjustment, positive and negative events do affect tedium differently. To test this finding further, we tabulated for each individual the number of positive and the number of negative events. These two numbers were then correlated with the tedium score. Results of this analysis showed that the greater the number of undesirable events, the greater the tedium. The number of desirable events was also significantly related to tedium but in the reverse direction; the greater the number of positive events, the less the tedium. These findings, point to the importance of separating positive from negative events, as the two kinds of events have different effects. Though all life events may require readjustment, their relationship to tedium is affected by the nature of the event.

A cross-cultural perspective: tedium in Americans and Israelis

The social-psychological perspective emphasizes environmental influences on people's behavior. Cross-cultural comparisons are one way to investigate influences that create, intensify, and maintain such experiences as burnout and tedium. We have discussed working and living with people as causes of burnout; we have talked about working in large organizations as a cause of tedium. These are stressful environmental influences. Environmental influences also go beyond one's home and work to include one's social and cultural environment. In one study we investigated the social and cultural dynamics of tedium by a comparison between Israeli and American subjects.[32] A total of sixty-six Israeli managers and sixty-six American managers participated in the study. They were questioned about their lives and work, their tedium, and their coping strategies.

Life is more stressful in Israel. There are physical stresses due to political tensions and military service, and economic stresses due to inflation, which recently hit an annual rate of 120 percent, Despite these stresses, the Israelis reported significantly lower tedium scores than the Americans. The comparison showed more significant differences between Israelis and Americans in their lives outside of work than in their work. The role of a manager may have stresses and rewards built into it that overshadow the cultural differences, which are therefore more evident in the life outside work. In terms of their life features, Israelis reported significantly higher levels of positive features such as a sense of significance, success, and appreciation than the American sample. Their social relations were described as better; they reported more emotional reciprocity, more sharing, feedback, and influence. On the other hand, Americans reported more negative features such as guilt and anxiety, overload, conflicting demands, and difficulty in decision making.

Similar findings were evident in the comparision of work features. Americans reported significantly higher levels of negative features such as overload, guilt and anxiety, emotional overextension, conflicting demands, and responsibility. Israelis reported more bureaucratic interference but more perceived freedom and more sense of success. Furthermore, Israelis reported less conflict between their life and work. They also had more life and work features significantly correlated with tedium. One possible interpretation of this last result is the greater awareness among Israelis of the relationship between tedium and environmental features or, interpreted in a different way, the tendency to find outside reasons to explain their subjective experience of tedium. Americans, in contrast, may look for explanations for their tedium in themselves or their organizations and thus feel more guilt, anxiety, resentment, and overload. These differences between Israelis and Americans in reported tedium were replicated in subsequent samples of managers, social workers, and nurses.[33]

Israel exists in a volatile social climate due to continual threats to its survival. In addition, it is a small country where people know each other better than do most American city dwellers. As a result, in Israel there is a greater sense of social unity and mutual fate and a feeling that every person is significant. Some Israeli psychologists contend that the Israelis' emotional stability and high morale are the result of an adaptation mechanism that developed out of necessity and that enables them to function normally in spite of constant dangers and stresses.[34] Israelis also are part of intimate and stable social systems of family, friends, and neighbors, more so than most Americans. These social systems protect them from pressure and support them in times of stress and failure. The cohesion that characterizes Israeli society may be one source of the good social relationships, the high levels of emotional reciprocity, and the sharing of stresses reported by the Israeli managers. The American culture tends to emphasize competition, individual achievements, and personal excellence. Malcolm Arth, who studied the phenomenon of friendship in the American culture, believes that the United States, with its competitive institutions and its values that emphasize achievement and status, might well produce a spirit not conducive to friendship.[35] The American culture values individualism and encourages introspection and self-consciousness. Such a competitive system makes failure a source of personal shame, generates guilt and anxiety, and may indirectly cause difficulty in decision making. Developmental psychologists have shown that American children will maintain a competitive strategy even in situations where cooperation is more profitable.[36] By contrast, the Israeli society still emphasizes the socialistic ideals of equality and shared national achievements. In Israel children and adults are not often faced with competitive situations in which they are supposed to show their ability and skill relative to others. As a result, Israelis also have less chance to experience failure. In addition for the Israeli, goals are less individualized, better defined, and more realistically attainable. Israelis are thus more likely to achieve what they set out to attain and to feel successful.[37]

One can also hypothesize that the American culture, with its emphasis on youth, puts an extra burden on professionals during their mid-life crises. The managers who particpated in the study were close to that stage of their life cycle; the average age of the Americans was 38, that of the Israelis 39. The differences in their tedium levels could have been caused in part by that fact.

The prevalence of negatives and absence of positives in the lives and work of the American managers could account for their tedium levels being higher than the Israelis'. Another explanation could be derived from the cultural differences in their coping strategies.[38] The Israelis reported more active, outward-directed coping techniques aimed at the source of their stress, such as changing the source of stress, confronting the source of stress, and trying to find positive aspects in the situation. The Israelis also perceived these coping techniques as more successful against the experience of tedium than did Americans. The Americans reported more passive coping techniques, such as ignoring the source of stress, avoiding it, or leaving the situation. More than the Israelis, the Americans also used inner-directed coping techniques, such as talking about the stress or becoming involved in other situations. These were aimed at changing themselves rather than changing the source of their stress.

There are other responses to stress that are negative responses: these change neither the source of the stress nor the person but merely postpone and numb the pain associated with the stress. American managers reported more frequent use of these negative responses than the Israelis. They reported, for example, drinking, getting sick, and collapsing physically or emotionally. Because the Israeli coping techniques were more effective in changing the stressful situations, they may be responsible for the lower tedium reported by the Israelis.

It should be emphasized that this cross-cultural study only documented that the Israelis *reported* less tedium than the Americans. Such reports may not accurately reflect the respondents' actual tedium. One might argue, for instance, that because Israelis see tedium as an undesirable indication of weakness and incompetence they are less willing to admit it and therefore they report it less often. And indeed we found that after being told that it's the best people who burn out, the level of tedium reported by Israeli managers increased almost to the level of their American colleagues.[39] Not to discount these results as culturally biased, our conclusion is that reported tedium is culturally related and thus can be influenced by external social forces.

The cross-cultural orientation emphasizes the search for situational forces and societal conditions that increase stress. The search for situational forces, if successful, can be used to prevent these stresses before they occur as well as to explain their casualties. The cross-cultural perspective can also shift the focus off the individual worker and the individual organization to the social context. This could help alleviate guilt, anxiety, and overload and free emotional energy for better coping.

Summary

In the first chapters of this book we defined tedium and burnout, described their phenomenology, and suggested some typical outcomes. The third, fourth, and fifth chapters described some of the antecedents and correlates of burnout and tedium in working with people, working in bureaucratic organizations, and among working women. The next three chapters of the book were devoted to discussion of what to do about burnout and tedium. Coping strategies and coping techniques were presented on three levels: the organizational level, the social level, and the individaul level.

The present chapter discussed antecedents of burnout and tedium in the home and life sphere. The chapter centered around three themes: the life cycle, stresses at home, and the cultural perspective. The life-cycle discussion focused on stresses inherent in certain stages of adult development and their relation to tedium. Postadolescent college students and middle-aged professionals were discussed at some length because they demonstrate two extremes in the continuum between environmental pressures and life-stage pressures. The discussion of stresses at home focused on marriage and parenthood as the two roles most likely to cause burnout from continual intimate involvement with people. The cultural perspective focused on Israeli and American cultural values as they intensify tedium.

Appendixes I and II describe in detail the two focuses of both our work and this book, namely, the burnout workshop and the research.

Notes

1. L. Bloom, ed., *Psychological Stress in the Campus Community (New York:* Behaviorial Publications, 1975).
2. R. H. Seiden, "The Problem of Suicide on College Campuses," *Journal of School Health*, 5 (1971): 243–248.
3. F. R. Timmons, "Research on College Dropouts," in *Pyschological Stress in the Campus Community*, ed. L. Bloom (New York: Behavorial Publications, 1975).
4. T. G. Caraskadon, "Help Seeking in the College Student: Strength and Weakness," in *Psychological Strain in the Campus Community*, ed. L. Bloom (New York: Behavioral Publications, 1975).
5. The mean value of tedium for students was $\bar{x} = 3.9$, for human service professionals it was 3.1, for business 3.2, science 3.3, and art 3.2. In addition, 8 percent of the students, and only 25 percent of the professionals, experienced the highest levels of tedium.
6. The mean values of variety were: for students $\bar{x} = 4.2$, for professionals $\bar{x} = 5.0$; autonomy, for students $\bar{x} = 4.1$, for professionals $\bar{x} = 5.0$; significance, for students $\bar{x} = 4.1$, for professionals $\bar{x} = 5.3$; innovation, for students $\bar{x} = 3.8$, for professionals $\bar{x} = 4.7$; self-expression, for students $\bar{x} = 4.1$, for professionals $\bar{x} = 4.9$; demand to prove oneself in competitive situations, for students $\bar{x} = 5.0$, for professionals $\bar{x} = 4.7$, influence on decision making that affects one's life, for students $\bar{x} = 3.3$, for professionals $\bar{x} = 4.0$; personal relationships, for students $\bar{x} = 4.9$, for professionals $\bar{x} = 5.5$; sharing, for students, $\bar{x} = 3.5$, for professionals, $\bar{x} = 4.4$. It is important to mention the possibility that, for some unknown reason, students were more honest in their response to the

questionnaire than the professionals and were thus willing to admit to higher levels of tedium and more negative environmental features (more on this point in the footnote in Chapter 2, p. 16).

7. When students described their life outside of school as compared to their school life, the following means were obtained: variety, in life $\bar{x}$ = 5.3, in school $\bar{x}$ = 4.2; autonomy, in life $\bar{x}$ = 5.4, in school $\bar{x}$ = 4.1; significance, in life $\bar{x}$ − 5.3, in school $\bar{x}$ − 4.1; innovation, in life $\bar{x}$ = 4.9, in school, $\bar{x}$ = 3.8; self-expression, in life $\bar{x}$ = 5.8, in school $\bar{x}$ = 4.1; self-actualization, in life $\bar{x}$ = 5.8, in school $\bar{x}$ = 4.5; bureaucratic interference, in life $\bar{x}$ = 3.4, in school $\bar{x}$ = 4.4; administrative hassles, in life $\bar{x}$ = 3.0, in school $\bar{x}$ = 4.2; influence in decisions that can affect one's life, in life $\bar{x}$ = 5.0, in school $\bar{x}$ = 3.3; appreciation, in life $\bar{x}$ = 5.0, in school $\bar{x}$ = 4.3; personal relations, in life $\bar{x}$ = 5.7, in school $\bar{x}$ = 4.9; support, in life $\bar{x}$ = 5.3, in school $\bar{x}$ = 4.2; sharing, in life $\bar{x}$ = 4.6, in school $\bar{x}$ = 3.5.

8. The study was done in collaboration with Liz Lopez, a University of California–Berkeley student.

9. W. Bridges, *The Seasons of Our Lives* (San Francisco: The Wayfarer Press, 1977).

10. The mean value for conflict between school and life for students was $\bar{x}$ = 4.6; for professionals the conflict between work and life was $\bar{x}$ = 4.2.

11. D. Levinson et al., *The Seasons of a Man's Life* (New York: Knopf, 1979).

12. Bridges, *Season of Our lives*, pp. 7–8.

13. For example, in one study subjects were asked to rate the relative importance of life and work for themselves on a scale of 1 to 7 with 1 = only work and 7 = only life. For 84 students the mean was 5.6; for 205 professionals the mean was 5.3.

14. For example, in a sample of 205 professionals the correlation between life satisfaction and tedium was r = −.56, the correlation between work satisfaction and tedium was r = .39. For a sample of 84 students life satisfaction and tedium were correlated r = −.69, work satisfaction and tedium were r = −.50. All correlations are statistically significant at p < .001 level of significance.

15. For example, A. H. Cantril and C. W. Roll Jr., *Hopes and Fears of the American People* (New York: Universe Books, 1971).

16. For a detailed description of the study see D. Kafry and A. Pines, "Life and Work Tedium," *Human Relations*, 1980, in press.

17. In the study that was done in collaboration with Steven Weinberg and the Management Training Program at the University of Alabama, life/work overlap of stresses was correlated r = .42 (p < .01) with tedium, while life/work overlap of pleasures was correlated r = .08.

18. B. Sutton-Smith and B. G. Rosenberg, "A Scale to Identify Impulse Behavior in Children," *Journal of Generic Psychology* 94 (1959): 211–216. The correlation between children's impulsivity and mother's burnout was r = .49, p < .001.

19. The correlation between tedium and being burned out as a parent was r = .70, p < .001 for thirty-three fathers, r = .31, p < .01 for seventy-three mothers.
20. R. E. Helfe and E. H. Kempe, *The Battered Child* (Chicago: University of Chicago Press, 1978).
21. L. Morrow, "Wondering if Children are Necessary," *Time,* March 5, 1979, p. 42.
22. We have interviewed several "parental stress" workers about the relation between burnout and child abuse and talked at particular length with Irene Melnick.
23. The study was conducted in collaboration with Teresa Ramirez, a University of California—Berkeley student. The mean tedium for abusive parents was 4.4, while the overall mean tedium (N = 3650) was 3.3.
24. "Attraction: Why Do People Like Each Other?" in E. Aronson, *The Social Animal,* (San Francisco: Freeman, 1973), chap. 7.
25. M. French, *The Women's Room* (New York: JOVE/HBJ, 1977), p. 558.
26. H. Selye, *The Stress of Life* (New York: McGraw-Hill, 1956).
27. T. H. Holmes and R. H. Rahe, "The Social Readjustment Rating Scale," *Journal of Psychosomatic Research* (1967): 213–218.
28. T. H. Holmes and M. Masuda, "Life Change and Illness Susceptibility," in *Stressful Life Events* ed. B. S. Dohrenwend and B. P. Dohrenwend (New York: Wiley, 1974).
29. A Kanner, D. Kafry, and A. Pines. "Stress Results from the Absence of Positive Experiences As Well." Paper presented at the annual meeting of the Western Psychological Association, Honolulu, Hawaii, May 1980.
30. For a description of the measure as well as its validity and reliability, see Appendix II.
31. Mean tedium for people who had the negative experiences of operation, injury, or illness was $\bar{x}$ = 3.9. Mean tedium for people who had the positive experience of positive change at work was $\bar{x}$ = 3.5. The correlation between the number of positive events and tedium was r = −.22, p < .001. The correlation between the number of negative events and tedium was r = .30, p < .001.
32. A. Pines, D. Kafry, and D. Etzion, "A Cross Cultural Comparison Between Israelis and Americans in the Experience of Tedium and Ways of Coping with It." Paper presented at the Western Psychological Association Convention, San Diego, Calif., April 1979.
33. All these cross-cultural studies were done in collaboration with Dalia Etzion of Tel Aviv University.
34. For example, E. L. Gutman, "The Israeli's Mood Is Stable—with No Unrealistic Expectations and No Disappointments" (Y. Shavit), *Yediot Achronot* 3.11 (1977): 11, 20.
35. M. Arth Jr., "American Culture and the Phenomenon of Friendship in the Aged," in *Social and Psychological Aspects of Aging,* ed. C Tibbitts and W. Donohue (New York: Columbia University Press, 1962).

36. M. C. Madsch and A. Shapiro, "Cooperative and Competitive Balance of Urban Afro Americans, Anglo Americans, Mexican Americans and Mexican Village Children, *"Developmental Psychology* 3 (1970): 16–20.
37. A. Pines and P. G. Zimbardo, "The Personal and Cultural Dynamics of Shyness: A Comparision between Israelis, American Jews, and Americans," *Journal of Psychology and Judaism* 3, no.2 (Winter 1978): 81–101.
38. Pines, Kafry, and Etzion, "Cross-Cultural Comparison."
39. See note 29 in Chapter 2.

appendix I

Burnout workshops

What is a burnout workshop? It's a situation in which we bring together all of the things we know about burnout, including much of the material presented in the preceding chapters. We present this material to groups of participants in the context of experiential learning—that is, not only do we explain what burnout is, we provide participants with the opportunity to become increasingly aware of the specific stresses in their own occupation, to discuss these stresses with other individuals in similar or identical occupations, and to utilize some of our findings on various coping strategies in a highly personal and individualized manner. One of the great benefits of a workshop is that it enables participants to take time out from their usual activities, focus on serious problems they are experiencing, and arrive at tentative solutions in collaboration with other individuals who are in a similar circumstance. Thus, while we believe that the material contained in this volume can be of great benefit to the reader, we also feel that the benefit is increased by the focus, the individualized guidance, and the social support—the hallmarks of the workshops we conduct.

In this appendix we will describe in detail the impact of one workshop that we investigated in a systematic way. Most of the other evidence we have that these workshops are effective is contained in the responses that participants share with us afterwards, especially when they tell us about changes they have made in their lives as a result of participating in the workshops. This feedback has been particularly rewarding in those cases when we came back to the same group of people a year or two later and heard about the changes that were implemented as a result of our workshop and their long-term impact. Other feedback is in the form of letters expressing appreciation of the impetus for change that the workshops provided.

There is nothing magical about the actual activities in a burnout workshop. It is our belief that the workshops are effective because they represent a focused and concrete attempt to deal with burnout in a growth-producing way. Thus it is our hope that this appendix, as well as the rest of the book, will encourage the reader to try out concrete ideas about doing "workshop-like" activities in their own settings. The key variables in such activities are: they should be done during "time out" of work, together with other people who share the same stresses and could potentially become a social support group, and they should focus on concrete, positive ways of coping with burnout.

Between 1976 and 1980 we conducted over one hundred burnout workshops in Israel and throughout the United States (Alabama, California, Colorado, Florida, Georgia, Illinois, North Carolina, North Dakota, Michigan, Missouri, and Texas). These workshops ranged in size from 12 to 500 participants, with most including 50 to 100 participants. Some were open enrollment workshops, others were special offerings during professional conferences, and others were part of in-service training provided by various organizations.

Organizational settings in which workshops were held included: child-care centers, elementary schools, junior high schools, high schools, community colleges, colleges, university extension programs, special education schools, a school for the blind, a language school, departments of public health and welfare, departments of health, social service agencies, vocational service units, community mental health centers, home health and counseling centers, departments of rehabilitation, departments of human resources, departments of social services, Social Security offices, psychiatric clinics in and out of hospitals, a state hospital, veterans administration hospitals, community hospitals, medical centers, emergency units, dialysis units, departments of nursing, psychiatry departments, a prison, probation departments, management training programs, a career planning and placement center, and the army.

Professions that participated in the workshops were: psychiatrists, psychologists, counselors, physicians, nurses, dentists, dental hygienists, dental assistants, dialysis worker, perinatal social workers, occupational therapists, physical therapists, social workers, welfare workers, child welfare attendants, mental retardation workers, community mental health workers, alcoholism workers, child abuse workers, prison personnel, probation officers, child-care workers, teachers, college professors, career planning and placement counselors, student personnel administrators, labor management administrators, Social Security supervisors and staff, vocational service workers, special education teachers and counselors, superintendents of mental retardation facilities, business managers, lawyers, policemen, organizational development experts, priests, nuns, and army psychologists.

Unsolicited feedback of workshop participants, immediately following the workshops, both written and verbal, has been consistently very positive. We have made numerous attempts to evaluate this feedback more systematically. In one department of public health and welfare, for example, 132 participants responded to the department's own training activity evaluation. The overall ratings of the workshop were: 80 participants rated it "excellent", 41 rated it "very good," 11 rated it "good," 0 rated it "poor," and 0 rated it " very poor."

In another department of social services in the Midwest six months after a workshop, participants were asked to rate its effectiveness for defining the problems of burnout and for combating it. Thirty participants responded to this postworkshop questionnaire. All respondents rated the workshop very highly on both effectiveness questions: the average response to both questions was "very good." Two years after this workshop a second burnout workshop was conducted with the same participants. Informal feedback from participants indicated that support systems that were established as a result of the first workshop were still functioning and effectively combating burnout two years later.

The specific content of the workshops differed according to the composition and needs of the participants. This appendix presents a detailed description of one workshop in which we attempted to evaluate the short-term and long-term impact of a one-day burnout workshop.

The evaluation study of this workshop used a non-equivalent control group design.[1] This design involves an experimental group and a control group. Both groups are given a pretest and posttest. The control group and the experimental group do not have preexperimental sampling equivalence, rather, the groups constitute naturally assembled collectives, as simlar as availability permits yet not so similar that one can dispense with the pretest. The assignment of the experimental manipulation, the burnout workshop, to one group or the other is assumed to be random and under the experimenter's control.

A total of fifty-three social service employees from two different offices participated in the study. The two offices were chosen because they were considered similar in location, size, clients, and performance. Twenty-three employees (3 men and 20 women) participated from the "experimental" office and 30 employees (10 men and 20 women) participated from the "control" office.

All the employees in the experimental group participated in a one-day burnout workshop. A questionnaire was administered to all employees. It included the 21-item tedium measure (see self-diagnosis instrument in Chapter 2) plus a description of work features, attitudinal variables, satisfaction, and stress from work activities. Employees in the experimental and control groups filled out the questionnaire three times: (1) pretest: one week before the workshop to establish a base line; (2) short-term posttest: one week after the workshop; (3) long-term posttest: six months after the workshop. In addition, a short feedback questionnaire was administered to the experimental group immediately after the workshop.

The workshop had four major goals:

1. Introduction of the concepts of burnout and tedium, clarification of their symptoms, and discussion of how people experience and express them. This was done in an attempt to make participants aware of the problem, as the first step in developing adequate coping.

2. Identification of work stresses commonly causing tedium and burnout in social service workers, in an attempt to help participants take responsibility for action directed toward postive change.

3. Development of cognitive clarity in the distinction between two categories of stressful work features: those that are under the control of the individual and that can be modified; and those that are an inherent part of the work and must be accepted as such.

4. Development of tools for coping such as the improvement of individual adjustment via more flexible utilization of different coping strategies and the modification of work features that are under the individual's control. A central topic is the development and use of support systems; other topics include the focus on positive work aspects and the development of positive attitudes as buffers against tedium.

It was decided not to include management personnel in the one-day workshop to assure that participants would feel free to talk openly about their job stresses. The day started with a theoretical presentation of the concepts of burnout and tedium and their danger signs. Participants were able to identify their levels of burnout. Antecedents and correlates of burnout in one's work environment and within specfic work activities were discussed. Participants were encouraged to talk about their goals and expectations from their work and their stresses, especially those resulting from their frustrated expectations, as a way of getting in touch with feelings of hopelessness and helplessness and becoming aware of the problem. Through lectures and small-group discussions, employees had the opportunity to increase their understanding of common aspects of their work that could cause burnout and tedium, and take responsibility for doing something about them.

Emphasis was put on achieving some degree of cognitive clarity in distinguishing between those stresses that are within the employees' control and those that cannot be modified. In order to develop new tools for coping and to improve the range and quality of old tools, a variety of coping resources and coping skills was introduced aimed at modifying work features within one's control. Participants were urged, after identifying their major cause of stress, to make concrete plans for changes. In general, participants were encouraged to use flexibility in their coping with stresses; to use a variety of coping strategies *when appropriate:* active-direct coping (e.g., changing the source of stress), active-indirect coping (e.g., talking to friends), and inactive-direct coping (e.g., ignoring or avoiding the source of stress). They were discouraged from using inactive-indirect coping (e.g., drugs and alcohol). Emphasis was put on techniques for recognizing, establishing, and using support systems among colleagues. Recommendations included employee-oriented staff meetings, open communication, active listening, providing of technical support and technical challenge, open discussion of disruptive emotional experiences, looking for positive aspects in the interaction with clients, and work sharing. The power of positive attitudes and a sense of humor as buffers against tedium and burnout on the individual level was discussed. Specific recommendations included acknowledging time as a valuable resource, compartmentalization between work and home, "decompression" at the end of stressful days, awareness of danger signs, acknowledgment of vulnerabilities, and the setting of realistic, achievable goals. The day ended with a summary session in which the relevance of burnout and tedium to one's life as well as work was discussed.

The effects of the burnout workshop were assessed by an immediate feedback questionnaire and by two posttest questionnaires collected one week and six months after the workshop. Responses to the feedback questionnaire given immediately after the workshop indicated that the participants viewed the workshop very favorably and positively evaluated the introduction of concepts, suggestions for solving problems, and their hopes for future solutions.

The immediate feedback questionnaire also included open-ended questions. To the question, "What was the most important informative aspect of the workshop?" participants emphasized recognizing the shared nature of their work stresses and the importance of using support systems on the job. Some of the responses were: "finding out that all of us have basically the same problems," "finding ways of helping one another and getting to know the other person," "stress on co-workers as support system," "don't always rely on management to give you encouragement, get encouragement from each other." Other comments dealt with specific suggestions of the workshop: "controlling work load," "being given positive ways of combating problems and positive ways of looking at problems," "stating you have a problem and a solution." Still others appreciated the opportunity to talk openly, especially without their supervisors present.

The last part of the questionnaire asked for general comments. Responses were of two kinds: evaluation of the workshop and suggestions to management on work improvement. Comments of the first kind included appreciation of the workshop in general, need for a two-day program, suggestions for specific topics to be covered, and requests for similar workshops for management personnel.

Suggestions to management included ideas about improving work relations: "employees need to talk out their problems without being afraid of management," "management should communicate with all employees," "individuals can withstand many negative aspects of their job when bosses are aware of and appreciate their effort," "be more supportive to employees. It's not sufficient to say it during quarterly discussions and evaluations, " "have more 'team work' between mangement and employees," "have many sessions like today, maybe once a month."

Short-term posttest

One week before the workshop, the pretest was administered to all employees to establish base line. One week after the workshop, employees in both the experimental group and the control group were given the first posttest. This questionnaire was given for the second time to assess the short-term impact of the workshop.

Preexperimental responses to the questionnaire were compared to postexperimental responses, with the assumption that those changes that occurred only in the experimental group were the result of the burnout workshop. Only 15 employees out of the 23 who participated in the workshop completed both the pre- and postquestionnaire. Subject loss is especially serious with such small samples as ours and it raises questions about the validity and the generalizability of the data.

Results for the employees who completed the questionnaire twice show that tedium in the experimental group decreased slightly ($p <$ .10) and satisfaction from coworkers went up significantly ($p < .01$). Employees in the experimental group were also more satisfied with their supervisors, their contact with the public, and their clients after the workshop. Employees in the control group, who did not participate in the workshop, did not show this consistent and positive attitude change. The workshop had negligible impact on such internal work features as variety, autonomy, significance, success, underload, and overload. These work features are part of the reality of the job and as such were beyond the control of the individual worker. The workshop had more impact on the external personal aspects of the work: personal relations, relations with supervisors, and feedback from colleagues were all evaluated more positively in the experimental group than in the control group.

Experimental-group employees also described themselves as more adequately rewarded after the workshop. Two of the external, impersonal work features, bureaucratic interference and administrative conflicts, increased after the workshop, but the difference was not statistically significant. These features had been identified in numerous workshop discussions as inherent to the job and unchangeable. As a result they could be perceived as more stressful by the workshop participants. In summary, the comparison of the pretest and posttest indicated that the major effect of the burnout workshop was to increase satisfaction; it had no effect on those internal and external work features that are beyond the individual's control.

In the pretest/posttest comparison we also looked at work features and satisfaction as correlates of tedium. In the experimental group, several variables were associated more with tedium following the workshop. In the control group there was no such change. These changes may suggest that as a result of the workshop the experimental group became more aware of the relationship between such features as overload, feedback, and especially personal relations with coworkers and the subjective experience of tedium.

This increased awareness, which was the first goal of the workshop, is also evident when one examines the satisfaction measures as correlates of tedium in pretest and posttest. Although the negative correlation of tedium with general work satisfaction increased for the experimental group, it changed much less and in the opposite direction for the control group. The correlation between tedium and satisfaction from clients and from the department increased dramatically for the experimental group and decreased for the control group. The correlation between satisfaction from supervisors and tedium increased very dramatically for the experimental group and remained unchanged for the control group. We interpreted these changes in the correlation between satisfaction and tedium to reflect on increased awareness of the concept of tedium. All these interpretations must be taken with caution due to the small sample on which the correlations are based.

In summary, the comparison of the pretest and the first posttest suggests that the burnout workshop had impact in two areas: an increased awareness of the relationship between various work features and tedium; and a slight decrease in tedium and an increase in satisfaction from supervisors, the department, the public, clients, and coworkers. Of these relationships, only the improvement with coworkers was statistically significant. Although the workshop had an impact on awareness and satisfaction, it had a negligible effect on internal, stressful work features such as lack of autonomy and sense of overload. The workshop also did not have an impact on such impersonal features as administrative conflicts, bureaucratic interference, and lack of "time outs."

Long-term Posttest

Six months after the burnout workshop the experimental group and the control group were given the second posttest. The questionnaire was given for the third time to assess the long-term impact of the workshop. Preworkshop responses to the questionnaire and short-term posttest responses were compared to the long-term postworkshop responses, with the assumption that those changes that occurred only in the experimental group were the result of the burnout workshop. The changes that were in evidence in the second posttest were assumed to indicate the long-term effects of the workshop.

Due to the high attrition rate of participants in the study, a comparison of the pretest and the two posttests is not scientifically sound. Only 8 experimental-group employees of the 23 in the workshop completed all three questionnaires, and only 14 of the 30 control-group employees did so. Such small samples make any sophisticated statistical analysis meaningless and raise serious doubts about the validity and generalizability of the data.

Because the workshop had little effect on work features inherent to bureaucracies, such as variety, autonmy, significance, success, underload, and overload, these variables will not be discussed. The major impact of the workshop was on the social aspects of the job, and some of that impact, though weakened, remained after six months. For the experimental group, satisfaction from coworkers, clients, and the public remained higher six months after the burnout workshop than it was prior to workshop. The one satisfaction measure that did not show the impact of the workshop after six months was satisfaction from supervisors. There was a slight increase in satisfaction in personal relationship in the experimental group but not in the control group.

Despite the limitations of a very small sample, after six months the correlations of tedium with the different variables seem consistently higher for the experimental group—this suggests the continuing impact of the workshop on the participants' awareness of the relationships between these variables and tedium.

In summary, a cautious comparision of the pretest and the long-term posttest in both experimental and control groups suggests that the burnout workshop had lasting impact after six months in two areas: a slight increase in satisfaction from the public, clients, and especially coworkers, and increased awareness of the relationships between various work features and tedium.

The burnout workshop had impact in some areas and not in others. It had no impact on features of the job that are inherent to large complex organizations, such as overload, lack of autonomy, lack of rewards, and lack of a sense of significance. It did have impact on work relationships and on satisfaction from coworkers, clients, and the public, effects still evident six months after the workshop.

Many workshop participants told us the workshop was too short to be most helpful. Not surprisingly, the effects of the workshop weakened after six months. Thus, a burnout workshop can be seen as the start of a process that will continue on the job in one- or two-hour meetings once or twice a month. The workshop itself teaches communication skills that employees can use in those meetings.

In the workshop described here it was decided not to include management in order to create a comfortable atmosphere for personal expression. Yet some participants said they could have benefited more from the workshop if management had been included, even at the price of less comfort. One exchange in particular demonstrated the value of management participation: the employees were saying that no matter how hard they tried or how much they produced, their supervisors' feedback always had some criticism. A supervisor who participated in the workshop explained that she had been instructed to give positive feedback when deserved but always to find additional negative feedback that will suggest possible improvement. The employees then understood the supervisor's conflict and could empathize; the supervisor understood the impact of her feedback. The participants felt that communication had been improved.

There are two types of burnout workshops. One workshop is for employees from different jobs who have similar work roles and work stresses. In these groups participants can discuss stresses and rewards unique to their position and could establish support systems with people outside of their own jobs. These workshops can be particularly helpful for those management personnel who, because of their position, feel they cannot confer with others or use a support system. These occupation-specific workshops can be helpful in breaking the asymmetry of feedback and rewards in organizations. Many social service employees expect their rewards to come from management; they rarely look to their coworkers for feedback and as a result feel demoralized. These expectations create much pressure on management personnel. During a workshop an effort can be made to change this pattern by teaching employees how to be effective support systems for each other.

The second kind of workshop is for people from one organization. These workshops can be especially useful where lack of communication, hostility, and inadequate cooperation are affecting the office's proper functioning. This kind of workshop is similar to the one described in this appendix and is likely to have similar effects.

Note

1. D. T. Campbell and J. C. Stanley, *Experimental and Quasi Experimental Designs for Research* (Chicago: Rand-McNally, 1973), pp. 47–50.

appendix II

The research

Ditsa Kafry

Our research on tedium, centered at the University of California, Berkeley, involved 3,916 people. Participants were students and professionals from the United States, Canada, Japan, and Israel. They were studied from 1976 to 1980. This appendix describes the tedium measure and the samples studied and presents some of the research findings. It should be emphasized that the usual problems associated with correlating self-report data apply to much of the research reported below (see footnote in Chapter 2, p. 16).

The tedium measure

Definition

Tedium is the experience of physical, emotional, and mental exhaustion. It is characterized by emotional and physical depletion and by the negation of one's self, one's environment, one's work, and one's life. (Burnout is identical to tedium in terms of definition and symptomology but is unique to people who work with people in situations that are emotionally demanding.)

Description

Tedium is measured by a 21-item questionnaire. The items represent its three aspects:

1. physical exhaustion: being tired, being physically exhausted, feeling wiped out, feeling rundown, being weary, feeling weak, feeling energetic
2. emotional exhaustion: feeling depressed, being emotionally exhausted, feeling burned out, feeling trapped, being troubled, feeling hopeless, feeling anxious
3. mental exhaustion (negation of one's life, self, and others): being happy, being unhappy, having a good day, feeling worthless, feeling optimistic, feeling disillusioned and resentful about people, feeling rejected

These items are presented in random order and are each evaluated on a 7-point frequency scale. The scale has the following anchors: 1 = never, 2 = once, 3 = rarely, 4 = sometimes, 5 = often, 6 = usually, 7 = always. The overall tedium score is the mean value of the responses to the items, with four items reversed (feeling energetic, being happy, having a good day, feeling optimistic).

Reliability

Test-retest reliability of the measure was found to be .89 for a one-month interval, .76 for a two-month interval, and .66 for a four-

---

The tedium measure

How often do you have any of the following experiences? Please use the following scale:

1	2	3	4	5	6	7
Never	Once	Rarely	Sometimes	Often	Usually	Always

_____ 1. Being tired
_____ 2. Feeling depressed
_____ 3. Having a good day
_____ 4. Being physically exhausted
_____ 5. Being emotionally exhausted
_____ 6. Being happy
_____ 7. Being "wiped out"
_____ 8. Feeling "burned out"
_____ 9. Being unhappy
_____ 10. Feeling rundown
_____ 11. Feeling trapped
_____ 12. Feeling worthless
_____ 13. Being weary
_____ 14. Being troubled
_____ 15. Feeling disillusioned and resentful about people
_____ 16. Feeling weak
_____ 17. Feeling hopeless
_____ 18. Feeling rejected
_____ 19. Feeling optimistic
_____ 20. Feeling energetic
_____ 21. Feeling anxious

---

month interval. Internal consistency was assessed by the α coefficient for most samples studied; the values of the α coefficient ranged between .91 and .93.

The samples studied

The study of tedium included 30 samples of participants. The groups varied in size from 9 to 724 people; they also varied in profession and location. The samples are described below:

1. 205 (96 men and 109 women) professionals from the San Francisco Bay Area, recruited by students who participated in a group research course. They represented a variety of areas: human services, science, business, art, and homemaking.
2. 220 (47 men and 173 women) professionals who participated in a burnout workshop in the San Francisco Bay Area. They represented different areas of human service and management.
3. 322 (56 men and 266 women) professionals who participated in a burnout workshop in the San Francisco Bay area. They represented different areas of human service and management.
4. 277 professional women from the San Franciso Bay area, recruited by students who participated in a group research course. They represented a variety of areas: human service, science, business, art, and homemaking.
5. 129 (19 men and 110 women) social service workers who participated in a burnout workshop in Colorado.
6. 198 (166 men and 32 women) mental retardation workers who participated in a burnout workshop in Georgia.
7. 66 (17 men and 49 women) social service workers who participated in a burnout workshop in Colorado.
8. 89 (11 men and 78 women) teachers who participated in two burnout workshops in northern California.
9. 53 (13 men and 40 women) employees of two offices of public social service agencies in northern California.
10. 724 (275 men and 449 women) human service professionals who were sampled randomly from 14 state residential facilities for the developmentally disabled in: North Carolina, South Carolina, Indiana, New Jersey, Colorado, Montana, West Virginia, Texas, Virginia, Louisiana, and New York.
11. 29 (1 man and 28 women) nurses who participated in a burnout workshop in the San Francisco Bay area.
12. 45 (23 men and 22 women) probation officers who participated in a burnout workshop in the San Francisco Bay area.
13. 12 (1 man and 11 women) parents suspected of abusing or neglecting their children.
14. 73 mothers of school children who participated in a research project in the San Francisco Bay area.

15. 33 fathers of school children who participated in a research project in the San Francisco Bay area.
16. 72 mothers of school children who participated in a research project in the San Francisco Bay area.
17. 50 fathers of school children who participated in a research project in the San Francisco Bay area.
18. 39 female nurses who participated in a reseach project in southern California.
19. 25 (9 men and 16 women) who participated in a one-month course on burnout in the San Francisco Bay area.
20. 9 (2 men and 7 women) supervisors and administrators in a health-care facility in the San Francisco Bay area.
21. 84 (35 men and 49 women) undergraduate students from the University of California, Berkeley.
22. 147 (49 men and 98 women) undergraduate students from the University of California, Berkeley.
23. 294 (106 men and 188 women) undergraduate students from the University of California, Berkeley.
24. 118 (12 men and 106 women) human service professionals in three hospitals and one community center in Canada. The sample was randomly drawn from employees of intensive care, emergency, and long-term care wards.
25. 81 (10 men and 71 women) social workers from Israel.
26. 181 (26 men and 155 women) telephone operators from Israel.
27. 66 (59 men and 7 women) managers who participated in a managerial seminar in Israel.
28. 55 male managers who participated in a management development program in Israel.
29. 21 (17 men and 4 women) managers who participated in a burnout workshop in Israel.
30. 199 Japanese students from Rissho University in Tokyo.

Tedium for the various samples

Table A.1 presents the mean values and the standard deviations for all samples studied. The mean values ranged from 2.8 to 4.2 and the standard deviations from 0.4 to 1.0. The overall mean value of tedium was found to be 3.3.

TABLE A.1.   Sample size, mean values, and standard deviations of tedium

SAMPLE	N	MEAN	STANDARD DEVIATION
1	205	3.2	0.6
2	220	3.7	0.6
3	322	3.6	0.7
4	277	3.1	0.6
5	129	3.3	1.0
6	198	3.1	0.6
7	66	3.7	0.7
8	89	3.2	0.9
9	53	3.6	0.7
10	724	3.1	0.9
11	29	3.6	0.6
12	45	3.5	0.5
13	12	4.2	0.6
14	73	3.1	0.8
15	33	2.9	0.9
16	72	3.1	0.5
17	50	2.9	0.5
18	39	3.0	0.6
19	25	3.1	0.9
20	9	3.0	0.4
21	84	3.4	0.7
22	147	3.4	0.7
23	294	3.3	0.8
24	118	3.3	0.6
25	81	3.1	0.6
26	181	3.1	0.7
27	66	2.8	0.5
28	65	2.8	0.6
29	21	3.5	0.4
30	199	3.5	0.9

Tedium by sex

Table A.2 presents the mean values of tedium for men and women for almost all samples studied. The overall mean value of tedium was 3.2 for men (N = 1,188) and 3.3 for women (N = 2,529).

TABLE A.2.   Mean values of tedium for men and women

SAMPLE	MEN		WOMEN	
	N	*Mean*	*N*	*Mean*
1	96	3.1	109	3.3
2	47	3.5	173	3.8
3	56	3.6	266	3.6
4	0	–	277	3.1
5	19	3.3	110	3.3
6	166	3.1	32	3.2
7	17	3.8	49	3.7
8	11	2.7	78	3.2
9	13	3.7	40	3.5
10	275	3.1	449	3.2
11	1	3.2	28	3.6
12	23	3.6	22	3.5
13	1	3.5	11	4.3
14	0	–	73	3.1
15	33	2.9	0	–
16	0	–	72	3.1
17	50	2.9	0	–
18	0	–	39	3.0
19	9	2.9	16	3.2
20	2	2.9	7	3.0
21	35	3.6	49	3.3
22	49	3.3	98	3.5
23	106	3.2	188	3.3
24	12	3.0	106	3.3
25	10	2.8	71	3.2
26	26	2.9	155	3.1
27	59	2.8	7	3.0
28	55	2.8	0	–
29	17	3.5	4	3.5

Tedium by profession

Table A.3 presents the mean values of tedium by profession. Due to the large variety of professions, not all the participants are presented in this table.

TABLE A.3.   Mean values of tedium by profession

SAMPLE	PROFESSION	N	MEAN
1	Human service	63	3.1
	Business and management	36	3.2
	Science	39	3.3
	Art	13	3.2
	Homemaking	14	3.2
	Technical and clerical	40	3.4
2	Social work	48	3.8
	Counseling	38	3.7
	Therapy	26	3.6
	Nursing	35	3.8
	Education	27	3.8
	Administration and management	28	3.4
3	Human service	260	3.7
	Technical, clerical and administration	46	3.4
4	Business and management	56	3.1
	Education	21	3.1
	Social work and nursing	36	3.3
	Science	46	3.0
	Technical and clerical	45	3.0
	Homemaking	18	3.5
5	Professional homemaking	17	3.0
	Case work	94	3.4
	Supervision	16	3.2
7	Professional homemaking	18	3.6
	Case work	44	3.8
8	Teaching	89	3.2
9	Public social service	53	3.6
10	Administration and management	256	3.1
	Professional direct care	244	3.1
	Nonprofessional direct care	224	3.1
11	Nursing	29	3.6
12	Probation	45	3.6
20	Students	84	3.4
21	Students	147	3.4
22	Students	294	3.3
24	Nursing—Canada	55	3.4
	Nursing aide—Canada	27	3.0
	Social work—Canada	23	3.3
25	Social work—Israel	81	3.1
26	Telephone operators—Israel	133	3.2
	Telephone supervisors—Israel	33	2.9
27	Managers—Israel	66	2.8
28	Managers—Israel	55	2.8
29	Managers—Israel	21	3.5
30	Students—Japan	199	3.5

Tedium and other variables

SATISFACTION MEASURES

Table A.4 presents the mean values and correlations with tedium for three satisfaction measures: satisfaction from work, life, and self. Satisfaction was measured by Kunin's Faces Scale.[1] Most correlations were negative and significantly different from zero ($p < .05$).

TABLE A.4. Mean values and correlations with tedium for satisfaction measures

	WORK		LIFE		SELF	
SAMPLE	Mean	Correlation	Mean	Correlation	Mean	Correlation
1	5.1	− .39	5.7	− .56		
2	4.7	− .53	5.3	− .58	5.4	− .54
3	4.7	− .63	5.5	− .62	5.5	− .62
4	5.3	− .38	5.7	− .38		
5	5.0	− .58				
6	5.5	− .52				
9	4.8	− .58	5.5	− .44	5.6	− .45
10	5.4	− .45	5.9	− .43	5.1	− .43
11	5.3	− .37(NS)	5.4	− .53	5.3	− .34(NS)
12	4.5	− .45	5.5	− .55	5.3	− .59
14	5.4	− .41	5.8	− .61		
15	5.5	− .43	5.7	− .56		
16	5.6	− .63	5.8	− .51	5.9	− .54
17	5.6	− .31(NS)	5.9	− .37(NS)	5.9	− .60
18	4.8	− .53	5.9	− .70	6.1	− .68
21	4.7	− .50	5.6	− .69		
22	4.8	− .52	5.6	− .56	5.6	− .73
23	4.9	− .38	5.7	− .46		
24	5.4	− .24	5.9	− .34	5.7	− .40
25	5.6	− .30	5.6	− .46	5.6	− .41
26	4.7	− .53	5.7	− .47		
27	5.4	− .26	5.7	− .32		
28	5.1	− .39	5.5	− .54	5.1	− .32
30	3.7	− .35	4.8	− .61	4.3	− .35

(NS)−not significant.

PERCEPTION OF PHYSICAL HEALTH AND
REPORTS OF SLEEP PROBLEMS

Table A.5 presents means and correlations with tedium for perception of physical health and reports of sleep problems for a number of samples. All correlations were significantly different from zero ($p < .05$) and in the predicted direction: positive for sleep problems and negative for perception of health.

TABLE A.5. Mean values and correlations with tedium for perception of physical health and reports of sleep problems

| SAMPLE | PHYSICAL HEALTH | | SLEEP PROBLEMS | |
	Mean	Correlation	Mean	Correlation
1	5.6	−.39		
4	5.4	−.33	2.7	.30
5			3.0	.33
6			2.8	.32
10	5.5	−.26		
14			2.8	.33
15			2.4	.47
23	5.4	−.40	2.9	.30
24	5.4	−.20		
25	5.4	−.38		
26	4.0	−.46		
28	5.5	−.28		
29	5.4	−.25		

CONFLICT BETWEEN LIFE AND WORK

Table A.6 presents the mean values and the correlation with tedium of conflict between life and work for a number of samples. All correlations were positive and significantly different from zero ($p < .05$).

TABLE A.6. Mean values and correlations with tedium for conflict life-work

SAMPLE	MEAN	CORRELATION
1	4.2	.36
4	3.6	.22
10	3.6	.33
21	4.6	.32
23	4.1	.26
24	4.1	.38
28	3.7	.28
29	4.0	.24

HOPELESSNESS

A subgroup of sample 3 (N = 130) responded to the 20-item hopelessness questionnaires designed by Beck, Weissman, Lester, and Trexler.[2] The correlation between tedium and hopelessness was .59 ($p < .001$).

TARDINESS

Information about tardiness (the number of days in a year in which employees were late for work) was available for sample 26. The correlation between tardiness and tedium was .30 ($p < .001$).

MAJOR LIFE EVENTS

Participants in sample 3 listed the life events they experienced during the six months prior to responding to the questionnaire. Twenty-two life events were included, representing the following areas: physical health, mental health, economic situation, family condition, work, and other experiences. The number of positive and the number of negative events were computed for each respondent. The number of positive life events was significantly and negatively related to tedium with the correlation of −.22, while the number of negative life events was significantly and positively related to tedium with the correlation of .30 ($p < .001$ for the two correlations).

TENDENCY TO LEAVE THE JOB

Table A.7 presents the mean values and the correlations with tedium of the tendency to leave the job for four samples. All correlations were positive and significantly different from zero ($p < .05$).

TABLE A.7. **Mean values and correlations with tedium for tendency to leave the job**

SAMPLE	MEAN	CORRELATION
5	3.6	.58
6	2.6	.40
10	3.0	.33
24	3.2	.27

EXPERIENCING WORK BURNOUT

Participants of sample 7 were asked several questions about their experience of work burnout. Forty-eight percent of the respondents felt work burnout at the time of the study; 29 percent had felt work burnout in the past but not at the time of the study; and 23 percent had never felt work burnout. Those who had never felt burnout had significantly lower mean value of tedium relative to those who reported work burnout ($p <$ .05).

PERCEPTION OF TEDIUM BY OTHERS

Participants of samples 8 and 11 responded to the tedium measure themselves; in addition, other members of their groups also assessed their level of tedium. The correlation between self-assessment and assessment of tedium by colleagues for the two samples combined was .37 ($p <$ .001).

WORK AND LIFE PRESSURES

Participants in sample 1 were asked to list their most important pressures in life and at work. These pressures were content-analyzed into eight categories. Analysis of the results presented in table A.8 showed that the mean value of tedium had a significant overall effect ($p <$ .05) for the types of life pressures but not for the types of work pressures mentioned by the participants.

TABLE A.8. Percentage of participants indicating the most important pressure in life and work and their mean value of tedium—sample 1

| | LIFE | | WORK | |
PRESSURE	Percentage	Mean	Percentage	Mean
Financial problems	14	3.1	3	2.8
Interpersonal problems	39	3.2	18	3.3
Lack of time	13	3.3	17	3.3
Decision and planning problems	2	3.3	17	3.1
Hassles	4	3.2	15	3.2
Self-actualization problems	12	3.6	13	3.3
Negative feelings	9	3.4	13	3.4
No problems	7	2.8	4	2.9

PRESSURES AND JOYS

Table A. 9 presents the distribution of 564 pressures and 527 joys mentioned by participants of sample 22. Analysis of correlations with tedium showed that the number of pressures mentioned was not significantly related to tedium (r −.08), while the mean intensity of these pressures was (.42, $p < .05$). Both number of joys and mean intensity of joys were negatively and significantly related to tedium ($r = - .21$ and $r = - . 23$ respectively, $p < .05$).

TABLE A.9.   Percentages of pressures and joys by category—sample 22

Category	Percentage of Pressures	Percentage of Joys
Finance	10	0
Interpersonal relations	33	40
School	28	13
Self-actualization	10	5
Future	8	2
Work	6	3
Health	5	1
Hobbies and activities	0	34
Relaxation	0	2

WORK AND LIFE FEATURES

Table A.10 presents the means and the correlations with tedium for 12 work features for samples 5 and 6. Table A.11 presents equivalent information for life features for samples 4 and 23 . Table A.12 presents the means and correlations with tedium for work and life features for samples 1 and 10.

TABLE A.10.   Mean values and correlations with tedium for work features

WORK FEATURES	SAMPLE 5		SAMPLE 6	
	Mean	Correlation	Mean	Correlation
Variety	5.4	− .14	6.2	−.23*
Complexity	5.1	− .03	5.8	−.16*
Autonomy	5.0	− .15	5.4	−.32*
Significance	5.5	− .13	6.3	−.18*
Feedback	4.8	− .31*	5.0	−.15*
Success	5.2	− .16	5.9	−.15*
Opportunity to take off	4.2	− .27*	4.4	−.15*
Facility effectiveness	4.4	− .30*	5.4	−.18*
Work sharing	4.2	− .28*	5.1	−.22*
Work relations	5.2	− .32*	5.2	−.28*
Social support	5.9	− .29*	5.4	−.26*
Social feedback	4.1	− .36*	4.2	−.32*

*$p < .05$

TABLE A.11.   Mean values and correlations with tedium for life features

LIFE FEATURES	SAMPLE 4		SAMPLE 23	
	Mean	Correlation	Mean	Correlation
Variety	5.5	− .32*	5.1	− .35*
Complexity	5.5	− .05	5.6	.01
Autonomy	5.6	− .29*	5.4	− .24*
Significance	5.4	− .13*	5.2	− .23*
Success	5.1	− .47*	5.1	− .47*
Overextension	4.1	.21*	4.4	.20*
Opportunity to take off	4.4	− .27*	4.4	− .15*
Family relations	5.7	− .30*	5.6	− .17*
Friends relations	6.0	− .30*	5.8	− .32*
Support	5.4	− .25*	5.5	− .27*
Social overextension	3.8	.35*	4.0	.24*
Distraction by work	3.6	.33*	4.3	.28*

*$p < .05$

TABLE A.12. Mean values and correlations with tedium for work and life features

	SAMPLE 1				SAMPLE 10			
	Life		Work		Life		Work	
	Mean	r	Mean	r	Mean	r	Mean	r
Variety	5.2	− .23*	5.0	− .21*	5.2	− .22*	4.8	− .20*
Complexity	4.9	− .11	5.1	− .20*	4.9	− .09*	5.2	− .03
Autonomy	5.7	− .15*	5.0	− .28*	5.8	− .19*	4.7	− .19*
Overextension	4.1	.22*	4.2	.23*	3.8	.23*	4.4	.31*
Overload	3.8	.13	4.0	.13	3.9	.27*	4.5	.35*
Underload	3.2	.29*	3.3	.15*	3.3	.22*	3.5	.20*
Decision load	3.4	.21*	3.9	.19*	3.2	.18*	4.1	.30*
Innovation load	4.7	− .15*	4.7	− .17*	4.9	− .12*	5.0	− .08*
Significance	5.2	− .22*	5.3	− .21*	5.7	− .18*	5.9	− .15*
Feedback	4.9	− .23*	4.7	− .15*	5.0	− .21*	4.4	− .15*
Success	5.2	− .48*	5.2	− .24*	5.4	− .28*	5.2	− .17*
Negative consequences	4.3	− .07	5.0	− .19*	4.6	.00	5.3	.04
Self-expression	5.6	− .31*	4.9	− .22*	5.7	− .15*	4.9	− .20*
Self-actualization	5.5	− .28*	4.7	− .22*	5.4	− .24*	4.7	− .20*
Self-worth demand	3.6	.11	4.2	.00	3.8	.08*	4.6	.17*
Guilt	3.2	.51*	3.1	.29*	3.3	.41*	3.6	.42*
Physical danger	2.0	− .03	1.9	− .06	2.2	.10*	2.9	.12*
Environmental pressures	2.5	.26*	2.8	.27*	2.4	.19*	3.3	.21*
Comfortable environment	5.6	− .35*	4.6	− .29*	5.5	− .20*	4.4	− .24*
Bureaucratic pressures	3.0	.20*	4.2	.11	2.7	.10*	4.6	.24*
Administrative hassles	2.8	.20*	4.5	.06	2.5	.10*	5.1	.26*
Policy influence	5.2	− .24*	4.0	− .15*	5.5	− .16*	4.1	− .18*
Rewards	5.0	− .41*	4.4	− .33*	4.9	− .17*	4.0	− .17*
Opportunity to take off	4.4	.18*	4.2	− .11	4.5	− .16*	4.3	− .09*
Social overextension	4.4	.28*	4.2	.16*	3.7	− .33*	3.9	.38*
Support	5.0	− .29*	4.5	− .27*	5.1	− .12*	4.6	− .17*
Personal relations	5.7	− .32*	5.5	− .27*	5.9	− .26*	5.6	− .25*
Sharing	4.7	.28*	4.4	.13	5.1	− .20*	4.9	.23*
Conflicting demands	3.8	.38*	3.9	.27*	3.5	− .30*	4.0	.31*
Appreciation	5.0	− .31*	4.6	− .32*	5.1	− .13*	4.3	− .16*
Responsibility	4.4	− .12	4.1	− .06	4.3	− .01	4.3	− .07*
Emotional reciprocity	5.2	− .29*	4.5	− .18*	5.2	− .22*	4.2	− .18*

*p< .05

Sex differences. Table A.13 presents the mean values and correlations with tedium for work and life features for men and women who participated in sample 1.

TABLE A.13.   **Mean values and correlations with tedium for work and life features of men and women—sample 1**

		MEN		WOMEN		MEN/WOMEN
		Mean	*r*	*Mean*	*r*	MEAN COMPARISON t
Variety	Life	5.4	− .17	5.0	− .22*	1.98*
	Work	5.3	− .19	4.8	− .20*	2.10*
Complexity	Life	5.1	− .04	4.9	− .11	0.35
	Work	5.4	− .02	4.9	− .30*	2.52*
Autonomy	Life	5.8	− .02	5.7	− .18	0.40
	Work	5.4	− .20*	4.7	− .30*	2.99*
Underload	Life	3.1	.19	3.2	.32*	− 0.63
	Work	3.1	.03	3.5	.21*	− 1.75
Overload	Life	3.9	.17	3.9	.12	0.25
	Work	4.3	.21*	3.9	.10	1.57
Decision Load	Life	3.5	.14	3.3	.30*	1.44
	Work	4.1	.22*	3.8	.17	1.20
Overextension	Life	4.1	.20*	4.2	.27*	− 0.41
	Work	4.4	.20*	4.1	.25*	1.56
Self-worth demand	Life	3.7	− .05	3.7	.19	0.06
	Work	4.5	− .07	3.9	− .03	2.44*
Innovation load	Life	4.7	− .14	4.7	− .12	0.04
	Work	5.2	− .02	4.4	− .25*	2.97*
Significance	Life	5.1	− .22*	5.3	− .21*	− 1.20
	Work	5.3	− .24*	5.3	− .22*	0.15
Success	Life	5.3	− .41*	5.2	− .48*	0.48
	Work	5.3	− .22*	5.1	− .23*	0.76
Feedback	Life	4.7	− .29*	5.0	− .17	− 1.34
	Work	4.8	− .17	4.6	− .11	0.75
Self-expression	Life	5.5	− .09	5.6	− .42*	− 0.51
	Work	5.2	− .09	4.6	− .28*	2.62*
Self-actualization	Life	5.5	− .18	5.5	− .29*	0.27
	Work	5.1	− .15	4.5	− .24*	2.49*
Guilt	Life	3.0	.43*	3.5	.57*	− 2.28*
	Work	3.0	.30*	3.2	.25*	− 0.64

		MEN		WOMEN		MEN/WOMEN
		Mean	*r*	*Mean*	*r*	MEAN COMPARISON t
Environment	Life	2.3	.15	2.6	.33*	'— 1.60
pressures	Work	2.6	.11	3.0	.37*	— 2.04*
Bureaucratic	Life	3.0	.22*	3.1	.18	— 0.27
pressures	Work	4.2	.08	4.3	.13	— 0.23
Administrative	Life	2.9	.20*	2.8	.18	0.44
hassles	Work	4.7	.06	4.5	.03	0.50
Comfortable	Life	5.7	— .42*	5.5	— .30*	— 1.28
environment	Work	4.9	— .25*	4.2	— .31*	2.97*
Responsibility	Life	4.3	.05	4.3	.16	— 0.34
	Work	4.1	— .19	4.2	.00	— 0.44
Policy influence	Life	5.2	— .22*	5.3	— .28*	— 0.61
	Work	4.5	— .13	3.7	— .12	3.16*
Rewards	Life	5.1	— .34*	5.0	— .44*	0.18
	Work	4.7	— .24*	4.2	— .36*	1.96*
Opportunity	Life	4.5	— .14	4.3	— .21*	0.78
to take off	Work	4.5	— .09	3.8	— .05	3.08*
Support	Life	4.8	— .31*	5.2	— .31*	— 2.13*
	Work	4.4	— .28*	4.6	— .27*	— 0.93
Appreciation	Life	5.0	— .34*	5.1	— .27*	— 0.47
	Work	4.8	— .25*	4.4	— .33*	1.56
Emotional	Life	5.1	— .31*	5.4	— .30*	— 1.74
reciprocity	Work	4.4	— .20*	4.5	— .13	— 0.43
Sharing	Life	4.6	— .27*	4.9	— .30*	— 1.05
	Work	4.1	— .20*	4.6	— .11	— 2.19*
Personal relations	Life	5.6	— .21*	5.9	— .42*	— 1.96*
	Work	5.4	— .24*	5.6	— .30*	— 1.10
Social	Life	4.0	.16	4.7	.34*	— 2.76*
overextension	Work	3.9	.04	4.6	.21*	— 2.16*
Conflicting	Life	3.7	.30*	3.9	.44*	— 1.38
demands	Work	4.0	.29*	3.8	.25*	1.05

*$p < .05$

Cultural differences. Table A.14 presents the mean values and correlations with tedium for work and life features for United States and Israeli managers.

TABLE A.14.   Mean values and correlations with tedium of life and work features for United States and Israeli managers

| | UNITED STATES | | | | ISRAEL | | | |
| | Life | | Work | | Life | | Work | |
	Mean	r	Mean	r	Mean	r	Mean	r
Variety	5.5	− .08	5.7	− .12	5.0	− .12	6.0	− .14
Complexity	5.1	.01	5.5	.03	4.6	12	5.9	− .12
Autonomy	5.9	.04	5.6	− .04	5.7	− .31*	5.8	− .21*
Overextension	3.9	.16	4.8	.33*	4.2	− .07	5.3	− .08
Overload	4.0	.30*	4.4	.29*	3.2	.26*	3.8	.16
Underload	2.9	.16	2.7	− .06	2.8	.20	2.6	.15
Decision load	3.5	.18	4.2	.37*	2.9	.33*	3.8	.20
Innovation load	4.8	− .18	5.5	− .01	4.6	− .17	5.7	− .37*
Significance	5.1	− .05	5.8	− .07	6.0	.01	6.0	− .27*
Feedback	4.8	− .17	5.2	− .06	5.5	− .17	5.8	− .16
Success	5.3	− .30*	5.5	− .21*	5.6	− .43*	6.0	− .26*
Negative consequences	4.3	.03	5.4	− .05	4.9	− .00	5.6	− .27*
Self-expression	5.6	− .25*	5.6	− .10	5.5	− .27*	5.7	− .34*
Self-actualization	5.5	− .15	5.4	− .17	5.1	− .19	5.2	− .16
Self-worth demand	3.8	.09	4.9	.09	3.2	.15	5.1	− .06
Guilt	3.1	.53*	3.3	.48*	2.4	.38*	2.3	.36*
Physical danger	2.0	− .08	1.8	− .05	1.7	− .11	2.2	.05
Environmental pressures	2.2	.12	2.6	.17	2.2	.13	3.2	.16
Comfortable environment	6.1	− .14	5.2	− .14	5.7	− .17	4.8	− .22*
Bureaucratic pressures	2.7	.13	3.9	.05	2.6	.31*	4.5	.31*
Administrative hassles	2.7	.16	4.6	.15	2.4	.37*	4.5	.40*
Policy influence	5.3	− .17	4.9	− .15	5.8	.04	5.4	− .40*
Rewards	5.2	− .28*	5.1	− .29*	5.5	− .14	4.7	− .35*
Opportunity to take off	4.7	− .06	4.7	.11	4.1	− .06	4.3	− .07
Social overextension	4.3	.13	4.5	.31*	4.4	.15	3.7	− .12
Support	5.1	.24*	4.7	− .16	5.3	− .09	4.9	− .15
Personal relations	5.8	− .25*	5.6	− .28*	6.1	− .25*	5.5	− .34*
Sharing	4.5	− .37*	4.3	− .01	5.2	− .16	4.1	.07
Conflicting demands	3.7	.32*	4.4	.31*	3.2	.26*	3.7	.26*
Appreciation	5.1	− .30*	5.2	− .22*	5.6	− .21*	5.3	− .16
Responsibility	4.4	.13	4.6	.06	4.2	− .02	3.8	.06
Emotional reciprocity	5.3	− .24*	4.7	− .16	5.8	.19	4.6	− .36*

*p<.05

COPING STRATEGIES

A two-dimensional taxonomy of coping strategies: direct/indirect and active/inactive was investigated. These two coping dimensions interact and generate four types of coping strategies, each one of them represented by three actions. The frequency of use of these coping strategies, their level of success, and their relationships with tedium were studied for sample 2. The results, presented in table A.15, showed that active strategies were most often used and were the most successful. Inactive strategies were used less frequently and were the least successful. The correlational analysis showed that the frequencies of use of active strategies were negatively related to tedium and the frequency of use of the inactive strategies were positively related to tedium. The correlations between tedium and the success of strategies were predominantly negative, half of them reaching statistical significance at the .05 level.

TABLE A.15. Mean values and correlations with tedium for frequency and success of coping techniques—sample 2

	FREQUENCY		SUCCESS	
	Mean	*Correlation*	*Mean*	*Correlation*
Direct-Active				
Changing the source	3.4	− .09	3.4	− .26*
Confronting the source	4.1	− .32*	4.4	− .40*
Finding positive aspects in the situation	4.5	− .19*	4.2	− .33*
Direct-Inactive				
Ignoring the source	3.3	.05	2.7	− .26*
Avoiding the source	3.6	.21*	3.1	− .03
Leaving the source	3.4	.15*	3.8	− .08
Indirect-Active				
Talking about the source	5.2	− .09	5.2	− .25*
Changing self	3.6	− .03	3.6	− .17*
Getting involved in other activities	4.5	− .09	4.9	− .13
Indirect-Inactive				
Drinking or using drugs	2.6	.21*	3.0	− .09
Getting ill	2.6	.35*	2.4	.19*
Collapsing	2.1	.33*	2.4	.13

*p< .05

Sex differences. Table A.16 compares men and women from sample 2 on the coping techniques. Analysis revealed signficant differences ($p < .05$) on the frequency of use of four coping techniques: ignoring the source, talking about the source, getting ill, and collapsing. Women had a lower mean on the first one and higher means on the last three strategies. The evaluations of success showed two significantly ($p < .05$) different means: ignoring the source and talking about the source. Women had a lower mean on the former and a higher mean on the latter strategy.

TABLE A.16. Mean values of frequency and success of coping techniques for men and women—sample 2

	FREQUENCY		SUCCESS	
	Men	*Women*	*Men*	*Women*
Direct-Active				
Changing the source	3.5	3.4	3.5	3.3
Confronting the source	4.3	4.1	4.5	4.4
Finding positive aspects in the situation	4.5	4.5	4.4	4.1
Direct-Inactive				
Ignoring the source	3.7	3.1	3.2	2.6
Avoiding the source	3.4	3.6	3.2	3.1
Leaving the source	3.5	3.3	4.2	3.7
Indirect-Active				
Talking about the source	4.7	5.3	4.8	5.3
Changing self	3.8	3.6	3.9	3.5
Getting involved in other activities	4.4	4.6	4.6	4.9
Indirect-Inactive				
Drinking or using drugs	2.5	2.6	3.0	3.0
Getting ill	1.8	2.8	2.5	2.4
Collapsing	1.5	2.3	2.3	2.5

Cultural differences. The frequency and use of coping techniques were compared in the United States sample 2 and the Israeli sample 27. Results, presented in table A.17, showed that the Israelis use more direct-active coping techniques such as changing the source of stress, confronting it, and trying to find positive aspects in the situation. The Americans used more direct-inactive coping techniques such as ignoring the source of stress, avoiding it, and leaving the situation. They also used more indirect-active coping techniques such as talking about the source, changing self, and getting involved in other situations, as well as more indirect-inactive activities such as drinking, getting sick, and collapsing.

TABLE A.17.   Mean values of frequency and success of coping techniques for Israelis and Americans

	FREQUENCY		SUCCESS	
	Israel	*US*	*Israel*	*US*
Direct-Active				
Changing the source	3.7	3.4	4.2	3.4
Confronting the source	4.8	4.1	4.7	4.4
Finding positive aspects in the situation	4.7	4.5	4.9	4.2
Direct-Inactive				
Ignoring the source	2.6	3.3	3.7	2.7
Avoiding the source	2.8	3.6	3.5	3.1
Leaving the source	2.5	3.4	3.3	3.8
Indirect-Active				
Talking about the source	3.9	5.2	4.2	5.2
Changing self	2.9	3.6	3.5	3.6
Getting involved in other activities	4.0	4.5	4.7	4.9
Indirect-Inactive				
Drinking or using drugs	1.1	2.6	2.6	3.0
Getting ill	1.5	2.6	2.0	2.4
Collapsing	1.3	2.1	2.4	2.4

Summary

The appendix presented our research on tedium and its major findings. It presented the mean value of tedium for the different samples, professions, and for men and women, as well as its relationships to other variables. The interested reader is referred to the list of articles following this appendix for further information about these studies.

Notes

1. T. Kunin, The Contruction of a New Type of Attitude Measure, *Personnel Psychology*, 8 (1955): 65–77.

2. A. T. Beck, A. Weissman, D. Lester, and L. Trexler, "The Measurement of Pessimism: The Hopelessness Scale," *Journal of Consulting and Clinical Psychology, 42 (1974): 861–865.*

Relevant references

ETZION, D.; KAFRY, D.; and PINES, A. "Tedium among Managers: A Cross-cultural American-Israeli Comparison. *Journal of Psychology and Judaism,* in press.

ETZION, D.; PINES, A.; and KAFRY, D. "Coping Strategies and the Experience of Tedium: A Cross-cultural Comparison Between Israelis and Americans." *Journal of Psychology and Judaism, in press.*

KAFRY, D., and PINES, A. "Coping Strategies and the Experience of Tedium." Paper presented at the American Psychological Association Convention, Toronto, Canada, August 1978.

KAFRY, D., and PINES, A. "Tedium in Life and Work." *Human Relations,* in press.

KANNER, A. D.; KAFRY, D.; and PINES, A. "Conspicuous in its Absence: The Lack of Positive Conditions as a Source of Stress. " *Journal of Human Stress* 4(4) (1978): 33–39.

KANNER, A. D.; KAFRY, D.; and PINES, A. "Stress Results from the Absence of Positive Experiences As Well." Paper presented at the Western Psychological Association Convention, Honolulu, Hawaii, May 1980.

MASLACH, C., and PINES, A. "The "Burnout" Syndrome in Day Care Settings." *Child Care Quarterly* 6, no. 2 (1977): 100–113.

MASLACH, C., and PINES, A. "Burnout,' the Loss of Human Caring." In *Experiencing Social Psychology,* by A. Pines and C. Maslach, New York: Random House, 1979, pp. 245–252.

PINES, A. "Burnout and Life Tedium in Three Generations of Professional Women." Paper presented at the American Psychological Association Convention, San Francisco, California, August 1977.

PINES, A. "Characteristics of Burnout in Human Service Workers." Paper presented at the Twenty-first Annual Clinical Conference, Asilomar, California, June 1978.

PINES, A. "Emotional Involvement of Helping Persons—Where Do We Draw the Line?" Paper presented at the Annual Conference on Child Abuse and Neglect, Houston, Texas April 1977.

PINES, A. "How to Develop Detached Concern and Prevent Burnout." Paper presented at the Second Annual National Conference on Child Abuse and Neglect, San Antonio, Texas, October 1977.

PINES, A., and ARONSON, E. *Burnout.* Schiller Park, Ill.: M.T.I. Teleprograms Inc., 1980.

PINES, A., and ARONSON, E. "From Burnout to Personal Growth." Paper presented at the American Psychological Association Convention, Montreal, Canada, September 1980.

PINES A., and KAFRY, D. "Tedium in the Life of Three Generations of Professional Women." *Sex Roles*, in press.

PINES, A., and KAFRY, D. "Occupational Tedium in the Social Services." *Social Work* 23, no. 6 (1978): 499–507; also in *On Becoming a Social Worker: Issues in Career Development,* edited by J. Herrick and D. Bargal. Columbus: Collegiate Publishing, in press.

PINES , A., and KAFRY, D. "Tedium in College," Paper presented at the Western Psychological Association Convention, Honolulu, Hawaii, May 1980.

PINES, A., and KAFRY, D. "Tedium in the Life and Work of Professional Women as Compared to Men." *Sex Roles*, in press.

PINES, A.; KAFRY, D.; and ETZION, D. "A Cross-cultural Comparison between Israelis and Americans in the Experience of Tedium and Coping with It." Paper presented at the Western Psychological Association Convention, San Diego, California, April 1979.

PINES, A.; KAFRY, D; and ETZION, D. "Job Stress from a Cross-cultural Perspective." In *Burnout in the Helping Professions*, edited by K. Reid. Kalamazoo: Western Michigan University Press, 1980.

PINES, A.; KAFRY, D.; and ETZION, D. "Tedium: The Dangers Facing People at Work." Working paper, 581–78, Tel Aviv University, Faculty of Management, November 1978; also in *Shurot* (Hebrew) (April 1979): 12–16.

PINES, A., and MASLACH, C. "Characteristics of Staff Burnout in Mental Health Settings." *Hospital and Community Psychiatry* 29 (1978): 233–237; also in *Innovations* 6, no. 2 (Summer 1979): 40.

PINES, A., and MASLACH, C. "Combating Staff Burnout in a Child Care Center." *Child Care Quarterly* 9, no. 1 (1979): 5–16.

PINES, A., and SOLOMON, T. "Perception of Self as a Mediator in the Dehumanization Process." *Personality and Social Psychology Bulletin* 3, no. 2 (1977): 219–223.

Index